HOMESTEADING in the CALM EYE of the STORM

HOMESTEADING in the CALM EYE of the STORM

A Therapist Navigates His Complex PTSD

A Memoir and Companion to *COMPLEX PTSD: From Surviving to Thriving*

Pete Walker

Author of *COMPLEX PTSD: From Surviving to Thriving* &
THE TAO of FULLY FEELING: Harvesting Forgiveness from Blame

HOMESTEADING in the CALM EYE of the STORM
AN AZURE COYOTE BOOK/ 2017
www.pete-walker.com
First Edition

Cover Art: Pete Walker

Copyright 2017 by Pete Walker
ISBN-13: 9781974029150
ISBN-10: 1974029158
All Rights Reserved
Printed in the United States of America

Dedication

To everyone who got a bad deal from the *Parenting Deck*.

Do I contradict myself?
Then, I contradict myself!
I am large.
I contain multitudes.

— Walt Whitman

I won't take the easy road…
Show me my silver lining

— Song by First Aid Kit

Table Of Contents

Acknowledgements xv
Introduction xvii
    An Emblematic Snapshot. xviii

PART I	Discovery: Looking Outward For Answers. 1	
Chapter 1	Born Into the Wrong Tribe 3	
	Shut Up and Don't Ask 3	
	The Thought Police. 5	
	Out of the Frying Pan 7	
Chapter 2	Home Improvement With Uncle Sam's Family 12	
	An Officer and Gentleman by Act of Congress 12	
	War Games in the Okefenokee Swamp 16	
	The Blind Leading the Blind 17	
	Teaching Korean Soldiers How to Eat. 19	
	Tempting Fate on the DMZ. 19	
Chapter 3	A Jack Kerouac Attack 21	
	The Road Less Travelled 23	
	Emily Post Would Have Died 25	
	Sweet Home Alabama…I Don't' Think So 27	
	Cultivating a Ride 28	
Chapter 4	Full Tilt Detour. 30	
	Bear County Jail 32	
	The Unholy Hole 33	
	Manny and Pablo Lose the Spelling Bee 36	
	Doing a Rumba with Moochigumba. 37	

	All Hail the Public Defender 39
	Austin City Limits 42
	Cherry Jubilee. 43
	My Thumb has Miles To Go Before It Sleeps 46
Chapter 5	A Love Affair with Life 51
	Vacationing in Skid Row 51
	Hate in the Haight. 53
	Getting Blood out of the Stoned 56
	Cataloging the Sins of Our Fathers 57
Chapter 6	Lucy in the Sky with Diamonds. 59
	LSD caveat 63
	St Anthony and the Argonauts 63
Chapter 7	On The Road Again 68
	Full Frontal Living 69
	Love the One You're With. 70
	Bed-bugged 72
	The Weird Tribe 73
	The *Djama el Fna* 74
	Looking for Traces of Dr. Livingstone. 76
	FEZ 80
Chapter 8	Pilgrimage to an Unholy Land. 83
	Pain on the Plain in Spain 83
	Scalped in the Alps. 85
	Dave's on First. 87
	Tiptoeing Through Tehran 89
	With Friends Like These... 91
	The Stans. 92
	Dave Steals Second. 95
Chapter 9	Tick Tock in Attock Prison 99
	Reverend Peanut Butter 103
	Fling Ding in Sing Sing 105
	Never the Twain Shall Meet .108

	The Lurch That Sunk the Love Boat	109
	Dave Rounds Third	111
	Goa: Lost in Paradise	112
	And Zen, What Do I Do?	116
	Dave is Out at Home	117
Chapter 10	Pitch Black Flight-Into-Light	120
	Annihilated by Amoeba	122
	Death of a Quest	123
	Whither Now?	125
Chapter 11	Darwin – A Taste of Evolution	130
	3 Wells Street	130
	Going Back to Basics	132
	Herbie Monroe	134
	Working for the Aussie Dollar	135
	Warm Leatherette	136
	Instant Family	137
PART II	Recovery: Looking Inward For Answers	141
	Glossary	141
Chapter 12	Sanctuary Thy Name is Sydney	143
	Getting Real Down Under	145
	Dietary and Somatic Salvation Fantasies	147
	Getting Schooled	148
	Demonizing Introversion	150
	True Alchemy: Grief Morphing into Relief	151
	Angering is Grieving Too	152
	Rajneesh	155
	Jody Steps Out	156
Chapter 13	Working with Real Live Clients	158
	Sometimes It Is Easier To Die	160
	Kicking It with Sat	161
	Going Back to the Dry Well	162

	Meditate Don't Medicate 164	
	Out of My Body, But in My Mind 165	
	How Many Times Can I Step into the Same Hole. . . .168	
	Astrology: The First Psychology 171	
	Opening a Client to Grieving 173	
Chapter 14	Onward and Inward 176	
	Raging into Love. 178	
	Spiritual Chiropractic 179	
	Love and Anger Couples Workshop. 182	
	Debbie 185	
	Look Homeward Angel 187	
	Debbie Seals the Deal 189	
	California Here I Come 190	
Chapter 15	Home is Where the Depth Work is 192	
	The Encounter Group Maestro. 192	
	Declaring War on the Critic. .193	
	Bearded Nanny. 195	
	Tantruming as a Healthy Developmental Stage 196	
	How can Self-Esteem Exist in a Mind Poisoned	
	Against Itself?. 197	
	Mommy Dearest 198	
Chapter 16	Flight Into Darkness 203	
	Spiritual Bypass University 204	
	Fugitive from the Law of Averages. 206	
	Finding Tribe in Berkeley 209	
	Duck and Cover Jim 211	
	Psycho-Spiritual Sports Therapy. 211	
	Everything Flowers from Within 213	
Chapter 17	Incubating a Therapist 216	
	Self-Validation Eludes Me 218	
	Marie. 219	
	Repetition Compulsion and Reenactment 221	
	Fawning as Reenactment 222	

	Disarming the Homicidal Client 224	
	Rosen Work. 225	
	The Imposter Syndrome 226	
Chapter 18	Out of Abuse into Neglect 230	
	Brenda. 230	
	Licensed and Free. 231	
	Praying with Bearheart 232	
	Singing Bird's Vision Quest. 235	
	Ameliorating Sexual Abuse. 239	
	Like Parent, Like Partner 240	
	My Mother the Men's Group 242	
Chapter 19	Writing the Tao of Fully Feeling 245	
	Challenging Mainstream Psychology 247	
	Busyholism: "Don't Just Do Something, Stand There!". . . 250	
	Running on Empty 253	
	Minding the Body 257	
Chapter 20	Dating: the Dragstrip Between Abandonment and Engulfment 262	
	Poverty Consciousness Fades Away. 262	
	Good Enough Love. 264	
	Relational Therapy 265	
	Dating Co-Counseling 266	
	Learning What To Want 268	
Chapter 21	Volunteer Work 270	
	Zen and Laguna Honda Hospice 271	
	Betty not-Boop. 272	
	Therapist Heal Thyself 275	
	Roy Bleeds Out. 275	
	Deafening Silence. 277	
	A Clarion Call for Euthanasia 279	
Chapter 22	A Marriage and Family Therapist Gets a Marriage and Family. 282	
	Sara Cheech & Chongs Her Way into My Heart. 285	

	Jaden: The Ultimate Creativity 288
	Keeping My Vow: The Buck Stops Here 289
Chapter 23	Regenerating At The Hub Of Relational Healing. 296
	Meandering into the Role of Therapist. 296
	Not Toeing the Line of Melanie Klein 300
	Mutual Relational Healing. 301
	Writing COMP*LEX PTSD: From*
	Surviving to Thriving 305
Chapter 24	Thriving Surpasses Surviving .308
	My Introvert Emerges from a Chrysalis of Extroversion. . .311
	The Right to Feel Bad 312
	Countering Counterphobia. .315
	Not As Good As I Hoped – Better Than I Expected. . .317
	A Final Parental Appraisal. 319
	Onward and Where-ward? 320
	Narrative Therapy 321
Appendix 1	Navigating CPTSD: My Top 10 Practices 323
	Milking Self-Kindness and Self-Protection
	out of Grieving 323
	Whittling Down the Critic. 325
	Flight-into-Light 328
	Bibliotherapy. 329
	Writing that Helped Me To Right Myself 331
	Meditation: There's No Boogeyman in
	My Inner Closet 331
	Getting and Giving Individual & Group Therapy 332
	Self-Reparenting: Finding an Inner Mom and Dad. . .336
	The Created Family: Healing the Loss of Tribe. 336
	Gratitude: A Realistic Approach 338
Appendix 2	Three Dimensional Relational Healing *. 341
	Self-Compassion, Empathy, Mutuality 341
	Healing Developmental Arrests in Complex PTSD . .342
Appendix 3	Psychedelic-Assisted Therapy .347
	A Caution about Cannabis 349

Acknowledgements

I AM TREMENDOUSLY grateful to my team of editors. They gave me invaluable assistance and encouragement.

> I thank…
> My wife, Sara, and my son, Jaden, who let me run the book's phrasings and anecdotes by them endlessly. Thank you so much for your consistently helpful advice, and for tempering my crude Scottish sense of humor.
> Sara also helped me tremendously with written, paragraph-by-paragraph feedback on a near final version of the manuscript.
> My excellent, longstanding friend and writer, Bill O'Brien, also tweaked the book most helpfully in his detailed commentary on all sections of the book.
> My equally excellent, longstanding friend and writer, John Barry, also helped me greatly to improve the flow and rhythm of the story.
> My colleague, Julie Scheinman, read the manuscript and also gave excellent advice.
> My good friend, Ine Secivkulis, copy-edited the final proof, as she did with my CPTSD book, and caught many errors I never would have seen.
>
> I am also grateful to many *clients and readers* of my writing who powerfully stoked my motivation to write this book.
> I thank…

The many readers who took the time to rate my books positively on Amazon, and testify to how they helped them in their recovery.

The many readers who let me know that my writing made them feel *seen and understood* for the first time in their lives.

The many clients and readers who shared with me the relief that came to them from exploring their childhood trauma with my map and toolbox: *COMPLEX PTSD: From Surviving to Thriving.*

The many clients and readers who reported that distancing from parents, who were still abusive, accelerated their recovery. They emboldened me greatly to further promote the unpopular position of putting blame and distance on parents who were grossly abusive and/or neglectful.

I am also extraordinarily grateful to the many therapists and theorists who helped me build my eclectic approach – those named within and those whose contributions I may have inadvertently failed to cite.

Introduction

WELCOME, AND I hope reading my memoir is a worthwhile, enjoyable and emotionally rich experience for you. Herein, I tell my story in a more playful, easier to read style than in my other books – much less dense and relatively free of psychological jargon. Yet, I hope you find many helpful takeaways.

I started this book in the army in 1966 with my first journal, *Chemical Hopes* – a response to being trapped in Combat Platoon Leader Training. I used this journal to help me process the dread of being Viet Nam-bound. I focused my hopes on earning a transfer from the Infantry into the less combat-oriented Chemical Corps.

When I got the transfer, I felt like the journal helped make it happen. Subsequently I embarked on a lifetime of journaling. My four foot stack of fifty years of journals has fertilized this memoir.

Part I is my *On-The-Road* style book, chronicling my world-wide search for answers. Part II details my journey of deprogramming myself from my parents' brainwashing. As a child, they continuously abused and neglected me into constant fear, toxic shame and despairing self-abandonment. Part II shows how I gradually healed my psyche by growing my self-kindness, self-care, and self-protection.

One of my editors thinks this is two books – two memoirs of different times in my life. I, however, see them both as central to understanding how I – a CPTSD survivor – rose out my rough start in life and gradually learned to thrive.

Nonetheless, I expect that some readers of my other books might want to skip or skim Part I and focus more on Part II – the meat of my psychological discoveries. Conversely, those of you who are not enamored with introspection may find that psychology-lite and easy-to-read Part I sheds light on how a fellow human being becomes a therapist.

An Emblematic Snapshot

It is 2001. As I leave my therapy office in Lafayette one night, I notice a small swarm of honey bees around the light by my office door. Afraid of bees all my life, I rush and fumble to get the key into the lock – to lock the door and get away as soon as possible.

But a bee flies underneath my glasses and stings me just below my right eye. I have never had a panic attack, but I feel sure I am about to have one. My heart pounds. Adrenaline seems to be pushing out of my every pore. Finally the door locks, and I spring away bracing myself for the pain of the sting.

But all I can feel is the mildest sensation of a pinprick – like a well-placed acupuncture needle on an insensitive point. I wait and wait, and sure enough, there is no physical pain.

Instead, I have a vivid flashback to being a toddler on my porch in childhood. I am terrified and crying. Mommy has yet again angrily pushed me out the front door to a place much worse than the closet under the stairs with the boogeyman in it.

It is summer and zillions of bees taste her flowers alongside the fence-enclosed porch. I am so scared of them.

Mommy screams: "You're a bad boy, Peter. You belong out here with those wicked bees." She sticks my heinie with a safety pin. "This is what it will feel like when they sting you. I hope when they sting you, you will decide to be good!" The door slams and I beat on it screaming and crying over and over: "Please mommy let me in. I won't do it again!"

As I attend to this flashback, my heart goes out to the petrified child that I was. For the first time I believe that all those vague images I have of my mother sticking me with a safety pin are actual memories – especially those times when she was ragefully changing my diaper.

I internally hear a long crying howl: "Yoowhhww!" and Helen yelling: "I told you if you didn't stay still I'd stick you with this, you nasty little devil. Now stop jumping round!"

I tune back into the bee-sting and I'm astounded that there's no pain. I go into the bathroom and I can't see any swelling.

I start to realize what my bee phobia has been about all these years. It's an emotional flashback to being stabbed with the safety pin. No wonder seeing someone armed with a knife in a movie always makes me wince. In the army I had little fear of being shot, but I couldn't bear the thought of being bayoneted.

When I reach the safety of my car, I open to the feelings of the flashback. I cry a great deal for the poor boy with the crazy mother. I love him even more because of how she tormented him. I show him my rage about her cruelty.

And then, my emotional intelligence produces this: "I wish I could go back in a time machine to protect you. I would do whatever it takes to stop her from ever hurting you again."

More tears percolate up about all those decades of unnecessarily feeling freaked out around bees, and knives and sharp pointy objects. I anger again at my mother for all that unnecessary pain.

I tell my inner child: *If she ever comes near us again, I'll bee-sting her with a pin!* He laughs…and relaxes, and my flashback melts into a feeling of safety and relief.

On the drive home I think: *Damn! This bee phobia has rained on my gardening pleasure for decades.* Suddenly, I feel buoyed by an epiphany springing into bloom: *I bet I'm not so afraid of bees anymore!*

But maybe that's just wishful thinking…silly new age "mind over matter." I test my bee salvation fantasy the next day while I'm weeding in my garden. WOW! I'm barely afraid of the bees. I remind myself: *Bee-stings barely hurt.* I can feel my whole body letting go as if I have just shed a wetsuit that's too tight. My pleasure at being surrounded by my garden's beauty subtlely but steadily increases.

Two weeks later, while deadheading some cornflowers, I accidentally pinch one off with a bee still in it. I feel a tiny prick in my palm. I'm not even sure that I've been stung until I find the tiny stinger in my palm. What a great sense of liberation from needless fear. I feel like I've been baptized in a religion that immunizes one against bee stings.

From hereon I routinely relax around bees. I increasingly mellow into the garden, even when there's a sudden large influx of pollinating bees. I stay and putter no matter how many bees are fattening on my honey.

And so, if you have had the misfortune of being raised on fear rather than love, I hope that this recollection and the many that follow, will help you understand that present time fear is often rooted in undigested but *resolvable* fear from the past.

This memoir however, is not a how-to-manual like my first two books. It is the progressive story of my half-century journey of recovering from Complex Post Traumatic Stress Disorder.

While everyone's recovery process is different, I hope that reading about mine will show you shortcuts and help you avoid the blind alleys in which I was sometimes lost. I also hope that seeing how long it took me will help soothe the shame and impatience that typically plagues this slow-paced journey. What's more, I pray that you will find the relief and growth that informed recovery work typically brings.

I see my recovery journey as composed of two parts. In Part I, *Discovery*, I escape from my dysfunctional family and backpack around the world. I consciously seek happiness while I unconsciously flee my suffering. Out of naiveté and desperation, I try to find meaning through a spiritual quest. On an unconscious level however, I look for human warmth and connection, despite my claim to be a loner who's vowed to never need anyone.

In Part II, *Recovery*, I wander in the jungles of psychological theory and technique. I shift my focus from global adventurer to inner world explorer. I detour from *On the Road* [Jack Kerouac] and embark *On the Road Less Travelled* [Scott Peck].

The therapeutic frustrations and accomplishments of the second half of my life are detailed herein. Largely hit and miss, I find effective help and gradually move from struggling to survive to discovering how to thrive.

My psychological health slowly improves as I interweave my cognitive and emotional selves. I rescue my thinking processes from the inner critic and my brain becomes user-friendly. Fear shrinks, toxic shame melts away, and peace of mind becomes my touchstone.

Very gradually I find meaning, belonging and fulfillment. I break the pattern of being attracted to painful relationships that mirror my experiences with my parents. This in turn frees me to find a number of truly intimate and comforting relationships.

PART I

Discovery: Looking Outward For Answers

CHAPTER 1

Born Into the Wrong Tribe

FOR STARTERS, I will confine the story of my childhood trauma to three emblematic incidents. There is much more in my first two books, and in Part II where I explore my recovery from daily childhood abuse and neglect.

Shut Up and Don't Ask

I look inward down the corridors of time which seem to stretch endlessly toward my early childhood. The downward curve makes me feel dizzy – like I am on Columbus's ship about to fall off the edge of the world.

I finally land on 13th Avenue in Queens, New York in 1953. My house is in the suburbs of NYC, and trees curl from both sides of the road to form a bower over the road. I am six – carrying a jar of live lightning bugs that I caught last night, when I wander into a big commotion.

Three tough Irish-American teenagers, the Carmody brothers, are fighting Italian-American Alfred Saturno and calling him a guinea wop. It is so hot and sticky that everyone has a sweat mustache.

They fight in front of Alfred's yard as his eight younger siblings and their goat cower and watch. Alfred is biting his lower lip with his own teeth, and it's bleeding. It hurts to look at.

They are all armed with stickball bats [sawed off mops and brooms]. Like swords, the bats swoosh down on Alfred's bat and slide into his knuckles making a cracking sound. The largest freckled boy calls him a goat-fucker.

Alfred's parents, immigrants from Italy, commit the sin of keeping a goat and chickens in their backyard. On better days, when his mother lets the little kids of the neighborhood ride her, everybody loves the goat.

All of Alfred's knuckles are bleeding. The surrounding mob of kids howl in delight. I'm so upset. Alfred is so brave, but it's three against one, and I can't believe my friends are laughing at him getting beat up.

Now I'm so embarrassed. Tears flow down my face like a tattle tale icing – not the kind anyone wants on their cake.

That evening at the dinner table, mom is laughing as she mimics her favorite comedian, W.C. Fields. She uses a carrot like she is smoking a cigar and says many times: "Anybody who hates kids and animals can't be all bad!"

She must be in a good mood. Maybe it's safe to talk about what happened to Alfred. I take a risk. "The Carmody brothers are so mean! They beat up Alfred…"

Momma quickly cuts me off. "Peter, why can't you stay out of trouble!?"

"But, Momma I didn't do anything!"

Daddy roars: "Shut up Dumbo. Just listen when you're being talked too!"

"But I…" Daddy reaches across the table and takes a full backhand swing and slaps me. I see a close-up of the back of his hand, until my eyes close and it smashes into my face. Then I feel flecks of his spit spray across my face as he yells: "For crying out loud, Peter! How dare you talk back to me?"

I hear my sister Patricia crying. He used one of his two-for-one smacks and hit her as well. "And you Patricia wipe that smirk off your face, or I'll wipe it off for you."

I'd like to say: "You already did," but I know that would be a mortal sin. The fourth commandment says: "Honor thy mother and father," and that means never contradict them.

I wish and pray so hard all the time to be good. On Good Friday, last week, I stuck thorns into my palm to be like Jesus…to make penance for my sins. Maybe things will change when I get to be an altar boy next year. Maybe then I won't be such a disappointment.

At night in bed, I can't stop thinking about Tar Baby, my beautiful cat. Where is she? She disappeared last week…two days after her eight little cutie-pie kittens had to go live somewhere else. I asked momma if she knew were Tar Baby was, and she got very mad. I'm so stupid. I should know better than to ask questions. Questions don't honor thy mother and father. Questions are bad.

Every night I have a terrible nightmare about Tar Baby. I see a steamroller squashing her. Terrible smushing sounds. Water dripping and plunking loudly makes me shiver. A booming raspy voice growls over and over: "You did it, you did it…" My body swells up to a huge size and then shrinks into tiny-ness and then swells up again and again.

Momma's right. There's something wrong with me. I do have the devil in me.

The Thought Police

I am thirteen, a roiling mess of sexual craving, guilt and self-disgust. Every day in catechism class the nuns remind me of what an abomination *impure* boys are in the sight of God.

The clergy preach endlessly about the numerous ways in which thinking is sinful. Thinking about sex is the worst – a mortal sin which will land me eternally in hell if I die before I go to confession.

I privately nickname the worst nun: *Sister Jean Therese of the Angry Face*. Her face is as red as the devil, and flushes when she shows us Hieronymus Bosch's torture-filled painting of purgatory. "Hell is a thousand times worse than this!" she laugh-snarls.

She sneers and bits of foam accumulate at the corners of her mouth. "And the best that any of you degenerates can hope for – especially you disgusting teenage boys – is hundreds of thousands of years burning in purgatory – if you're lucky enough to confess before you die."

"And you Antonelli, Heckman and Walker, keep up your shenanigans and you'll miss your chance for purgatory and go straight to Hell which is even worse...and forever."

I know sex is evil. I despise myself because I am helpless to stop thinking about it.

I rarely even get absolution [God's forgiveness] in the confessional anymore. Usually when I come out, I see a teenage girl and impure thoughts pop into my mind like someone has thrown corn kernels on a hot skillet.

I need a confessional with a revolving door, so that if I see a girl when I come out, I can go right back in and re-confess.

What is wrong with me? Everyone says I'm the most devout altar boy, and I know that God wants me to be a priest, but I'm setting a record for impure thoughts.

Today, Father Connolly pulls me out of Father Matter's confessional line. No one wants to go to him because he repeats your sins in a loud voice so that anyone within a ten pew-radius can hear.

Sure enough I finish confession and he barks: "If you just pray a little harder, Jesus will clean up that dirty, disgusting mind of yours." I'm mortified when I exit the confession, especially as I am with my eight grade class and all my female classmates are sitting within earshot.

When I get home I tell mom about my bad experience at confession, skipping the sexual details. She also carefully avoids Father Connolly, but instead of sympathizing with me, she tears into me: "What's wrong with you, Peter? Why can't you be good? Now everyone knows you're rotten to the core. You're such a disgrace!"

"They must have given me the wrong baby at the hospital. How in God's name do you think you'll ever get accepted for the priesthood? I wish I could smack you! Wait 'til your father gets home!"

She can't hit me anymore because: "It hurts my arthritis more than it hurts you." But her angry words make me feel worse than her slapping.

She changes the subject. "Why don't you shave that hair between your eyebrows? You look like you have a mustache on your forehead. I'm going to rename you *FrankenPeter*. Get out of my sight, FrankenPeter. You make me sick. Go on! Go up to your room and wait for your father to get home."

And, *wait* I do – in a cesspool of feeling ugly. Why was I ever born? I feel like I'd be better off dead. Maybe I could have a heart attack in the confessional right after I get absolution, and beat my fate of going to hell.

I'm walking down the street and *Oh No! Here comes Joan Pliza strolling right toward me*. I am gut-wrenchingly shy. I am sure everyone – especially girls – can read my mind like momma, and I cannot stop thinking impurely about her.

Jesus, Mary and Joseph, I won't know what to do with my eyes and my voice when we meet. So I pretend I don't see her, reverse direction and go around the block. *Real smooth, Pete!* She and her girlfriends will be laughing about this for months.

Today, I unexpectedly run into another crush in the hall at school as I turn a corner. *Oh No! Too late to turn around and flee!* When we reach greeting distance, excruciating embarrassment turns my face as red as Sister Jean Therese's. I beg my tongue for a greeting but fear, like a frog, gobbles up my words and I gawk myself past her, a sinking ship of shame.

Thank God for my dog, Ginger! She is always thrilled to see me. She makes me feel like I'm not so bad. Why can't anyone else see me like she does?

Out of the Frying Pan

I am 19 in my sophomore year of Pre-Med. Catholicism has sloughed off me like a sunburned, cancerous skin. My parents think I am living in the dorm at the University of New Hampshire, but instead I am living in heaven with my lover, Ruth. I am ecstatic about no longer being a virgin, and sex is a thousand times more wonderful than making out, which I thought was sliced bread itself. I feel so free and so in love with her...with my friends...and with Life.

Liberation came last month when we fell madly in love at a party. In our first experience of making love, a Beatles' song played: "In the beginning I misunderstood. But now I got it, the word is good. It's the word Love. It's so fine, it's sunshine, it's the word Love."

It's true, I thought. *Love is the answer. This is so Good, so Pure! Catholicism clearly took a wrong turn somewhere! I surrender to you Ruth. I am yours. Do whatever you want with me. I only want to be with you.*

Ruth is a bright, beautiful, vivacious twenty-three-year-old widow with a two-year-old son. I not only love her, but I love Frankie as well. I am so relieved to see that, unlike my parents, I never feel cranky with him. He is icing on the cake – so easy to love that I don't even mind changing his diaper.

Christmas vacation has closed the dorms and I have to return to my home asylum. I would have to be suicidal to tell my parents about Ruth. Thankfully, I still get to see her every day, but I have to be home by 11PM.

It is two days before Christmas and I wake up at 4 AM and I am still in Ruth's bed. We fell asleep after making love and I forgot to set the alarm.

"Oh, my God!" I wail to Ruth. "They are going to kill me. I should have been home five hours ago."

We rush out to Ruth's car and she drops me at the end of my parents' block. As I open the front door Charlie roars at me: "Where the hell have you been? You're mother's been up all night worried to death. You're such a disgrace...you never think about anyone but yourself!"

I just can't lie anymore. Trying to hide my joy and pride in having a lover, I tell them. My mother looks like she's about to faint. "I can't believe it...you're living in sin with a woman."

"It can't possibly be sin, Mom, it's too beautiful!"

Charlie pulls back his arm for a backhand slap and then thinks better of it. He's probably remembering how I got up after the last time he hit me, and glowered down at him from my new height advantage. Since then, he hasn't had the guts to touch me.

"That does it Peter, you lousy excuse for a son. You're nothing but a goddamn ingrate…through and through. I've had with you. Pack up your stuff and get out. I can hardly wait to see what a mess you'll make out of trying to support yourself!"

I happily move out. Being with Ruth is my salvation. For the next two months however, I'm up and down like the storm-driven surf – cresting in the ecstasies of new love and crashing into the troughs of worrying about paying my tuition.

My money problems are crushing me. Washing dishes in the dorm kitchen is misery. It pays a pittance and decimates my study time.

I am no longer on the Dean's list, and I am pissed off that the pre-med curriculum prohibits me from taking anymore psychology classes. I easily aced my Psych 101 course, and passionately explored subjects outside the syllabus.

Even worse, my savings are gone and I don't have next year's tuition. It's the height of Viet Nam, my student deferment is coming to an end and The Draft, like a spider, is ready to pounce.

My good friend Jim Dowe comes over to try to cheer me up – sporting a quart of whiskey. I've only had beer before, but after the awful burn of the first few sips, this stuff is going down like cream soda.

In short order, my whole being expands in a thrilling surge of feeling powerfully and happily pissed off. Dowe and I stir up each other's fury about parental and societal injustice.

All the neighborhood adults and teachers at school see me as the model youth, but my parents are never pleased – nothing is ever enough. Rage swells up in me about perfectly meeting their civic and academic expectations but never getting their approval.

We are walking by the admin building, and my reflection in the window looks too much like my father, so I reach out and punch it. The shattering and sound of the glass breaking is intoxicating in itself, and what do you know…another window, and my mother is staring back at me. "Screw you bitch. You always side with him!" I scream as I let her have it.

Dowe grabs my arm. "All right, Pete. We're gonna get caught if you don't stop. That's enough. Let's get out of here"

"Catch ya later, Jim. I couldn't stop if I wanted to." Every time I punch a window, life feels a little fairer to me. My hands are getting pretty bloody, but it looks and feels kinda cool. I flash back to my History of Civilization class and think: *So that's why those medieval guys used bloodletting to cure people. I've never felt better!*

By the time the score gets to Pete 20 Windows 0, I see two cops hurtling toward me. I take off running, thinking: *They'll never catch me. I'm a cross country runner and they look like they've got beer kegs under their uniforms.* I get away easily.

But this is too rich. I gotta go back for more. I jog 180 degrees around the campus and come back at the building from the other side – jogging and punching windows, feeling like I could take out Cassius Clay… when all of a sudden the two cops tackle me high and low.

In my desperation to get up and get away I grab and rip open one of the cop's jackets, buttons popping off like bottle caps. The other one grabs my wrist and twists it behind my back. I am under arrest – malicious damage and *assaulting an officer.*

My father comes to bail me out. I'm still drunk and I have some delicious moments critiquing his 19 years of fathering. He says: "Ok smart ass, I'm getting Father Maloney to talk to you." It takes me a good thirty seconds to stop laughing and let him know I'm not Catholic anymore. "I hate Catholicism!"

He leaves in huff. "Jeezzz! You Goddamn, good-for-nothing lout. I'll be back when you sober up."

He comes back in the morning, and I have reverted to my old contrite and shameful self.

He resumes command. "So here's your choices, you incredible ingrate: the police chief says that assaulting an officer is a felony, so you can spend two years in jail, or they'll drop the charge to a misdemeanor, if you enlist. Maybe the goddamn army can make a man out of you!"

CHAPTER 2

Home Improvement With Uncle Sam's Family

I AM RELEASED into the custody of my parents and have a week to make my choice. I sneak out the cellar door one afternoon and hike to a hill above a nearby freeway where I contemplate unofficial choice number three. I could hitchhike to refuge in Canada and dodge the military like so many other young men. The war is a travesty and I want no part of it.

The gravity of my situation pulls me to the ground and to my great surprise I rage and cry for half an hour. I have not cried since I was six, and my tears deliver me into clarity. I cannot risk my eventual freedom by becoming an outlaw living in Canada. I won't shrink my world by rendering America off limits.

Way down deep an inner knowing tells me that I can handle the army. And if I do not get killed, I will be free to search the world for the many wonders I read about in Walt Whitman's *Leaves of Grass*. Walt Whitman – an unparalleled Humanist with an almighty heart.

An Officer and Gentleman by Act of Congress

The bus from the induction center dumps us into barber chairs where my longish hair is unceremoniously buzzed off. Even my head is cold in this cold-hearted place.

Twenty of us are herded into a room where we have to face the wall, bend over and drop our pants. A doctor comes in to inspect our nether regions. Almost all of us peek upside down through our legs to check out the proceedings. Not a pretty sight. Twenty hairy anuses with scrotum and balls hanging down behind them. The antithesis of a garden!

Excruciatingly startling is the giant swollen testicle of one poor guy. It is easily five times the normal size and very inflamed. We all watch as the doc comes up to him and says: "How long has it been swollen son?" With great indignance he answers: "How long has what been swollen?" I think I read something about "denial" in my psych 101 text. This sure seems like a textbook case, as everyone tries not to laugh at the poor bastard's expense.

We are housed in a crowded barracks of bunk beds and every morning a macho, highly pissed off sergeant awakens us by screaming: "Drop those cocks and grab those socks!"

Army Basic Training is a rude awakening from the nightmare of my family. Life here seems even worse than home. The drill sergeants torture us with contempt and exhaustion. I am squashed into "name, rank and serial number" through the regimentation of perpetual exercise.

Fortunately half of my platoon are draftees, and like me, none of them want to be here. Sardonic humor about our situation gradually makes the whole ordeal palatable.

I disguise my simmering case of bad attitude, but it is as plain as dog's balls to Sergeant Jeter. He is a fierce African American drill sergeant who is six inches shorter than me and six times as strong. One morning he picks me up one-handed by the front of my shirt and pins me against the wall. "I know ya fuckin' off, Walker! I can see ya got more in ya than that. Straighten up boy, or I'm gonna whup ya ass!"

This is very motivating to me. *I mean, Damn! I could ruin my future... short-circuit into a dishonorable discharge, which is effectively a felony.* Now that would seriously hinder my travelling plans.

My despair and resentment gradually ebb, and my survival instincts kick in. I do not want to die in Vietnam because I am ill prepared. I apply myself to training, and am pleasantly surprised that my striving is occasionally rewarded. More and more, I am spared the kind of arbitrary punishment I got so often at home.

I have my first experience of the *imposter syndrome* when they award me two trophies: one for fitness and the other for military skills. They have to call my name three times at the graduation ceremony before the guy behind me pushes me forward into a stumble. Startled, I realize there is no other Pvt. Walker and this is not some sadistic setup.

As an unexpected bonus, I also beef up and gain twenty pounds which assuages my shame about being skinny. To my dumbfounded amazement, Sgt. Jeter recommends me for Officer's Candidate School [OCS].

In my interview, I am told that I will get out of the army six weeks early if I volunteer for this assignment. Moreover, I can choose a less hazardous branch than the Infantry, such as Engineers or Artillery. So I sign on the dotted line.

I guess I missed the fine print however, as the dotted line coughs me up into the Infantry Branch of OCS – which bears the intimidating moniker: "Combat Platoon Leader's School." When the time comes to report, a corporal tells me I can renege, but I will be sent immediately to Vietnam as a machine gunner, lugging a twenty-five pound machine gun through the jungle. He says: "Machine gunners are Charlie's [the Viet Cong] favorite targets. They got the highest mortality rate."

When I arrive at OCS, I learn in the orientation that the sixty percent of us who survive training will be commissioned as *officers and gentlemen by Act of Congress*. This tickles me as I have been in open rebellion against the notion of acting like a gentleman for almost two years.

OCS is six months of West Point-like hell. Arbitrary punishment is back in spades, and the philosophy of the trainers is: "We can't simulate the stress of combat – which causes nervous breakdowns in the weak – so we'll use other creative ways to try to stress you into cracking up before we send you to Nam."

For the first three months, we do not have walking privileges. We run everywhere. On bad days, running privileges are suspended, and locomotion is limited to crawling.

Crawling downstairs is even worse than crawling up them. Crawling to the bathroom is disgusting, and crawling across the barracks floor that we spend countless hours spit-shining, wrecks the polish and takes hours to re-shine.

The training standard is: "Pain is weakness leaving your body," and pain is on the main menu night and day.

"Push-ups forever" is the training cadre's favorite mantra. If you are tired, you are told: "You can rest when you're dead" or you are allowed to rest in "the front-leaning *rest* position," A.K.A. the pushup starting position. One day I have to duck walk everywhere because an inspecting officer finds a pubic hair on my soap.

About eight weeks into the training, one member of my company is kicked out of the program when he goes berserk and launches himself through the dayroom picture window.

Here is a journal entry from when my suffering was at its worst.

> The days drag like syrup
>   slicing their bellies across
>   the broken glass-littered
>   paths of smog confusion.
> With every certainty challenged by its opposite
>   and every belief disemboweled by doubt
> My dying self
>   mourns the loss
>   of having known what it was once about.

Rereading my journal now as I write, I feel nauseous as I recall the horror of my recurring nightmares in Officer's Candidate School. In most of them, I am leading a patrol through the jungle. I turn a blind corner, panic and open fire on a threatening silhouette. Horrified, I see that the misperceived threat is a child or an old woman – now crumpled in a bloody mangle on the ground.

War Games in the Okefenokee Swamp

We are on maneuvers in the Okefenokee Swamp where we often train. The captain divides us up into two forces to wage mock battle against each other. On an early morning patrol, we see a soldier with a blue arm band [we wear red] squatting next to a tree. We sneak up, point our rifles and yell: "Drop your weapon, Rodriguez! We are taking you prisoner!"

His weapon turns out to be a roll of toilet paper, and the poor guy is in the middle of a non-military evacuation.

We aren't cruel – he is a platoon member friend of ours – but we just cannot stop laughing. I don't know which is worse for him: his humiliation at being captured or his fear that the story will accompany him in perpetuity.

I begin to feel warmth and appreciation for some of my co-sufferers, especially ones like me who can sometimes laugh about the cruel farce in which we are trapped. We especially enjoy satirizing our gung ho, dimwitted leader who we secretly call Captain Pizza Face. Terry Falk pretends he's talking to the captain: "Sir, I love this 'Follow Me!' patch that we wear on all our uniforms, but when we actually get into combat, instead of yelling 'Follow Me', I'll be sure to scream: 'After You!'."

On another excursion, we are maneuvering to attack the base of the blue team. We are armed with blanks, which are real bullets without the bullet projectile. They are filled with the same amount of gunpowder as live ammo and sealed with a small BB-sized wad of cardboard. A blank can be lethal when fired at close range.

On this cold, almost pitch black night, we advance on line against their position. On line means we walk abreast of each other, so that no one gets in front of anyone else – so that no one wanders into the line of fire of the soldiers adjacent to them.

When we receive the command: "Fire!" my friend, Gary-the-Bear Stevens, twists his ankle and lunges in front of me just as I let loose a blast from my machine gun. The burst runs right up his back as he pitches sideways. I feel pins and needles of terror. I almost throw up as I see him go ass over tip by the light of the descending flare that supports our attack.

My mind explodes – invaded by images of him dead and of me court-martialed in the stockade.

Gary is lying face down and I let out a strangled scream when I see a row of ragged, layered holes evenly spaced across the back of his jacket. Squeamishly, I put my forefinger into the central hole and feel a huge relief when it doesn't feel wet – when it comes back out the same color.

Gary is relatively unscathed thanks to the thick winter fatigue jackets that the cold night has forced us to wear. When he comes out of being stunned, he finds the whole thing hilarious, despite finding a string of nasty bruises tattooed on his back the next day.

I get some cardboard and make Gary a fake *Purple Heart* medal – the one given to soldiers who are wounded in combat. He sports it around our barracks for an evening of unusually upbeat rep-artee and banter.

The Blind Leading the Blind

I graduate and am now officially an officer and gentleman. Eleventh hour luck serves me up a branch transfer to the Chemical Corps. Good Riddance Infantry!

It is the winter of 1967/68 and the old saw: "Join the armed services and see the world" coughs up a palatable overseas trip. Spared the evil of Vietnam, I am sent to Korea. Several "lifers" tell me it is the army's best kept secret.

Just twenty-one years old, I am somehow the key field advisor on a huge project. *Talk about imposter syndrome. How can the powers that be think I can advise anyone about anything?*

My assignment is to supervise the defoliation of a strip of dense vegetation one hundred yards wide across the one hundred and fifty mile long Korean Demilitarized Zone [DMZ]. [Now in 2017 two million troops are still perched on opposite sides of the DMZ – anticipating the possibility of a North Korean attack].

With my Katusa [Korean soldier] driver, I scrutinize key points and outposts along the DMZ, and oversee the dispersal of defoliants. I am here to insure that the defoliation only occurs adjacent to the DMZ fence and not inside it. My boss, Colonel C., intimidates me with a warning that using defoliants inside the DMZ could create an international incident. The North Koreans could propagandize it as chemical warfare.

About a month into the operation, I find irrefutable proof that the DMZ fence, and hence the defoliated land, is hundreds of yards inside the demilitarized zone. I am simultaneously scared and excited about this huge violation, but when I report it to the colonel he rebuffs me with a stern "Don't worry about it, Lieutenant."

"But sir, you told me…"

"What part of DON'T are you having trouble understanding! Just continue coordinating with our allies, Lieutenant, and stop playing with your map! The only thing more dangerous than a Lieutenant with a Map is a Private with a Clipboard. Do you hear me? Is that clear enough?!"

"Yes, Sir."

Little wonder the old army acronym, SNAFU, enjoyed so much usage. It translates: "Situation Normal, All Fucked Up." Needless to say I not only do not win a medal, I worry for months afterward that I am in danger for seeing something that I should not have recognized.

Teaching Korean Soldiers How to Eat

I am visiting a remote mountain outpost of South Korean soldiers. A daring young private engages me while I sit in my jeep eating C-rations. He is very struck by my mustache as most Koreans, except for the old men, have little or no facial hair.

My sleeves are also rolled up and he cannot get over the amount of hair on my arms. Like a little kid he asks my permission to touch it. He pets it as if I am a cat or a dog, and his fierce fellow shoulders shriek in delight. I call them fierce because the U.S. paid the Korean government mightily to get a division of these elite troops to fight in Viet Nam. They are the only soldiers the Viet Cong fear.

Twenty pairs of eyes are now glued on my every move. I take a chocolate biscuit out of its C-ration tin, break off a narrow quarter-inch strip, and nonchalantly insert it in my ear.

A great hush! Jaws drop, eyes widen – and then much squealing delight, as I laugh and let them know that I am pulling their chains.

Word apparently travels fast on the Z, as I start getting much warmer receptions at all the outposts I subsequently visit.

Tempting Fate on the DMZ

My orders clearly state that: "under no circumstances will you enter the DMZ." Yet, two Korean Colonels with whom I hope to build credibility and rapport invite me to visit a listening post far inside the DMZ.

Oh my god, I think. Reports of North Korean cruelty abound in this bloody year, in which 50 Americans, 200 South Koreans and 600 North Koreans are killed in DMZ skirmishes. In the worst of these, two South Korean troops are found dead in their outpost – castrated with their penises sewn up in their mouths.

Competing thoughts scrimmage in my brain: *I have to go* vs. *Don't go you idiot*. Frozen in indecision, I let my driver follow the colonels' jeep.

Utter fear tightens my body like a ball of rubber bands. I pull out my revolver, anxiously scanning the bushes that nearly overwhelm the road – that limit our view to less than three feet.

I'm wacked out in the spin cycle of fear. Will I fight back if we are ambushed – or surrender – or put a round through my own head to avoid capture and torture?

Fortunately, I don't get to find out.

CHAPTER 3

A Jack Kerouac Attack

I COMPLETE MY service and I am free at last! The army didn't drive me crazy, and I have survived without killing or hurting anyone. I even had two supportive commanding officers.

Although I would not go back and relive a minute of it, I feel richer for the experience, and have made more than a few excellent friends.

In fact, I have thrived to a small extent. My confidence has grown, even though my self-esteem remains abysmal. *And Total Surprise! It seems I'm a bit of a leader.* I am usually cool and collected under pressure, and a quick study in emergencies. It is only after a crisis resolves that self-doubt floods me with a maze of self-critique.

So, it seems I am a walking, talking paradox. I feel confident when practical problems arise but uptight and self-effacing in most social situations.

The richest gift from Uncle Sam is that I have tantalizingly tasted *Travel* – the travelling I've been yearning for these last five years. I glance at Robert Frost's words inscribed on the cover of my Army journal for the umpteenth time:

Two roads diverged in a wood, and
I took the one less travelled
And that has made all the difference.

I think back to when the singular desire to travel exploded within me. It was when I graduated from High School and met my first mentor, charismatic Jim Dowe.

Jim often regaled me with hilarious stories of his hitchhiking adventures. He lent me his copies of the Jack Kerouac books *On the Road* and *Dharma Bums*. Before I knew it, I was hooked by the Muse of hitchhiking.

Jim was a genius and raconteur – fond of quoting Walt Whitman, especially his epic poem "Song of the Open Road":

*From this hour I ordain myself loos'd of limits and imaginary lines,
Going where I list, my own master total and absolute...
Gently, but with undeniable will, divesting myself of the holds that would hold me.*

What a great day it was when Dick Michaud and I took off from the University of New Hampshire [UNH] over winter break and hitchhiked to visit a friend in Washington D.C. Thirteen rides to get there and twelve to return.

Everyone who picked us up was friendly – interesting samplings from a wide cross-section of society. Only one ride was disturbing. Two "rocks" who reminded me of the Carmody brothers momentarily scared the hitchhiker out of me with their sawed off baseball bats on the back floor of their car.

Their rough, expletive-ridden banter had Dick and me up against the wall of the backseat trying to merge with the upholstery. It took too long but we finally won them over with our humor, and they did not roll us "Beatle-haircut pussies."

My first hitchhiking trip was an unparalleled adventure. From then on, I obsessed about being permanently on the road. Despite excelling in Pre-Med at UNH, the call of *The Road* steadily ate away at my mother's design for me to be a doctor.

Ironically my mother fueled my wanderlust by attacking me whenever I was not being entertaining and energizing. I grew to hate everything in me that was not exciting.

Consummate extroversion – or *good bullshit* as Dowe called it – became my new salvation fantasy. *Who could believe in heaven anymore!*

Through travelling, I would accumulate adventures and juice up my song and dance. Surely such adventures would build my bullshit – my bravado bluff – into something that made people want me around.

The pipedream of hitchhiking also helped get me through my army captivity. For the entire three years, I frequently travelled in my mind, fabricating a fable that I was born wearing a backpack. Sometimes I heard Dowe's voice echoing Whitman in my mind:

> *Afoot and light-hearted I take to the open road,*
> *Healthy, free, the world before me,*
> *The long brown path before me leading wherever I choose.*

The Road Less Travelled

> *…let me pretend I'm a player*
> *with an ace in the hole.*
> *because I know I have nothing,*
> *but sometimes only nothing*
> *can open the door to something else.*
>
> —— Barbara Hambry

I can finally pull my dream of *On the Road* out of the ethers and put some miles on my thumb. And who knows, maybe I'll have enough rich experiences to write my own version of *On the Road*.

I leave Korea and fly to Seattle for my formal discharge. I then begin a hitchhiking trip to circumnavigate the United States. In the words of Whitman:

> *Henceforth I whimper no more, postpone no more, need nothing,*
> *Done with indoor complaints, offices, querulous criticisms,*
> *Strong and content I travel the open road.*

I hitch to New Hampshire for a joyous reunion with old friends. I cannot sit still for long however, and I am soon Florida-bound to visit Jim Dowe at his mother's summer house.

As I wait for a ride on the side of the road in Dover, I remember the summer I worked with him at a brickyard doing slave-like labor, earning ninety cents for every thousands bricks we made. Jim made the ordeal bearable and often orchestrated it into fun. Even better, he turned the summer into a twelve credit course that could have been called Expanding Walker's Horizons.

Jim single-handedly rescued me from the fundamentalist form of Catholicism in which I was still imprisoned. I couldn't stop myself from laughing at his brilliant satire…and his cold hard facts about Catholic travesties like corrupt popes, the Inquisition, the pathologizing of sex and the buying of indulgences to get out of purgatory.

I remember his tongue-in-cheek, tide-turning-riff: "Pete! Just imagine a spaceship with more evolved beings coming here and wandering into Sunday Mass at St. Mary's Church. What do you think they would make of that giant crucified Christ over the altar with the bright red blood coming out of his many wounds…and of the walls covered with gruesome paintings of the Fourteen Stations of the Cross depicting him being tortured? Don't you think they'd see the churchgoers as members of a sado-masochistic cult that exults in human sacrifice? No wonder other intelligent life forms never try to make contact with us. They probably see us as too primitive, bloodthirsty, and dangerous to get involved with!"

Jim's brilliance shifted my search for meaning from the mental shackles of Catholicism to the soul-enhancing wisdom of Walt Whitman. In his wondrous epic poem, *Song of Myself,* he wrote:

> *I see something of God each hour of the twenty-four, and each moment then,*
> *In the faces of men and women I see God, and in my own face in the glass,*

I find letters from God dropt in the street, and every one is sign'd by God's name,
And I leave them where they are, for I know that wheresoe'er I go,
Others will punctually come for ever and ever.

Over the next year I also bought into Jim's notion of becoming a modern day Renaissance Man. He inspired me to pursue learning for its own sake…for the reward of discovering the treasures of human knowledge, art and accomplishment.

This was as easy as breathing, for I never wanted to parlay an education into a perky wife, two and a half kids and an oversized house in an affluent suburb. Before long I became the dean of my own university without walls, minoring in philosophy.

I also carried a dictionary as a companion to vocabulary-challenging novels like *Moby Dick* and *Look Homeward Angel*. Soon I started reading the dictionary whenever I looked up a word. Often I underlined every word I didn't know. Smitten with words, I regularly browsed through the underscored ones to try to own them.

Emily Post Would Have Died

A cornucopia of hitched rides culminates with me getting dropped off two blocks from Dowe's Daytona Beach home. Within fifty feet of the front door, I hear pounding rock music. Jim greets me and says: "I didn't know you were coming, so I baked a cake." He immediately conscripts me to join his friends in the feverish finishing touches of a feast. There is a turkey with trimmings and I get put on blender duty to help with the many varieties of mashed vegetables and pureed fruit.

We gorge for an hour, and seconds and thirds render most of us into food comas. Hawk – Jim's best friend – takes action to re-enliven the event. In his best High English, he says to Jim: "Jolly good my fine fellow! Have you sampled the mashed, cream-cheesed sweet potatoes?" When Jim shakes his head, Hawk flicks a spoonful genteelly at his mouth. An excellent shot, except for the tendrils that go up his nostrils!

Jim responds with a flick of his own. "Try some of this twice-chewed turkey, Chappie!"

Well, as one thing leads to another the compulsion to *share* food becomes instantly contagious. All eight of us air-mail tastes of everything to everyone. Bellyaching laughter, tears of joy and the symbolic anger-release of breaking every food taboo my parents ever assailed me with – make this a more wholesome emotional release than punching windows.

At the height of this culinary massacre, several of us are so food-splattered as to be unrecognizable in the Polaroid photos that Hawk takes. My joy peaks as I fantasize my parents looking in the window horrified to the point of fainting. I have well and truly defied and defiled the Congressional Act that tried to make me a gentleman.

—ɯ—

Wonderful days pass, and it's time to re-embark on the road. As I leave, Jim says: "I'm proud of you Pete. It's neat as hell to see you walking the talk. The only place I let the *Road* take me was back and forth between new Hampshire and my mother's house here in Florida.

"And whatever you do man, please don't follow my lead with drinking. I've really gotten screwed up on booze. I'm only drinking beer, but I've been drunk every night since High School. And I'm sure you can see that my 'good bullshit' ain't what it used to be."

I protest: "Aw c'mon Jim that's not true. Man, you're still the smartest, wisest, funniest person I know...by lightyears!"

"Yeah, Pete, well I'm feeling like an oil refinery gas vent. I can still flare some impressive plumes of insight when I'm beginning to buzz, but its taking less and less time before I'm farting black smoke. I feel like I'm entering the brain damage zone."

A tear rims in my eye. I feel pretty sad because it's true, but I love him and want to encourage him. "Hey Jim you're still brilliant, man, but you're starting to look unhealthy. Why don't you try taking a break?"

"I can't man. I wish I could. I think I'm turning into an alcoholic like my old man."

"Man, I hope not. Why don't you try Alcoholics Anonymous? A friend of mine in the army really got his life turned around through AA."

"Yeah, sure Pete. Maybe I'll give it a try."

Sweet Home Alabama...I Don't' Think So

"Parting is such sweet sorrow," and I move on. Long haired and bearded, I stick out my thumb to start hitchhiking across the hippie-hating South.

Rides are as scarce as well-adjusted teenagers. One morning some good old boys come by vilifying me with volume – warning me: "Ya'll better not be here on the road tonight, hippie-faggot!"

That night, after not getting a ride all day, I walk a mile back down the road away from my destination, thinking: *It's less likely they'll look for me in this direction.* I then scramble off into the woods to find a secluded, if not comforting, place to sleep.

Waiting for a ride in the South is like waiting for approval from my parents. Some days I only get as far as I can walk.

I treat this kind of boredom with myriad memorized songs. I know the lyrics to a cavalcade of Beatles and Dylan songs, and I sing each one until I wear it out. I also read and journal, but after a few days I'm barely buoyant above my depression.

The worst part of this Southern excursion is a stretch in southern Louisiana, where swamp sandwiches both sides of the road. One rideless day, I walk six miles to find a slightly elevated meadow that looks dry enough for sleeping.

Worrying about possible alligators in this part of the state prevents me from stacking any Z's.

I write this at first light:

Nightmares billow out of color-speckled night like warped cartoons
My mind is a rumble of fist-fighting selves
My heart is heavy with a phylum of unsated desires
My life is as empty as a scoreless scorecard.

Almost all my rides are with gay men on the prowl. One guy keeps stopping and spreading a road map out over my lap, but everyone else easily accepts my polite lack of interest.

A silver lining: I am happily disabused of the homophobia with which I was raised. I authentically like most of my new gay acquaintances – and not just because they get me across the deep draconian South.

Cultivating a Ride

Having a large army-supplied repertoire of jokes helps me get the most out of my rides. I've just scored a ride with Farleigh, a traveling salesman from Corpus Christi. A large bug hits his windshield, and feigning a philosophical bent, I say: "What do you think was the last thing that went through that bug's mind?"

In a deep Southern drawl he answers: "I don't really think bugs can think"…to which I reply: "Well yeah that's true, but I think the last thing to go through its mind was its asshole." He laughs so hard that he snorts like a pig, and we are in instant rapport. Too bad he's only going to the next town, but he buys me a hamburger when we get there.

I'm also good at listening and asking enticing questions to get drivers talking. Now and then they reward me by taking me farther or to a better hitching spot.

Like Walt Whitman, I like getting to know people…once I break through my initial anxiety with them. I always look for something likeable in everybody new. Typically I probe for something that we have in common, which often fertilizes a conversation.

As an adolescent, I was taken with Will Rogers. His flagship statement: "I never met a man I didn't like" became canon for me and elevated my people-pleasing skills to a hazardous extreme.

On the positive side, following this aphorism encouraged me to look deeper to find a person's good side. Sometimes however it got me entangled with kids and adults I needed to see as too dangerous to like.

CHAPTER 4

Full Tilt Detour

I AM STILL creeping through mosquito ridden Louisiana when I get a real ride – a ride all the way to San Antonio. The truck driver is a self-absorbed Meth-head whose about to set the record for the world's longest monologue. At least the guy is smart and interesting. No way will I risk losing my ride through inattentive listening. I give this stoner a thousand "un-hunhs" and "mmm-hmmms."

He drops me off in downtown San Antonio in the early evening. I find the nearest payphone and call my buddy, Barry Denniston. Denny and I were training officers together at Ft. Bliss – putting raw recruits through the soldier-making sausage machine to feed the blood banquet in Vietnam.

Denny and I commiserated frequently about the dilemma of hating the war but feeling compelled to maximize the trainees' chances of survival. Miraculously, both of us were spared combat duty. We both passed Go and got out of the army without any serious scars.

I am buzzing with the thought of reconnecting with him and having a real house to stay in for a couple of nights. Sitting in his new red Mustang, Denny meets me on a corner – looking as scruffy and macho-hippie as me.

We sit in his car and he passes me a massive can of beer that he brought to celebrate our reunion. I have not eaten since the trucker picked me up, and before long I begin to feel quite drunk, even though I am sipping while he is slugging.

Laughing with abandon, Denny snorts: "How do you like this shit, Pete?"

I'm surprised to hear myself slurring: "I must be out of practice from the long dry, journey across redneck country. I'm feeling three sheets to the wind!"

Denny dissolves into raucous laughter. "What's a matter, Pete? Never had a beer with a *lude* in it before? I ground a couple up in each of our beers!"

"You asshole Denny, you spiked my beer! What's a lude, anyway?"

"It's a Quaalude, man. A downer – a barbiturate – a lude! Don't tell me you never heard of it. Where you been? Ludes relax ya out man – all soft and mellow. Makes ya kinda lewd too, dude. It goes real good with beer."

"What's wrong with you Denny? You know I don't do that kind of shit."

"Well that's not true man, you just did do it. Come on, we better not drive. Let's leave the car and head over to my friends' house. They live a few blocks past that taco shop over there."

I open my door, take a step and do a clumsy little pirouette onto my butt. "Goddamn, Denny! I can't believe you spiked my drink."

"Well don't get a cockroach up your butt. I spiked mine too, and if you haven't noticed, I'm not walking any better than you. Guess I shoulda only put one of those ludes in our cans."

We stagger down the street, take a right at the Mexican restaurant and get into a fight with two garbage cans. They tackle us low sending us head over heels, further humiliating us by cloaking us with their kitchen scraps.

Two cops materialize out of nowhere and throw us up against the wall. They find my forty cent Korean knife – a three inch switch blade that doesn't work. It is a conversation piece not a weapon.

I tell him: "Press the button, man. It doesn't work. I got it for the silver dragons on the sides."

"Tell it to the judge" says Officer Martinez. He laughs derisively at my souvenir. "You know, *amigo*, I bet this little baby is bigger than your dick. You're under arrest for being drunk and carrying a concealed weapon."

The other cop says: "This other hippie freak is only drunk. So I'm gonna let him go, but you, hippie-shit, are coming with us!"

Bear County Jail

I am petrified and somehow it sobers me up. Occasionally, when I am suddenly confronted with intense danger, everything slows down, gets pellucidly clear and courage and certainty well up in me – like I am in the calm eye of the storm. It's as if there is a spring of grace inside me.

When we get to the jail – the notorious Bear County Jail – I am thrown into the drunk-tank, which in this part of the world is all too scary in itself. A police sergeant gives me my phone call and I have nobody to call because my parents kicked me out for the second time when I recently returned to New Hampshire.

My plan to visit my parents for a week shrunk into two days when my father – incensed by my unshaven look – realized that I was not going back to school or work anytime soon.

When the door hit me in the ass as I left, he forewarned me that petitions for help or reversed telephone charges would not be accepted. *As If I had ever asked that tightfisted tyrant for anything!* He incessantly whined about having to feed and clothe me. From the age of nine, I hustled jobs in my neighborhood for spending money– deposit bottle-collector, dog-walker, snow-shoveler, lawn mower, hedge-trimmer and finally *the big money*: paperboy.

So I call Denny even though he is unlikely to be home yet and leave him a help-message to which he never responds.

Early the next morning, I am led deep into the bowels of the jail and shoved into a tiny eight bunk cell occupied by seven other guys. Most of them look like poster boys for *Felon of the Month* magazine.

There are four Mexicans, two black guys and one other poor white guy who looks as scared as I feel. They figuratively lick their lips, sensing they are in for a taste of some barbaric fun. "New meat!" someone guffaws.

After a more intense interrogation than the one I endured for my security clearance as an army officer, the cell honcho has the creative idea that the two honkies should fight.

"I'm not fighting him" I say. "He didn't do nothin' to me!" Two big guys pick him up bodily and throw him on me. "Whadda ya mean hippie? He just attacked you." He lands on me crumpling me up against the bars. In the struggle to get him off me, I push myself up and my nose luckily hits him in the chin and starts to bleed.

I say luckily because spilled blood momentarily sates their appetites. Said appetites soon prove to be only whetted. I don't bleed for long, and a group discussion rumbles and grumbles around the theme of "you call that fighting!" Internally, I claw for the calm eye of this hurricane as my terror rises up in my throat with a bilious taste.

Then, Johnson from another cell yells: "Who's the new dude?"

"He's some hippie white boy!" scoffs one of my cell mates.

"Hey, cracker, I'm gonna eat your French toast tomorrow."

There's no calm eye anywhere to be found. An army of cats have got my tongue, with nary a retort to be found.

Everybody in the cell starts goading me: "You gonna let him pussy-whip you like that!" In a moment of desperate recklessness, I blurt out "The only way you'll eat it is after I digest it and excrete it."

Johnson screams: "What'd he say. What the fuck he'd just say?"

From another cell comes: "He said you're gonna eat his shit, Johnson!"

"Ooooh-wheee! Dumb shit motherfuckah. White boy you gonna die. I will shove yo head so far up yo asshole, yo gonna see yo tonsils!"

Everyone starts laughing telling me how big and bad Johnson is. My terror peaks. *Oh what a moron I am! Why in the world did I say that!?*

The Unholy Hole

A prison guard suddenly appears. With a voice that a drill sergeant would envy he barks: "I warned you assholes about fighting in this holding cell. I told you motherfuckers this white guy [the other one who's curled up in the fetal position] is in transit to another jail and cannot be all beat up when he gets there. You fuckers are all coming with me to the Hole."

The Hole is another floor below this one and we are being sent there for ten days. As he locks the cell door, he spits: "You're on bread and water now. Three pieces for breakfast, three for lunch, and as a special treat, three for supper. And you can bet your sorry asses it don't come with jam and butter. If you screw up anymore, you'll get another ten days here in the Ritz."

There are eleven of us in this eight bunk cell. For reasons I don't understand, I get an upper bunk. Three teenage Mexican miscreants from some other part of the jail, get mattresses on the floor – mattresses that look like they could win a stain competition.

Of course I am blamed and vilified for the whole thing. Surprisingly, I am not immediately pummeled. Perhaps the camera covering most of the cell is my new guardian angel – as well as everyone's fear of ten days turning into twenty.

Nothing however stops them from pushing a new scapegoat into an off-camera corner – for a world of hurt. I try to hide my cringing and my upset as they punch Felix, a big but flabby Mexican guy, freely and frequently. I flash back to Alfred Saturno getting beaten by the Carmody brothers, but this is a hundred times worse.

My three years of high school Latin help me to decipher some of their Spanish. Apparently, in some previous cell, he buckled under harassment and gave blowjobs to everyone. His fellow countrymen despise him – like he defecated on the Mexican flag.

On the third horrific night in the Hole, after Felix is pretty much wall-to-wall black and blue, they hold him upside down with his head nesting in the single, seat-less chrome toilet. I bounce back and forth and sideways between empathic sorrow for him, shame about not intervening, and fear that he will be murdered. I shiver at the thought that if he dies, I will also be up for murder.

They flush the toilet on him over and over – telling him they are helping him wash the cum out of his mouth. Suddenly he starts choking so badly that they stop and leave him crumpled in the corner.

That night he messes himself so badly with diarrhea that the guard who brings the Holy Eucharist – three slices of Wonder Bread – gags, and gets him removed.

Now I am once again the main attraction. I wobble on a tight rope of speech. *Don't stir them up* I tell myself. *But don't be a pussy!*

I grasp for assertiveness – balancing between agro and wimpy. How can I curb my repressed rage from suicidally screaming: "Assholes" without brown-nosing a signal of "Sure, mess with me, I don't mind?" Somehow I hold my own verbally, talking on eggshells – minute after agonizing minute.

As often as it's practical, I use my inborn curiosity about everyone's story – and listen and elicit like an anthropologist. Jail does not seem to be all that different than anywhere else – almost everyone is dying to be heard.

Humor also helps. My encyclopedic knowledge of crude army jokes helps me dampen the tension. I am generating enough anxiety to power a rock band's sound system. I unconsciously channel it into my jokes and ask my cellmates: "Why was the dog licking his butt?" Apparently no one wants to dignify me with a response, so I supply one. "Because he bit a cop." Someone disparages me. "That don't make no sense, hippie."

"Sure it does," I reply. "He was trying to get the taste out of his mouth." I get a few titters.

Then I try another. "If you were in a room with Hitler, Stalin and Nixon, and only had two bullets, who would you shoot?" Once again, the sound of aloof silence is deafening, until I answer my own question. "Well, I'd shoot Nixon twice!" I get a couple of genuine laughs for that one and decide to go for best out of three.

"So," I say: "A cop comes across a farmer throwing a final shovelful of dirt on a grave. 'What are you doing there, amigo?' asks the cop."

"The farmer replies: 'Ya see that wrecked car over there, officer. I just buried the scumbag politician that was driving it.'"

"The cop then says: 'So he musta been dead, hunh?'"

"'Well he said he wasn't dead, but you can't believe anything them lying bastards say.'"

This one gets some laughs and some playful boo's.

Almost half of my cellmates are young Mexicans between sixteen and twenty – all convicted of murder. Before long I realize that they are not garden-variety murderers. Their homicides were committed during gang fights. They were all born with a mandate of gang warfare – a cultural imperative that they could not escape.

At heart, most of these kids and young men are decent human beings, much like the Mexican-American sergeants who worked under me when I was teaching Basic Training. Two of "my" sergeants – like several of these inmates – radiated archetypal Latino warmth.

One of the sergeants, Ramon Holguin, became a good friend even though officers were not supposed to fraternize with enlisted men. Ramon invited me to a number of family events, and I felt envious of the palpable warmth among his family members. To my great delight they also lavished me with this warmth. Nonetheless, Ramon was a fierce fighter in Vietnam, as were my fellow inmates when they were on the streets of San Antonio.

Manny and Pablo Lose the Spelling Bee

I sort of win over sixteen-year-olds Manny and Pablo just by listening to their disturbingly brutal war stories. I say "sort of" because their primal loyalty is still with their Mexican brothers, so there is no way they will be there for me in a fight.

I am on a joking, first name basis with these two, and gradually it spreads to a few others. The Catholic priest "wannabe" of my childhood must be helping with this. More than once I have the image-sensation of bending forward like a priest in the confessional.

One night Manny and Pablo stay up late tattooing each other. The tattooing is ingenious for there are no possessions allowed in the Hole. Someone however smuggled in a box and a book of matches.

The staple was taken out of the match book, straightened and placed between two match sticks. A long thread – separated from a mattress cover – was wrapped around the whole apparatus many times until the staple was tightly secured. The edge of the staple, protruding a quarter inch beyond the match sticks, was then sharpened on an edge of the concrete floor. *Presto!* A tattooing needle.

Next came the ink. The card board center of a toilet paper roll was burned in the corner of the cell and the ash put in the match box and mixed with a bit of water. *Voila!* Indelible ink.

Pablo uses these crude tools to tattoo letters on the middle three fingers of each of Manny's hands. He outlines the letters with the black ink, and then like a human sewing machine rapidly punctures the skin over and over to get the ink to set in at the right level.

I lose interest, but later when I look at Manny's fingers he has MON and DOD imprinted on them. When I ask him what it stands for, he scoffs "C'mon hippie! You not dumb. It's Mom and Dad." I almost give my face a charlie-horse trying not to laugh. But it's sad too. How much chance do they have with so little education?

Equally startling in the realm of jailhouse tattoos is the design adorning the back of Lucky, an older career criminal. A partial rendition of Jesus Christ is emblazoned there. His tattoo-er got paroled early and left Lucky with an unfinished crucifixion covering the right half of his back. He sardonically tells me: "I've sinned so much I needed another Jesus to die for my sins. But I guess he's never gonna get the job done."

Doing a Rumba with Moochigumba

There is one guy, Moochigumba, who is not dying to be heard. He resists all my attempts to elicit him. *No way I'm gonna crack his hard macho* veneer. He's so ossified in his sociopathic eyes that he's probably hardened veneer to his core.

Moochigumba baits me frequently and is revolted by anything vaguely empathic. When I say: "Sorry", he says: "'Sorry is a sorry word." The tightrope with him feels like balancing on the edge of a razor. I am sure he would pound me if this was not the Hole, and if most of the others were not warming toward me.

"Mooch" puts some gas on the fire. "Do you think you could take me, Hippie?"

Falling off the tightrope I retort: "Take you where, Mooch?"

"Very funny, asshole! Do you think you could kick my ass?"

I am bigger in those days. Six foot and beefed up to 185 pounds by the army. I am taller than him but not nearly as thick, and more relevant, not much of a fighter.

In childhood, I boxed and wrestled a lot with friends, but had only reluctantly been in two real fights. Once another kid sucker punched and kicked me in the face and bloodied my nose on the outside and inside. The other time I defended a younger friend who was being picked on. I sparred with the bully for twenty minutes until he finally gave up and left. But I felt deeply ashamed when he came to school the next day with two black eyes and a pair of swollen lips.

Both fights left me sickened and determined to avoid physical fighting unless forced to defend myself. I am therefore not an accomplished fighter, and I know this guy will make short work of me.

So I climb back onto the tightrope and lie: "I don't know, Mooch, but I'll sure as hell give you a good fight." We have versions of this alarming dance at least twice a day for the next few days.

I am terrified of being raped, crippled and/or killed. I'm filled with miserable memories of waiting for my father to get home from work to wreak my mother's promise: "You'll wish you were never born when your father gets here."

A favorite "friendly" game occurs when other inmates light my bunk on fire after I go to sleep. I wake up to group hilarity as a chorus of Mexican accents croon: "Sommmbodieees on firreerrr!" I beat the flames out with my hands and force myself to laugh at the joke. I try but can't always be the last one to sleep.

Every night I am tortured with the same repeating nightmare – a hyper-ambivalent roller coaster ride cycling back and forth between being released from jail and reinterred.

In the first part of the dream I am set free and start to celebrate when suddenly I wake up and realize I am still in jail. But then I wake up again and realize I am truly out. My joy is ecstatic. But then I reawake and I am back behind bars drowning in despair.

Each time I reawake to still being imprisoned, my anguish intensifies. The scenario cycles and recycles three, four and eventually five times in each dream – five revolutions of this cruel ascendancy into freedom that always crashes into the profound depression of actually waking up still trapped in hell.

This numbing ditty invades my brain like a heart murmur:

Let me dissolve into the deep
I've paid my dues
Let me cease and die asleep

Much later, I name this tune: *The Suicidal Ideation Blues.*

All Hail the Public Defender

On the ninth day, the gruesome routine is broken. A guard takes me to meet with a public defender. I never knew such a person existed. Suddenly I am flaring with hope. *Maybe I'll get released before tomorrow, when my time in the Hole is over, when I go back to the general prison population!* Maybe I can escape getting creamed by Johnson and other monsters who would love to take a white boy apart.

The public defender's name is Hurley Wasdon. He is obviously a newbie – a shavetail lawyer. He looks as appalled as I feel when I describe Felix's beating and the stories of rape I've heard from the inmates. I practically beg him to get me out.

I'm trembling but I burst into the articulate zone, mining my Irish gift of the gab and my high school debating skills. I proclaim my good character: "I don't belong in a place like this! I am a good person! I was an altar boy; I was on the Dean's list. I was an officer and earned a distinguished service medal. I always strive to do the right thing!" *Not a single lie in this pack of truths.*

Hope flickers as I see shock taking residence in his eyes. And, then to my utmost relief, I see that he believes me. He says he'll help me. I tell him I will get my Traveler's Cheques forwarded to me to pay him, and he trusts me enough to post bail for me.

I am released within the hour. I want to weep in relief but my tears are in a vault. Wasdon drives me to the Greyhound bus station, so I can catch a bus two hours north to Austin, where I will reconnect with my army buddy, Pete Hooper.

I promise him I will show up at my court date next week with his money. He believes me again, and I feel shame. I feel like a liar, even though I know indubitably that I will – even though I hold my integrity sacred. I can hear my mother branding me "Liar!" over and over.

I phone Hooper. How wonderful to hear his excitement. "Hooo! Weee! Walker! You made it. I about gave up on you." He welcomes me to come and stay with him.

The minutes while away like hours as I face a long, famished wait for the bus. Eight days of nothing but Wonder Bread have left me ravenous. I have money in my wallet – returned to me upon my release – but I am still shaking on the inside – too terrified to risk crossing the street to the store.

A voice in my head sardonically quips: "Great traveler – Pete Walker, the petrified pussy!" For the next four hours, the voice works overtime to scare me out of crossing the street…and intermittently mocks me for being too scared to get some food.

I try to shake off this neurotic Woody Allen-ish worrying. *But what if it's my intuition?* What if some crazy bad luck occurs and I get caught up in something that gets me re-arrested? It is after all, an all Mexican part of town where I stick out like a ghost in an exorcism.

As I think this I remember my army buddy, Puerto Rican Tony once saying to me: "Pete, you are the original white guy. You are literally so white, you make white look tan." [Decade later I join a basketball pickup game with a group of African American teenagers, and I am instantly dubbed "Casper", as in "Yo Jamal! You cover Casper here."]

So I hold my ground. The pain of this bread-and-water hunger is nothing compared to the fear and hopelessness in which I was just drowning. The snail's pace of the second hand on the big foyer clock is torturous, and the voice tries a new ploy: "You know, Dumbo, trouble could just as easily come in and find you here." The accordion of time is as stretched out as it gets.

Eureka! The bus arrives and without incident I am aboard. As we pass out of the built-up part of the city, I begin to feel some relief. *Thank Dog, I escaped Bear County Jail with my be-hymen intact.*

Looking back at my jail experience from the perspective of 2017, I see an ironic silver lining: my childhood helped me survive this experience. Growing up in Walkerville taught me subtle verbal protection skills. Unrelentingly trapped on the balance beam of hypervigilance and hyper-audience, I gained some skill at finding safe answers to my mother's verbal snares.

Outside my house In NYC, I learned to navigate the dangerous waters of *ranking out*. Ranking out was a sick sport – a slippery banter of dueling insults that could turn on a dime from friendly humor to instant fist-fighting. What was funny in one context could be a red flag to a bull...y. I saw many a fight ensue from over-ranking out, as well as endless scapegoating of those who didn't mock back.

This warped sparring also prepared me well for the army where sarcasm was common parlance. There, it was so polished that I never once saw a physical fight between the many who dueled verbally…and often quasi-warmly!

Austin City Limits

As my adrenaline ebbs, I dissolve into despair. Four measly months on the road, and my journey is over. I can't risk sticking my thumb out again on that menacing highway. Innumerable fantasies of all that could go wrong batter me like bugs smashing into a windshield.

Even worse, there is absolutely nothing else that seems remotely worth doing. *Nowhere to go and nothing to do!* I am sinking fast into a paralytic depression. Where the hell's the silver lining to this calamity? In the back of the bus, I journal this:

MAKE GOD LAUGH: TELL HIM YOUR PLANS

There is only void and turmoil,
    no bollards or moorings
        in this jet stream egress from grace.
Strand by strand the web breaks
    flagellates in the wind
        effetely grasping for an anchorage.
Insect skeletons mimic
    a macabre rosary lost in space
        empty shells of hopes and dreams
            mucho miles beyond their demise.

Pete Hooper picks me up at the bus station and takes me home. I feel momentary relief as I vent my harrowing experiences to him. But when I am done I have to say it: "I'm really sorry, man. I'm just too freaked out to get back on the road again." I feel even worse as he falls into my depression. He has been hanging out, waiting to join me on this adventure, and now there won't be one.

Cherry Jubilee

Hooper says to me: "You know what you should do, Walker? You should have a date with my friend, Cherry Miller. I have been talking you up to her since I got back from Korea, and she is keen to meet you. I showed her that photo of us in Pusan, and she thinks you're cute."

I feel like I am on the seafloor and he's just passed me an air hose. I can breathe again. Hooper sees hope restructuring my face and continues. "Yeah, Man! She's got two tabs of LSD that she wants to try with someone. You know I'm not game! But you're always saying how your mission in life is to try everything at least once."

Past experience has made me wary of blind dates, but Hooper has a picture of her, and she looks like a sweet person. An inner voice quips: *Hey one more blind date and you'll qualify for a free guide dog!* This makes me laugh, and ironically resolves my ambivalence.

Besides, I've been reading about LSD and think it might give me a consciousness-expanding experience, like what Walt Whitman wrote about:

> *And I or you pocketless of a dime may purchase the pick of the earth.*
> *To glance with an eye or show a bean in its pod confounds the learning of all time,*
> *And there is no object so soft but it makes a hub for a wheeled universe.*
> *And any man or woman shall stand cool and supercilious before a million universes.*

—⋙—

Cherry picks me up from Hooper's house. She is so easy to talk with. We do not talk formulas but there is a lot of chemistry, especially conversational chemistry. I am, in the parlance of the times, suddenly "in love…L-U-V…love!"

Within an hour, we decide to take an LSD trip on the spot. At first it intensifies my anxiety, but before long my aesthetic sensibilities increase dramatically. Colors pulse with pristine beauty, and everything in the room glows with a dazzling aura. Soon we are making out, and then making love with tender and sensuous delight.

Our rhythm is slow and comforting with little explosions of pleasure at every change in the way we touch and hold each other. Orgasm stretches out endlessly – definitely not a discrete event confined to our genitals or a distinct period of time.

I whisper: "Cherry, I hardly know you – and it sounds crazy as I say it, but I love you so intensely."

Pealing a sweet riff of sultry laughter she croons: "I love you too baby…with all my giant Texas-sized heart. I've never felt love like this."

I can only echo her: "Oh my God, my love for you feels absolutely sublime."

"Me too, baby! The only thing that's missing is some music…but all I've got is this hokey Johnny Cash album that my redneck uncle gave me for my birthday."

"Well Cherry, this acid seems to be enhancing everything – maybe it can even make a silk purse out of some Country Western."

Writing about LSD is like writing about sex. You can't contemplate the majesty of sex until you have good sex. Likewise with acid – a good trip is exponentially more splendiferous than normal consciousness.

The LSD enhances my perception and appreciation of the music to the nth degree. Every instrument, every note abounds with intricate auditory textures that expand into an ecstatic synesthesia.

Notes not only invoke colors, but also exquisite patterns and images. I am in awe…in an ecstasy of delightful emotion and sensation. Happy tears feel like silk as they soften my face.

> The drought is conquered by unseasonal tears
> The breeze waltzes sibilantly through the trees
> I praise the eleventh hour arrival of grace
> As beauty reawakens and paints
> Luminous mandalas on the far reaches of my sight
> Coloring my world with numinous delight

We play the album over and over all night long. It is the concert Johnny Cash did in Folsom Prison.

Numerous verses invoke the dread of my jail experience in a way that feels healing – in the way that good poetry can elevate pain to a transcendent experience. What magical synchronicity! Nothing else could help me so thoroughly metabolize my prison trauma.

Over the length of the evening, my fear-ridden alienation is salved by our tender lovemaking. My pain seemingly dissolves into the music. Somewhere in the heart of this psychedelic experience, new hope blooms like spring on steroids. I am reborn out of the death of my *On the Road* dream into longing to get back out there again. The Road is once again indubitably my calling.

Three days later Hooper's mother, Violet, is putting the hard woo on me. She greases up to me with incestuous, Southern charm. "You're such a handsome young man, Peter. I know how much Texas gals appreciate a tall drink of water like you. Why don't you just stay here in Austin? I'll help you and my son set up a coffee shop. I'll give you boys a thousand dollars to start it up. It'll be so much fun. I'll even party with ya' all. I can drink a whole bottle of that LSD."

Somehow this reminds me of an old army joke: "I know you're married to another man but will you still do my laundry, mom."

I let my laughter warm my tone, but for once in my life I don't feel guilty saying no.

I meet Wasdon at the courtroom in San Antonio the next day and he gets my charge reduced to a misdemeanor. I pay my fine and Wasdon's fee, and I am once again a free man.

This song is not recorded yet, but in my retrospectoscope, it feels like my soul is belting out a hard rock version of Willie Nelson's "On the Road Again."

Pete Walker

My Thumb has Miles To Go Before It Sleeps

Hooper and I are stuck on the last freeway ramp out of Tucson. Hooper says: "I feel like we're statues to freedom with our thumbs extended. Let's try to bend these drivers' minds into picking us up."

Seven hour later I quip: "You were right about the statue part. We *are* stuck in place. I feel like my feet are putting down roots."

The sun sets. Ride-less in the gloaming, we head to a nearby gas station. I ask the guys inside if we can sleep on the ground out back, hoping to use their restroom the next morning.

"Sure ya can, son. Them big rattlers love crawling into warm sleeping bags at night. I'm sure they'd appreciate bunking down with y'all." Cruel laughter resounds off us from three different directions.

We know from our army training that snakes do not move around at night. We spent almost a month sleeping in the snake-filled Okefenokee Swamp without ever encountering a snake at night. They are cold-blooded creatures and rely on the warmth of the sun to get moving.

Nonetheless, neither of us sleeps a wink that night. We can't help keeping our ears peeled for the sounds of slithering. We are flashing back to all those viper-filled jungle adventures we watched and read about as kids.

Like roosters we're back on the side of the road at the crack of morning. We stand for hours waiting for a Samaritan, singing and inventing endless verses of the Beatles' song:

Jojo was a man who thought he was a loner,
But he knew it couldn't last;
Jojo left his home in Tucson Arizona,
For some California grass.

Hooper quips: "If we wait here much longer, it'll feel like we're leaving home when we finally get a ride!"

Jack Kerouac is not dead yet, but it feels like his spirit is with us late that afternoon, when we score a ride with a hippie who takes us all the way to a beach on the north side of San Diego. We exit the car and are immediately welcomed into a *happening* beach party. The sunset aflame with color, Santana tunes blaring, people dancing around a campfire, and everyone – especially two sweet women – smiling away at us! One guy passes Hooper a joint and he jubilantly exclaims: "Whoopee! This must be California's welcome mat."

Hitchhiking in California is a dream. Hippies galore in their VW buses treating us like brothers. Although I look like one, I do not yet see myself as a hippie. My persona – to ensure maximum safety – is that of a "beat" with a lumberjack-mountain man macho-flavor. I wear work boots, dungarees, flannel shirt, leather vest, and a bandana headband.

I am not aggressive – never have been – but I have a glare with which I can arm myself in threatening situations. Still, the longish hair and beard look hippie enough to garner many peace signs from the passing cars, and when it is a busload of kids flashing them *en masse*, I feel a sweet flutter – and always sign back.

We take our time getting up the coast and meet many lovely people. We stop for a week and camp with a bevy of other travelers at a Big Sur campground. Two young guys are headed to Ft. Ord where they will be inducted. I really feel for them.

Another guy is a pseudo-hippie on the run from the law because of a drug bust that he swears he's been framed for. He has sociopath written all over him, and in the ensuing years I meet too many like him – criminals in hippie garb, who contribute greatly to the eventual ruination of the hippie movement.

Hooper and I are stocked up with food supplies from a ride that dropped us near a corner market in Pismo Beach. It is lunchtime and I am excited about my great score: sixteen cans of Japanese cat food for one dollar. Couldn't be any worse than my mother's cooking, and I've still got her thing about hating how much food costs.

We argue amiably about it for a bit. Hooper says: "We're not eating that shit!"

"C'mon man, you know I dance to the beat of a different drummer."

"Yeah it's more like you rock and roll to the color of a different smell!"

"Ah Mannn! They wouldn't put anything in there that would hurt a cat. Therefore, hence and *ipso facto*, it is a fine source of protein for us."

When I open the can, Hooper says: "Looks like a fine source of toe jam to me."

Inwardly I agree, but outwardly I fake bravado. "Where's that spork-thing you brought with you?"

Would that he had lost it! After one tentative bite, which my stupid macho conditioning forces me to swallow, I am forced to also eat crow instead.

"Well Hooper, I have to admit that this is beyond awful! I have finally found an extreme in the realm of human experience into which I can bite no further. Cat food does in fact *bite*! No way it'll be 'a hub for that wheeled universe' Whitman wrote about."

He replies: "Well I got a hub for your wheeled universe – right over there – the lid on that garbage can where all this shit belongs."

"I don't know, Hooper. Maybe we could donate it to the hospital as an emetic for people who swallow poison…or maybe we can take the rest of the cans to the potluck those guys in the green tent are hosting tonight."

"Walker, you're just plain weird!"

"Thanks man. It's good to be recognized. It took me a long time to get here, and I was afraid you'd never notice."

―◊―

I decide to hike up the side of the fjord-like ravine that towers above us. I'm sure it will be a glorious run down if I can get to the top.

I love running down steep inclines! Back in N.H., when I was 17, Jim Dowe and I ran rock-hopping down a steep, mile long ravine on Mt. Washington. Several adults screamed at us various versions of: "STOP THAT! You're gonna kill yourselves!" *Yeah, What'd you know,* I thought. *You have no idea how joy-inducing this kind of flying is.*

It is a long exhausting climb up the switch-back trail. At the top I run into a guy who amiably challenges me to race to the bottom. It looks like it is a mile down to the bottom. He bursts into the lead.

As we race, we hit patches of screed, and ski wobbly and out of control on the soles of our feet. I can't get past him because the trail is too narrow. The only way to get into the lead is to leave the trail and jump down to a lower level of the switch-back.

I hesitate for a micro-second because the hill is so precipitous that jumping could lead to major damage from an out of control tumble...*but I bet I can grab the branch of that tree eight feet below me.*

What the hell! I leap and catch the branch and swing onto the trail in front of him. *Cooolll!* Gravity is my friend. *Hot damn! I feel like an eagle.*

And I am off into the lead. But he instantly groks my strategy. He cuts off the loop of the next turn by jumping and sliding down the embankment to the next switch-back, grabbing handfuls of brush to stay in control. Thusly we plummet crashing through brush, changing the lead every turn or two.

I jump and lose my grip on a sapling. *God damn! Help!* I screed-slide down two more levels of the trail, barely catching a bush to prevent a totally out of control tumble.

We arrive at the bottom ecstatic, looking like we have been in a beastly fight. Our arms are covered in scrapes and cuts but we tingle with the thrill of the gravity-powered race. We must have descended this enormous hill in one twentieth of the time it took to climb. And who cares about first place? We both win this electrifying race.

And who cares if I won't be able to sleep tonight because of my injuries? I don't know it yet, but I am a trauma survivor. As such I spend most of my time in the frozen present. I am trapped here by a foreshortened sense of the future and a fear of my childhood misery catching up with me. When I am adrenalized and busy, I can distract myself from my underlying emotional pain. How I hate it when it percolates up without warning and engulfs me in anxious deadness and shame.

CHAPTER 5

A Love Affair with Life

Vacationing in Skid Row

WE GET ANOTHER long ride to San Francisco with hippies who playfully call themselves *heads, freaks* or *weirdos*. We arrive *On a Warm San Franciscan Night* [iconic song by Eric Burdon], but soon realize the Englishman never came here as every night thereafter is a refrigerator. Night after night, the fog relentlessly comes in on *giant* cat feet. [Apologies to Carl Sandburg].

I have been periodically ablaze for the last few years with the romantic notion that I am having a love affair with life. Like Walt Whitman, I want to see the beauty of life everywhere, and also like him, I feel pulled to look for splendor in the taboo sides of life.

Hooper and I are exploring the skid row area south of Market Street and I say: "I want to find *Meaning* living amongst the poor and dispossessed. Could there be a better place to start than living in this ten dollar a week flop house-hotel?" Hooper says: "I can get with that."

We check in and resume exploring. A wino slumps next to a dumpster on our street. Is that dirt on his face William Blake's "eternity in a grain of sand?" As he staggers off, I journal this:

> Sipping on liquid courage
> The wino wraps his *Vino Fino* sweetheart
>   in a brown paper bag.
> Fire-watered,
>   he sashays his two step fandango

down the wet neon-painted street.
Joyously he sings "Thishh must be East BeJesus...
Holy shit and fucken truth!"

We explore the city on foot. I pan the streets for things to write about in my *On The Road* story. Every day, we eat free lunch at *St Anthony's Dining Hall* with the outcasts of San Francisco. Many nights we dine at *The Jesus Saves and Cares Mission*. Here is a journal entry of an excursion to *Jesus Saves and Cares*.

A slanting drizzle, a coaxing spit – from the great Rainmaker– brings in a full house at the daily 7 PM "Praise the Lord" dinner. Saturday night and not an empty seat. God has welcomed the most desperate into his fold again.

We will be punished for our sins with sermons, anointed with hymns and several congregants will be saved. No food unless at least three stray lambs are saved.

A derelict in the front row, who is either schizophrenic or speeding on methamphetamines, waves his hands around his head fighting off imaginary insects.

Young derelicts under thirty giggle and fidget under the influence of one form of dope or another. Older derelicts howl in verse, occasionally puke, and testify to past "salvations", having jumped the gun by drinking the blood of Christ - transubstantiated from cheap wine: Red Mountain, Thunderbird, Ripple, Frazzle.

In the middle of a cacophonous hymn titled: "Come to Jesus", a wine-eyed front-rower turns to a laughing, hippieish hood and hoarsely growls: "Come! You cocksucker!"

The hippie-punk counters: "Hey old man! If I want to hear from an asshole, I'll fart."

Toward the end of the service, three drunks blaspheme while responding to the minister who asks us what number hymn we want to sing next.

"Hymn twenty-seven sucks; we sing that every night! I want number seventeen. It's my lucky number!"

"Fuck you Murphy! We're singing forty-four. I haven't had a fucken turn in a month."

"Screw you jerkoff! A scumbag like you don't deserve no turn."

A very wasted hippie loudly implores: "Hey you guys, Be cool! Let's all sing 'Give Peace a Chance.'"

Three drunks in counterpoint swear: "Fuck You Hairball!"

Finally the unbelievably blasé minister says "Gentlemen!" – which makes them all laugh and look around quizzically.

"Gentlemen, I shall choose...a very favorite of mine that brings peace to the most troubled of souls. Will you all please turn to Hymn number ninety-seven? We do not want our repast to be delayed any longer than necessary."

I look at Hooper and whisper: "Damn, I was just going to request the Mickey Mouse Hymn" – referring to an army insubordination hymn that goes: "Himmm. Himmm. Fucckkk Himmm." It was usually used when an obnoxious higher up gave an absurd order, and was now out of hearing range.

I simultaneously feel appalled and fascinated by this whole spectacle. A great deal of laughter punctuates the repartee. On some fundamental level it is uplifting to see how so many people in dire circumstances use laughter to soften their plights. God knows it helped me immeasurably to get through the army and Bear County Jail, not to mention countless Walker family dinners. Who cares if I got countless smacks for making jokes at the table? My parents were never able to extinguish my spiritedness. No wonder I seem to have a photographic memory for jokes.

Hate in the Haight

I am eating at St. Anthony's and a Hell's Angel clone sits down next to me. His facial expression and motorcycle colors accentuate the career criminal vibe that floods out of him. I rue the cutoff denim jacket that I am wearing. I found it in an alley the day before. Inside me, my mother scolds: "Real smart, Dumbo! Real smart...dress like crap and you'll attract flies!" Lamely I silently reply: *Hey, at least it was clean.*

This short, stocky biker is scary. He looks like a mechanic – who during a messy oil change – repeatedly pushed his hair behind his ears. His ears are potato fields, and his face slopes back from his nose like a rat.

This archetypal James Deanian hood leans way back in his chair teetering towards the horizontal. With his finest pissed off look, he relentlessly drags on his cigarette – puffing out huge volumes of smoke, like a car in desperate need of a ring job.

I know instantly that leaving would be a hazardous insult, so I default into listening and eliciting mode. He tells me: "My handle is Weeping Jesus." He emphasizes the two words of his name by jutting his chin up and out twice. Looking like an uprooted onion, his twenty-hair goatee chin then points at the ragged looking tattoo on his wrist: **Weeping Jesus**. Definitely jail-made. I repress a laugh when I notice that it is at least spelled correctly.

He also has this tattoo on the sizeable canvas of his swastika-befouled upper arm:

My Bike Is
My Life
My Wife
When It Dies
So Do I

He is condescendingly friendly in a controlled Doberman way. The writer in me manifests a genuine interest in him, but I am further disturbed when he joins me as I get up to leave.

Outside, Jesus offers me a tailor made cigarette – a nice treat and break from my roll-your-owns. As we walk down Market Street, I flick the butt of my cigarette with my thumb nail to dislodge the ash. To my horror the whole ember breaks off and sails like a mini-guided missile across the space between us – directly into his ear.

He screams likes a cat and hops like a swimmer dislodging water from his ear. I gasp and prepare and contract for pulverization. But he shakes it off and growls: "That's cool man. You couldn't have done that if you tried."

What a surprise! A bully with a touch of heart. I wonder what happened to him to turn him into such a poser. I wish I'd had the nerve to ask him how he got his name. I wonder if he was like me when he was younger – really wanting to be like Jesus. Who knows maybe he even got temporarily brainwashed into thinking he should be a priest?

Hooper and I are exploring the legendary Haight-Ashbury district. Hooper says: "What a sad place! How can the Summer of Love already be ancient history? It's only 1969?"

And indeed, as I look around I see heroin and speed junkies littering every intersection. He tells me the morning news said over forty people have been murdered here in the last six months. I nod my head at some creeps on the corner. "Yeah look at those drug-hustling sociopaths – all duded out like they're hippies."

Still, there are many lovely unique people cavorting around – garbed in a riot of color, an insurrection of style and an art show of unique self-expression. Although it's not always pretty, it's a relief to see people breaking out of the carbon copy fashion code of the 1950's. It's inspiring to see men dressing and coifing themselves with color and abandon.

My heart loves these people, but my brain imagines my mother sniping: "Surely one should have to a pay a fine for dressing like that!" She was a fashion Nazi. When we were driving in the car, the sight of someone imperfectly dressed, overweight, or unattractive was cause for her to blurt: "How come you can never find a gun when you really need it?" She got that line from two hardened, NYC policemen: her brothers. She hissed it out with five times the contempt that they did.

A guy decked out in banana yellow jeans, a bottle cap covered vest, a ginormous orange Afro and a "Kill the Machine" t-shirt complains loudly. "I hate these busloads of tourists polluting the Haight. These porky, crewcut-sporting straights think nothing of sticking cameras right in your face."

When he notices me noticing him, he gestures to a huge glittering psychedelic poster behind him advertising: *A Freaks' Bus Tour of the Suburbs*. He exclaims: "You dudes'll really dig this. It's far out, way cool and heavy!"

Like a carnival barker, he then bellows his spiel for us and anyone in earshot: "Watch the Straights manicure their lawns! See the women in curlers and men in Bermuda shorts drinking beer in the middle of the day. See their families with their two and a half children and their ticky-tacky boxes all in a row."

He focuses back on us at: "Man it's so groovy: The tour guide dude is this huge gorgeous hairy Viking freak and he stops the bus at every lawn with native straights on it. He pulls out his bullhorn and sociologically blathers about their strange customs, unhealthy eating habits and dreadful clothing.

"'Hippie tourists' then pop out of the bus laughing uproariously and photograph the stunned bourgeoisie with these super antique cameras."

Looking at me, he says: "I'll tell you what my man. I'll give you a special deal. If you come today, you won't even have to give us any bread."

"Man" I say, "That's some offer, but I gotta go make some bread givin' blood."

Getting Blood out of the Stoned

Just down from our hotel is a *Plasma and Blood Donor Station*. The vampirous station prays on the desperation of the alcoholics, druggies, and other indigents who populate Skid Row.

Without any training, I have become a professional plasma donor and donate my plasma twice a week. The blood collectors pay fifteen dollars a visit and throw in a tasty hot meal to sweeten the pot.

Hooper tries in vain to harass and shame me out of submitting to this gruesome, ninety minute process. "Wake the fuck up Walker! This is beyond stupid!"

A large needle is inserted in my vein and a pint of blood is extracted. In phase one the pint is centrifuged so that the liquid plasma rises to the top, making it easy to pour off. The precipitate of blood cells at the bottom of the pint is then combined with room temperature saline solution and mixed to make a new pint of blood. This pint is then transfused back into me making me shiver with cold. In phase two, this whole process is repeated again to get a full pint "donation".

As macabre as it is, I mostly like doing it. *For the experience...For the story.* Maybe I can spread the word about how poor people are being harvested for their plasma.

The money is also a motivation. I am in the process of redefining *frugal*, and anything I earn now will support my ambition of being jobless for as long as possible.

> My ambition – like a radiated homing pigeon –
>   is loose and lost in the dark.
> I can't find my locker
>   in the public change room of nine-to-five
>   where speed and efficiency
>   anxiously mine a dance of real engagement
>   to the rhythm of a year of weeks
>   who's prison bars are fifty.

Cataloging the Sins of Our Fathers

In San Francisco my experiences vacillate between the uplifting and the sordid. I look for the *holy* in both sides of *Duality* – in the continuums that stretch between sweet and bitter, belonging and lonely, succeeding and failing.

I am growing in my ability to sing and dance as I stumble through the blessings and curses of life's opera. Reading Walt Whitman has taught me to value both sides of life. Someday I'll marvel that he understood the explanatory power of Taoism's yin and yang.

I read like an addict from an explosion of novels written in a freer, more expansive style. In the parlance of the times, *my mind is blown* by Thomas Pynchon, Herman Hesse, Richard Brautigan, Kurt Vonnegut, Tom Wolfe, Ken Kesey, etc. One hilarious book by Richard Farina, *I've Been Down So Long, It Looks Like Up To Me*, helps me feel liberated from my encumbered past.

Free anti-establishment newspapers abound. Articles cataloging the sins of our hidden rulers steep me in enlightening political critique. I identify increasingly with the hippies who are exposing the crimes of our elders – especially those perched at the top of *The Military-Industrial Complex* [a term coined by President Eisenhower].

At the same time, I reject the counterproductive destructiveness of the naïve, temper-tantruming anarchists. Instead I gravitate toward the Utopian hippies who rave romantically about tribal love, dropping out and building a counter-culture.

The City by the Bay is rife with *Happenings*, consciousness-raising groups and free concerts in the parks. Big name groups like Santana, Jefferson Airplane and The Grateful Dead commonly play for free – dispensing the good vibes of their mind-expanding music just for the joy of it. Hugging is the new handshake and spontaneous group hugs are ubiquitous. We all luxuriate in the comfort of finally fitting in – of belonging to a tribe.

There is a revival of the human instinct to circle up. The large meadow in Golden Gate Park is a pastiche of groups hanging out, improvising music, dancing and wildly exercising Freedom of Speech.

Discussions about music, sex, cooperative living, going back to the land and ending the Vietnam War are hot topics. Nothing is too taboo to talk about. We rejoice about fully claiming our first amendment rights. How great to be free to challenge so many mindlessly held conventions of habit and thought.

CHAPTER 6

Lucy in the Sky with Diamonds

So far my love affair with life is looking like it will be a conventional love affair – rich, unpredictable and tumultuous.

I am reading *The Psychedelic Experience*, written by three Harvard professors: Timothy Leary, Ralph Metzner and Richard Alpert.

Psychedelic literally means *mind-expanding* – which translates in the vernacular as *mind-blowing*. Decades earlier in *The Doors of Perception*, Aldous Huxley described the psychedelic experience as a profound expansion of the faculty of perception.

Leary's book is a loose translation of the Buddhist classic, *The Tibetan Book of the Dead*. It is a practical guide for using LSD to have a spiritual experience…an experience of symbolic death and rebirth.

As I read I feel like parts of the old me are dying. I feel glimmers of the glorious spiritual awakening that it promises, especially as I recall my stunning acid trip with Cherry Miller in Texas.

I am ready for a solo flight on LSD! Hooper grants me sole use of the bargain basement apartment we are now renting on the edge of the Fillmore ghetto. I fast from eating all morning and read the short book again just before launch time.

I turn on the radio because music enhances the effects of LSD. Blessedly, there are three stations of commercial-free FM radio that play edifying music – counterculture musicians riffing on peaceful and loving themes and rhythms.

I lie down on the rug, swallow the tiny clear square of pristine *Windowpane* acid, and close my eyes. The waiting seems interminable, and my negative thinking makes me lousy company.

It seems as if an hour passes. A huge commotion grows inside me. Frightening images fill my inner sight picture…just as the book predicts.

I desperately want to open my eyes, but somehow I am able to stick with the authors' advice: "Do not shrink from the violent and repulsive imagery. It is a normal part of the process. Fully focusing on the frightening imagery will eventually resolve it."

Damn, this is ghastly! Fierce reptiles, razor blades, exposed viscera, bodies being pierced with sharp objects, slimy orifices – all increasingly marbled with demonic motifs. My senses of fear and danger crescendos, and just as I am about to panic and flee into distraction, the Beatles song: "Tomorrow Never Knows" comes on the radio:

> *Turn off your mind relax and float down stream*
> *It is not dying, it is not dying*
> *Lay down all thoughts, surrender to the void,*
> *It is shining, it is shining…*
> *Love is all and love is everyone*
> *It is knowing, it is knowing*

The images begin to morph into colorful patterns of ineffable beauty.

I startle when I hear myself gently laughing. The laughing grows into ecstasy as delicious tears roll down my face. Then suddenly like a silent, gentle nuclear explosion, my consciousness explodes out at the speed of light – centrifugally in every direction. I fill up all imaginable space, dissolving into All That Is.

I transcend into feeling loving oneness with everything. I merge with a magnificent, bodiless sense of spirit that is most certainly God. I perceive God as the loving beneficent energy from which all things emanate – and from which all things are made.

I merge with Oneness. Everything is sublime just as it is. Even the most awful aspects of human existence somehow make sense – part of an exquisitely intricate Whole. The cosmos is exactly as it should be. All pain and horror is a redeemable part of an exquisite pattern that is the blessing of a God of unsurpassable generosity.

I float in and out of lyrics and melodies that are celestial sacraments. All my questions generate instant transforming answers. I bathe in perfect understanding for hours. "Ask and ye shall receive!" is at my beck and call.

As the experience ebbs, I sit for hours digesting my journey and know that I am unalterably changed for the better. I feel unshakably certain that I will forever seek and cultivate attunement with a Higher Love – the underlying Oneness that connects all things.

Although this knowing eludes reason, George Harrison's words about his LSD experience convey a great deal. "I had such an overwhelming feeling of well-being that there was a God, and I could see him in every blade of grass. It was like gaining hundreds of years of experience in 12 hours." Paul McCartney later said: "The drug opened my eyes to the fact that there is a God…it explained the mysteries of life."

My LSD trip immediately releases me from my oath to never need anyone. I probably vowed to be a loner sometime in early childhood, but I didn't carve it into the stone of my heart until things didn't work out with Ruth.

I figured that although I generally liked people, I never felt comfortable with anyone. I found people alternately – and often simultaneously – frightening and fascinating. I believed there was no one who would not inevitably let me down.

But now I know that I am misinformed. LSD has shown me that pride in being a loner is indeed foolish pride. In response, I journal this:

> My heart like an anemone
> Closed its tentacles around
>   *the loner fantasy –*
>   one neuro-toxic fish.

>Like a lock-jawed oyster
>>I let in nothing
>>>with which to make a pearl.

>Now I unknot the filaments of my fear.
>>One by one, I shrink the cardiac freeze
>>>of my perpetual self-protection.

From here on in, I know it is all about Love. I will try to move towards rather than away from getting close to others. I am map-less and short on skills, but I will open more to connection.

My friend Lynn lends me, Erich Fromm's *The Art of Loving*. *What a guide book*! Each chapter opens me to a more multidimensional view of love.

Sadly, however, my social phobia is still huge. Learning to be in loving connection with others looks as if it will be a long drawn out journey. I pray to any Power that might be listening for roadside assistance. Perhaps introspection will be my tow truck.

Even sadder, I soon lose the specifics of how the tragic is a redeemable aspect of the Gift of Life. I guess normal consciousness cannot grok that everything has some value. Perhaps it is because there are awful things in life that it is Right Action to denounce and resist on this plane of existence.

I still, in 2017, feel that this LSD experience was the most transformative single event of my life. The perspective I acquired from this mind expanding event was the most profoundly *real* experience of my life. This sense of the Supreme Nature of Love was continuingly bolstered throughout my life via myriad meditations and thousands of caring human interactions.

LSD caveat

<u>So now for a vital disclaimer</u>: In my opinion, LSD and other psychedelics are not something to toy with. They can easily trigger disaster, especially when used in unsafe circumstances or in an anxious or depressed state of mind. Psychedelics can induce madness, and can be a springboard to suicide – especially if you have CPTSD. If you are contemplating ignoring this advice, please see Appendix 3, *Psychedelic Assisted Therapy*.

St Anthony and the Argonauts

A week after my trip, I am walking down Market Street headed for lunch at St Anthony's when a drunk asks me for a dime. I tell him I don't have one, and show him the nine cents in my pocket. My financial plan is to squeeze the blood out of one twenty dollar traveler's cheque every fortnight. Nine cents is all I have left for the next two days.

Instead of giving him my not-so-spare change, I tell him about the free lunch I am heading for, and invite him to join me. My progress is somewhat slowed by his drunken sashay, but we chat amiably along the way.

"I'm Pete" I say proffering my hand.

"My handle is Crash Daddy, and I am looking for a big old fattie." He is referring to a large sized joint.

"I can't help you with that either. I can roll you a cigarette though." I pull out my packet of Bugler rolling tobacco.

"Far out, man! That's heavy. Roll it fat would 'ya? I picked up the nickname, 'Crash-Daddy' in Nam 'cause I wrecked three jeeps in my first month there. Cost me my fucken driving privileges."

"I lucked out" I reply "and only spent four hours there. I took some military documents from Korea to Khe Sahn, and man that was scary enough for me. Everyone tells me Nam is a nightmare."

"I wouldn't know man. I did a full tour, but I was so high, it was like I wasn't even there. Got hooked up with some first class smack [heroin], and cruised the whole way. The withdrawal was hell though when I got back. I think I got that flashback shit from going cold turkey. I only do booze and weed now, but I'm still fucked up all the time."

We approach a bar, and he says: "Wait for me a minute, bro. I promise I'll be right out."

Sure enough he returns quickly, and hands me a quarter and quips: "I always score some change when I panhandle in there."

We enter the dining room at St Anthony's, grab a cafeteria tray and receive our victuals in the serving line. It is a red letter day because in addition to the usual fare: potatoes, beans and vegetable stew, we get a slice of ripe cantaloupe and a cob of corn.

We find a seat opposite a tall African-American hippie with a sweet face and a motor mouth. His visage is haloed by a huge Afro, which in turn is punctuated in the front with a red toothbrush. "My mustache comb" he quips as he pulls it out after dinner and restores his "stache" to something a long way from groomed.

Jimi [guess where he got that name] wears a green army dress coat with bells instead of eagle-emblazoned brass buttons. He has a mess of military ribbons with all major color tones duly represented.

He preaches: "I never go to *Jesus Saves and Cares* anymore – or any of those churches where attending the service is a prerequisite for dinner. I'll be damned if I'll do penance for my communion. Life is religion enough for me."

I've seen him before. Sometimes he wears a cape and simulates flight as he glides down Haight St. to the delight of all but the local "porcine enforcers of the law." He doesn't like to call them pigs for an undeclared reason. He tells us they've messed with him so many times that they're too bored to bother him anymore.

"They finally get I'm harmless. I'm gonna split now, and head down to City Hall for some free tobacco."

"Really, man? They giving out free tobacco there?"

"Yeah, dude, though they don't really know it. What ya got to be hip to, is exactly where and when to get it. I wait outside the courtrooms and people get called back in before they have time for more than a toke or two of their smokes. The ash trays are filled with stubs this long." His thumb and forefinger describe the length of an almost regular sized cigarette.

"I usually get a whole pocketful." He laughs an infectious baritone chortle. "And dude, I never heard of the man busting someone for shoplifting from an ashtray."

I take a poetry class at the Free University. I want a venue to focus more on my idea that poetry is either preserved emotion or vignettes of beauty frozen in time.

The course culminates when my friend, Lynn Peoples, and I publish a pamphlet of our poems. Entitled "Monday Moments," we sell copies for a quarter each outside The City Lights Bookstore in North Beach. One exhilarating evening we sell a hundred copies. Here's an e.e. cummings-style sample of my contribution:

> the scepter of golden gate bridge
>   slices the setting sun like butter.
> the windows of houses in the east
>   reflect its blaze –
>   tiny hearth fires
>   burning in the hills.
> i laze upon a marina beach
>   as the pacific fills the bay,
> fills my heart with greed to be aboard
> that freighter sneaking out of port.
> the sun suicides into the sea.
> the fires on the hill
>   become burnt toast.

Pete Walker

   alcatraz's lighthouse
       dares my yearning soul
            to surf the white wake
                  of the fleeing ship.

A hippie who is apparently trying to set a record for weird sits next to me at St Anthony's. He is either on speed or his own Bipolar brain chemicals. He is sporting a Mohawk that goes sideways from ear to ear – perpendicular to the traditional one that goes from front to back. He is actually quite handsome, but it is still an abominable hairdo.

People laugh spontaneously when they see him, but quickly cover it up if he looks their way. He's linebacker-sized with crazy fierce eyes, and you know at first blush that you don't want to piss him off.

He talks at the speed of light. Convinced that he is a trendsetter, he's winding up into a manic filibuster. "This style will be embraced by hippies all over as the next groovy thing. You mark my word man – you'll be seeing this haircut on TV before the end of the month."

The guy sitting across from us somehow gets a word in edgewise and takes a risk: "Yeah man, probably on a late night bail bond commercial."

"No, No Man! I'm not shitting you! I got this transmission directly from the Dog Star. I was meditating in the lobby of the Pyramid Building downtown. The apex is in exact alignment with Sirius, the brightest star in the sky. The Navahos say it's where the first people came from. And you know what man! Get this – the Pyramid Building is built on an old Miwok Indian burial site. Yeah man! And it's built right where the earth's mantle is at its thinnest. No shit! The electromagnetic energy of the molten core powers up through the building which is also on the exact spot on the earth where the six most powerful Ley Lines intersect. You know that the Ley Lines are the earth's acupuncture meridians – powerful energy pathways, man – and this spot is this incredible nexus because it corresponds with the earth's pituitary gland. When I got the visualization for this 'do', the magma intensified through this nexus and passed up through all seven of my chakras creating a visualization of this hairstyle in my mind. It then radiated this *Look* through my mind out into the unconscious minds of everyone in a fifty mile radius. When they see my 'do', the hip ones are all going to be activated into getting one…"

He's one of those self-obsessed people who frequently says: "…to make a long story short…" and really means: "to make a long story endless." I feel for him…he's radiating major pain and I sense that his loneliness dwarfs mine, but I have to rescue myself from his wacked out, grandiose rant or he'll drain me like low tide…leave nothing but mudflats. I stage a coughing fit and punctuate it with: "Let me let you let me go. I gotta go give some plasma."

My gradual morphing from *Beat* to *Hippie* is now a fait accompli. I value peace and love. I feel blessed to be part of a tribe of people who I instantly recognize, and who welcome me whenever we meet.

During this time, I shuck off mindless conformity and speak out against many harmful social norms, such as treating minorities, women and gays as second class citizens. My compassion grows for people living on the margins of society: the poor, the homeless, the mentally ill and other discards of capitalist society.

I reject crass materialism. I escape from the prison of always trying to look good – always trying to outperform others. My ability to be a good friend continuously grows. I increasingly care about other people and all planetary life. My expanding aesthetic sensibilities promote appreciating beauty over acquiring possessions. You don't have to own beauty to find it spread ubiquitously around you.

CHAPTER 7

On The Road Again

HOOPER COMES HOME with a paperback entitled: *The Book: On The Taboo Against Knowing Who You Are*. It is packed with the wisdom of philosopher, Alan Watts, and I am instantly immersed in his take on ancient Taoist, Buddhist and Hindu Thought.

Just having finished Bertrand Russell's *History of Western Philosophy*, I am blown away by how Watts' understanding of Eastern Spirituality turns Western Thinking a whiter shade of pale. Filled with practical advice for healthy living, it makes Western philosophy look like an arid intellectual exercise.

I vibrate with *knowing* when I read Watt's statement: *We cannot be more sensitive to pleasure without being more sensitive to pain.* LSD dramatically showed me that, especially as it helped me work through my jail trauma and face my inner demons. Since my glorious inner journey, I have felt much more put together.

I reverberate even more with this statement from Watts: *The only way to make sense of change is to plunge into it, move with it and join the dance.* Maybe I unconsciously attuned to this truth during my transition from student to soldier. And more recently, I was wowed by the jitterbug of going from beatnik loner to hippie tribe member.

My experiences on LSD resonate so thoroughly with Watt's writing that I dive into a passionate study of Eastern Spirituality.

I soon discover similarly minded acquaintances whose LSD trips also graced them with glimpses of what Eastern Ideology calls *Enlightenment*. We have many inspiring conversations, and I hear repeatedly that India is a new Promised Land.

"Spiritual" hippies imagine a populace that lives according to Eastern principles. Thousands of hippies are already there pursuing enlightenment and the freedom from suffering that so many Eastern pundits and gurus write about and promise.

I have many doubts, but I have to give it a shot. I will go to Europe and hitchhike the overland *Hippie Trail* to India. Worst case scenario, I will have more material for my book. And of course, I'll also allow myself to wander there lackadaisically…to check out any interesting diversions along the way.

The wisdom of Walt Whitman remains my essential fallback position. I paraphrase him in my journal: *I am not a lost soul searching; I am a lost soul delighting in the wonders of being lost.* Toasting Whitman, who loves to embrace contradictions, I also print J.R. Tolkien's insight on the cover of my current journal: "Not all who wander are lost".

Full Frontal Living

The world awaits, but how hard it is to leave! How can I leave my loving companion Susan Schmitt with whom I have been living the last three months? We have comforted and loved each other so tenderly. We have helped each other loose ourselves from the stifling bonds of our suffocating families.

Our favorite song is Bob Dylan's "All I Really Want to Do." We sometimes sing phrases from it to each other:

> All I really want to do
> Is, Baby, be friends with you
> I ain't lookin' to compete with you
> Simplify you, classify you
> Analyze you, categorize you
> Or disgrace you or displace you
> Or define you or confine you

I don't want to meet your kin
Make you spin or do you in
I ain't lookin' for you to feel like me
See like me or be like me
All I really want to do
Is, baby, be friends with you

I think back fondly to how we once sought lighthearted revenge for having too many experiences of Jimi Hendrix's famous line: "White collar conservatives pointing their plastic finger at me."

One day we decided to shock all the sexually uptight suits on the bus. Although we hippies were enjoying the dawn of the age of free love, premarital sex was still widely taboo. Even using the word "sex" in public conversation was scandalous.

So we boarded the 22 Fillmore bus, and I garnered the passengers' attention with my falling down the aisle act – stumbling to the rear with clumsy aplomb. Sliding into the back seat, Susan and I locked into a torrid embrace and loudly whispered sweet erotic nothings.

Three stops later, as we dismounted the bus, Sue said in mock sorrow: "I'm sorry, Pete, I couldn't afford to buy groceries this week because the birth control pills were so expensive." A highly perfumed business woman dressed to the nines scowled, and I fantasized that I could hear her pancake makeup crack.

What can say!? I was still developmentally stalled in adolescence.

Love the One You're With

Whoever you are come travel with me...
I swear to you there are things more
beautiful than words can tell...

--- WALT WHITMAN

I bid a bittersweet farewell to Sue with Hooper's favorite line of poetry: "Oh my sweet Susan! 'Had it been another lifetime.'" She replies: "Maybe we can meet up in Europe next summer." I agree: "I'd love that…and I hope it's in the cards."

I also have wistful goodbyes with Hooper and several other friends. Hooper says: "Hey Walker, you know how I love Kurt Vonnegut's line: 'Strange travel suggestions are dance steps from the gods'. Well I woke up with that in my head…AND that *Wizard of OZ* song was on the radio. It does seem strange indeed, but I think my intuition's telling me to travel back to Austin to see if I can 'find *it* in my own backyard.'"

We have one of those "manly hugs" with lots of back pats, but we both get a bit misty when I thank him for having been such a great Whitmanesque *companero*.

—m—

I have good hitchhiking luck all the way to New York City, but not much luck dodging the reemergence of that old hound dog, loneliness and depression. *How I miss and long for Sue.*

Thankfully, I find a Yugoslavian shipping line in NYC that offers "deck-class passenger space" on its freighters. I book passage on a tramp steamer that departs for Casablanca.

What a heartening surprise to board the ship on Thanksgiving Day, 1969 and discover that nineteen of the twenty-two passengers are of the hippie persuasion.

The cruise comes with three cafeteria-style meals a day. It is party-city for the whole cruise – hippie party style – laid back and mellow, with lots of wit, good conversation and jamming. Five of the travelers are accompanied by their instruments.

Carol, who teaches deaf children in San Francisco, teaches me sign language throughout the voyage. On the last night of the trip, she signs me: "Would you like to make love?" *Finally, being a good student pays off*. We find a private niche in the bow and make sweet love under the auspices of the Milky Way and a gazillion stars.

Our love-making initiates four rich months of hanging out together. We are further graced to be joined by her best friend, Jenny West – a born entertainer. Jenny is a professional actress on sabbatical from The American Conservatory Theatre in San Francisco.

Theatre flows out of Jenny as she dazzles us with her words, gestures, accents and famous lines. She loves to do Blanche DuBois from *A Streetcar Named Desire*. Mysteriously pulling a kilo-watt of energy out of the ethers, Jenny sultrily beams: "I have always depended on the kindness of strangers." Blanche is only one of the many characters into whom she fluidly morphs.

Bed-bugged

We arrive in Casablanca and share a room in a Less-than-Best Hotel. On the second night, we discover that we are covered with bedbug bites from the night before. Even worse, we are stuck in the room – too late to find alternate lodging, or medication for poison oak-like itching.

We move all the beds and furniture into the hallway. I make paste with water and *Goffio* [toasted corn flour cereal]. I spread the paste over hundreds of holes in the adobe walls to thwart the bugs from getting in.

We put on all our clothes to foil any bedbugs that might have secret passageways. Jenny pulls a double set of socks over each limb, and pulls her emptied cloth shoulder bag over her head. Carol and I look like eccentric war causalities with weird articles of clothing bandaging our hands and feet.

Our dread of being bug fodder for another night momentarily subsides as we cry with laughter at how ludicrous we look. Carol snorts: "You guys! I can't believe none of us has a camera!"

The Weird Tribe

Forsaking the *Marrakesh Express,* we hitch to its namesake the next day. Our Moroccan driver brings us to a large adobe house in the medina. We rent a five room wing of the second floor for three months at a guilt-inducing low price. Our friends from the ship soon fill all the rooms.

I think it was Nixon who first branded hippies as freaks and weirdos. To prove that these slurs could not hurt us, we ironically adopted the terms – kind of like gays co-opting "queer", techies "nerd" and African-Americans the "N" word.

Many of the hippies I know enjoy calling themselves "Hippie Weirdo Freaks." I love the Jimmie Hendrix song with the line: "I'll just wave my *freak* flag high, and say 'Hi! Hello!'"

So little by little by a lot, we become the Weird Tribe. I am Pee-Weird and my girlfriend Carol is Cara-Weird. She is twice named: once for Carol and once for the caraway seeds she sprinkles on her food to make her eyes glitter.

Rhea is Really-Weird, Sonya is So-Weird, Richard is Dick-Weird and Howard Cohen is How-Weird. He decks himself out in a vest fashioned from a *Made-in-the-USA* wheat sack. The words "Food from America" and "Not to be sold for profit" are emblazoned across its back. He says: "I bought the empty sack at the *Djama el Fna* Market for a dollar, and paid the same for a tailor to "in-*vest*" it for me."

How-Weird was a New York City underground radio disc jockey who organized an air pollution protest by getting his listeners to send their dirty snot to the president. Telling me all about it, he says: "It must have been pretty successful because one day two muscle heads in monkey suits visited me, and 'advised' me that my campaign needed to immediately cease and desist. I got so scared I decided to go native here in Morocco."

We are fifteen in all, not counting Cat-Weird – the marmalade cat that adopts us, and Mo-Weird [Mohammed], a young Moroccan who often hangs out with us. We amuse ourselves playing with the "Weird" concept a bit too long, but other travelers who visit us find it funny and often invent their own weird monikers.

We spend many hours reading, hanging out together and nude sunbathing on our private roof. This is my first experience with communal living, and I am happier than I have ever been. Weeks go by with rarely a ripple in my peace of mind.

After dinner every night, we read snatches of the things we've read or written. Everything imaginable is up for discussion. Being authentic feels like a drug, and using our voices as instruments in our jams, feels especially freeing.

We also like to riff on how our families would find our lack of productivity appalling. Years ago, Kerouac's *Dharma Bums* swayed me from worshipping at the Altar of Productivity. I now consider myself a Dharma Bum and I've identified "bumming around" and working as little as possible as key elements of my education and development.

At night we brag about how little we did each day. Making two excursions – like going to the post office *and* the market – is parodied as workaholic.

The *Djama el Fna*

We live a block from The *Djama El Fna*, a huge open square in the center of the city. Hundreds of local merchants lay large canvases on the ground from which they pedal their wares. There are snake charmers, snake oil salesmen and monkeys on short leashes that cavort for attention.

Ancient Arabic music twists and wends its entrancing rhythms everywhere. Sellers offer flotsam and jetsam that would be discarded in America – random machine parts, stacks of used eyeglasses, retired toothbrushes, exhausted kitchen implements and clothes that are fit for a skid row king.

One weathered old man – looking as if he just wandered in from a sandstorm – is a freelance dentist. His implements are a jar of alcohol, three pairs of pliers, and a dubious ball of something that might have once been cotton. Long rows of decayed, blood-encrusted teeth – so destroyed they look like they still ache – tell the tale of *A Thousand and One Arabian Extractions*.

There is also a pyramid of used false teeth. I squeamishly suffer empathy for an imaginary customer – teeth freshly pulled – trying to get his mouth around a pair of used choppers. I bet this neurotic fantasy relates to childhood damage from the nuns freaking us school kids out with gruesome stories of the Inquisition.

I revisit this stall periodically, ambivalently hoping to catch Dr. Pliers procuring his trade. Fortunately and unfortunately, I never catch him in the act.

My favorite stalls belong to the storytellers who nightly mesmerize large crowds. I cannot understand a word of their deep throated Arabic, but I make some sense of their impassioned oratory.

The emotional responses of the audience are richly complex – laughter, tears, wonder and brief moments of what looks like terror. I feel frissons of excitement shimmer through the crowd. Clearly these voyagers are being taken on wondrous journeys by these tale-telling wizards.

Occasionally I feel as entranced as the kids and adults who watch in hyper-focused entrancement. One night I have a brief scary presentiment that armored Knights are about to ride in any minute to slaughter Infidels like me.

Everywhere I walk in the market, friendly circles of men hail me over for a chat. They spout strings of French phrases, signaling a language where we might meet. When I join them, they pour me hot mint tea from a teapot held two feet above my glass and then offer me a bowl of kief to smoke.

They are master communicators and the scarcity of shared vocabulary is hardly a hindrance. Much mime, pigeon French and laughter elaborate our interactions. In the courtyard of the building where we stay, I see similar banter in the gaggle of women who do the household chores as if they are playing.

The harmony and bonhomie of these people is heartwarming. Even the few beggars look hearty, as they are universally treated with kindness, generosity and respect.

Looking for Traces of Dr. Livingstone

Our three month lease on the medina apartment is up. How disappointing that our traveling Muses pull us in different directions. I have had three months of almost perfect contentment here, by far my longest period without a nosedive into depression.

I'm uneasy about leaving this lovely created family. I hope that my new contentment lasts. Perhaps it's a reward from all my reading about Eastern spirituality.

Before travelling north to pick up the Hippie Trail to India, I want to see more of Africa. Six of us crowd into Ern-Weird's VW bus, which is painted with intricate Aztec hieroglyphs and symbols. Ern-Weird is a Viet Nam vet and aspiring writer who looks like a clone of the young Ernest Hemmingway.

We meander slowly down the African coast. On the third day, herbalist-wannabe Jenny slices a cactus to taste its juice. She instantly crumples to the ground screaming and writhing in pain – petrifying all of us. Feeling the awful shame of helplessness, I silently invoke the gods to "Goddamn do something!"

Only *Chronos* answers the call: the passage of a few hours alleviates Jenny's symptoms. Surfacing from her delirious fugue she quips: "I don't think I'll try that drug again. It can't be the one Carlos Castaneda wrote about." She's referring to his book, *Don Juan: A Yaqui Way of Knowledge,* the would-be shaman's bible for experimenting with psychedelic desert plants.

We camp on a tiny beach in the late afternoon. How-Weird and I jump into the rough surf, swim out a dozen strokes and are swept by a powerful invisible force to the south. We fight for our lives to resist being swept over to the jagged rocks where the surf is crashing viciously. Something nasty seems to be pulling at my legs.

When we finally reach the safety of the shore, an inner voice makes me shiver as it plaintively asks: *Why do you keep trying to kill me?* Marrakesh's utopian glow is crumbling fast.

Several nights later we pull up outside of Tan-Tan, the southernmost town in Morocco. I hate making camp at night, especially when it's moonless, but we have a date with some supply trucks that are leaving early in the morning. They will cross a three day stretch of the Sahara and take us to catch a ferry to the Canary Islands.

So we spill out of the van, unroll our sleeping bags and drift into sleep. When we awake the next morning, two large Arabs pass by perched precariously on top of tiny donkeys. From deep inside their voluminous robes, we hear them chuckling as if they are witnessing something wonderfully funny.

Perhaps they have not seen hippie weirdo freaks before. But then, three more Arabs with enigmatic smiles approach us and ask in pidgin French: "Why you sleep in garbage?"

I get out of my sleeping bag to look around and feel as embarrassed as if I had walked into a convent with my fly open. Fortunately there is no raw refuse in this desert dump, but the mummified carcasses of dead animals are quite alarming. Thankfully they are so desiccated that they do not smell. Even better they are not maggoty.

We roll up our sleeping bags alongside bleached bones, rusty tin cans and unidentifiable bits of detritus, and drive to the center of the small town to wait for the trucks.

When the trucks arrive, they are so old and ramshackle that I think: *You really do want to die don't you. Some century they'll find you and your friends mummified like crispy critters in the middle of nowhere.*

To which I silently respond with my standard: *Hey! You can't live forever.*

The two ton trucks are filled with supplies – mostly vegetables for El Aiuun, the capital of Spanish Sahara.

The truck beds are fenced in and covered with large tarps. We lounge on the tarps and are enamored with a goat that stands in an open space at the back. The pupils of his glowing yellow eyes are long narrow vertical slits. Mesmerized by his spooky placidness, How-weird can't resist. "Lets' call him Goat-Weird…I mean he really is *weird*. I like him but he's kind of creepy, in a soft satanic sort of way."

We follow an invisible track into desert that is nothing but sand and dunes, unlike any of the thinly vegetated American deserts I hitched across. We drive all day and into the night. Lying on my back on the tarp, I gaze at a sky replete with stars. Two crawling satellites – miming stars – write their signatures across my sight.

> The sky exults in a purity of black
>   free from the Judas city lights
>   that grey the black
>   and abandon the dimmer stars.
> Glittering ebony stretches
>   in dome directions
>   to all arcs of the horizon.
> I float in a boundless scintillating sky.
> Infinite dark sprouts a glut of stars.
> My eyes take me by the hand
>   into the 3-D stelliferous night.
> I am in heaven celebrating in a festival of stars.

The trucks head out again in the pre-dawn light. We soon come to sand so soft that the truck's wheels do nothing but spin. The drivers pull out long two foot wide planks of PSP [perforated steel planking], and lay them in front of the wheels. They drive across the narrow strips, stop, and move the long planks in front of the wheels again.

    It takes an hour to cross an area no longer than a football field. *Fear begins to "harsh my mellow"*. Will this be the pace for the rest of the trip? Are the drivers lost – high on kief and leading us to die of thirst in the middle of nowhere?

    Hours later the wheels find harder sand and we pick up the pace. When the day begins to cool, the drivers make camp in a wind sculpted valley of voluptuous dunes. With relaxed efficiency, they cook a delicious tagine and couscous meal over the campfire.

We eat with relish – and with our hands. Food prepared outdoors – no matter how basic – always seems to enliven my taste buds. Though I did nothing to get us here, I feel a self-congratulatory sense of satiation and accomplishment.

We are luxuriating in the sunset when Jenny wonders about Goat-Weird's whereabouts. She searches the small camp, thoroughly checks both trucks and finally asks a driver, who jovially points to her stomach.

Jenny takes a few seconds to get his meaning, and ever-dramatic, loudly vomits the delicious meal off to the side. The drivers act as if they have never seen anything so funny. The rest of us go macho and subdue our nausea to avoid the disgrace of chundering.

We arrive at El Aiuun's deserted beach on the third day and camp above the high tide line of marine debris. We want to drink in the negative ions of the waves as thoroughly as possible. No one knows what kind of ions they are – oxygen, water vapor, ectoplasm? But all good hippies know they are there and they are healing.

Late in the day we watch a sunset that redefines *glorious* and I journal this:

> With handfuls of color
> Purloined from the sunset sky
> Silver waves,
>   frothy fingerprints of the sea,
>   swath Turner masterpieces
>   upon the foamy shore

I awake in the wee hours to a wet sleeping bag. It cannot be raining. There is no way that I have I wet myself – but *way*: the surf is breaking on my feet and tugging on our packs and various unpacked possessions.

I leap up and raise the alarm. We rescue everything but Swedish Scanda-Weird's canteen and her copy of Tom Wolfe's *The Electric Kool-Aid Acid Test*. Scanda-Weird exclaims: "This is God telling me not to read your crazy hippie bible!"

To top it off, we learn that the ferry service was recently canceled. I feel frustrated but soon decide that it's okay because I've gotten too far off the road to India. *Besides cul-de-sacs can be fun.* I refocus on the prospect of enjoying the return trip through the stunningly monotonous Sahara desert.

FEZ

From Tan-Tan, we hitch back to Marrakesh. Feeling quite melancholic, I bid my fine companions adieu. I love Morocco so much that I take the long route to Europe by travelling east through the Atlas Mountains.

Wearing an all-white uniform, a ski soldier, who calls himself Mohammed Ski, responds to my thumb and takes me high into the mountains. Like so many Moroccan men, he is sweet and vibrantly alive. Small talk is not my favorite sport but he is so relational that we eke out a warm chat from our shared pigeon French.

Then, in the middle of nowhere, Mohammed drops me off as he detours to his remote outpost, up a road that only he can see.

I sit on my backpack in a starkly beautiful and forsaken place until nightfall, and *nary a car do I see*. It has not rained once in the five months that I have been in North Africa, and I no longer cover myself with my waterproof poncho when I sleep outside.

My shivering awakens me. I am dangerously drenched and on the verge of hypothermia. In an ongoing drizzle, my vain attempts to get a fire going almost exhaust my matches. Desperate, I climb up into the heart of an evergreen tree and find enough dry dead branches to get my fire going.

All this unfolds in quietude, but once again I come perilously close to dying. The drizzle turns to sleet and without a fire to dry me out, I would likely have succumbed to the elements.

Yet another vehicle-less day! Nothing passes me in either direction. Mercurial as my moods have always been, I am pleasantly surprised to find myself low-key content this dusk. I sit by my small fire and eat my emergency rations – crackers, sardines and foil covered triangles of processed cheese – the hardtack of my entire journey. For dessert I treat myself to the sumptuous view.

>Black clouds tumble in from the west.
>Bullying the mauves and purples out of the sunset.
>Tiny white ghosts – sun-bleached snail shells –
>>cling like acrobats to swaying lacey weeds.
>
>Like Lilliputian statues
>>the tiny specters claim thrones of glory,
>>>in a field of papery lilac flowers.
>
>The fields below glow purple, ecru, licorice, chartreuse
>>undulating in luscious wind-sculpted curves.
>
>I gaze into the bleeding out sunset and blow some loneliness on my harp.

Last night my blues felt mellow, but I wake up morbidly lonely. Alienation nags me incessantly as another day goes by without a ride. I am in withdrawal from my Moroccan feast of human warmth, and my hindsight rues the lack of research that would have saved me from getting stranded here.

My hitchhiking success suddenly zooms to one hundred percent as the first vehicle to come my way in four days picks me up. Three New Zealand freaks in a Landrover greet me: "You look like a Biblical prophet that the cat dragged in from the desert." God knows I am hairy enough to look like one.
 These three lovely Kiwis are a cornucopia of gab. We wear out language in a long meandering drive to Tangier. Three days pass before they

drop me at the ferry terminal at the Strait of Gibraltar. Nigel shakes my hand like a pump: "Ya gotta come visit us in Wellington, mate. We'll show ya some real mountains there!"

I feel so sad sailing across the Strait…so sad to see sweet Morocco shrinking into the distance. What an unparalleled loving experience I had living with the Weird tribe in Marrakesh. *Those people really liked me. They were really interested in knowing me and honestly showing themselves!*

I've never felt so thoroughly and generously accepted and appreciated, and not once in all that time did I pump myself up with alcohol to invoke a feeling of worthiness. Nor for that matter did anyone else.

CHAPTER 8

Pilgrimage to an Unholy Land

Pain on the Plain in Spain

When I disembark in Spain, a pack of customs agents dump my rucksack on the littered floor and rake through its contents. Finding nothing, they lead me into a back room where a guard who is as wide as he is tall growls: "Bend over and spread your cheeks, hippie!"

Two guards squat behind me for anal viewing – to see if I am butt-smuggling any drugs. *How I wish I could fart!* Visibly disappointed, they find nothing. As self-destructive as I am, I am not suicidal. I've heard too many stories of hippies wallowing in Spanish prisons for years for a single joint. One poor bastard reputedly got jailed for a single seed.

I graduate from customs and am soon on the road. I walk backwards all day with my thumb out in a ride-begging position trying to escape the city of Algeciras.

If looks could kill, I am exponentially dead. Countless drivers speed up to let me know they are passing me in a huff. Shades and whispers of the American Deep South. I feel lonely as a turnstile.

Thankfully shanks' mare gets me to the city outskirts before nightfall. Relieved, I find myself a place to bed down in a copse of small trees by the road.

Bob Dylan's "Rolling Stone" echoes and reechoes through my mind. "How does it feel to be on your own – like a rolling stone – with no direction home – like a rolling stone – how does it feel?"

It feels pretty damn awful right now. It sucks – if that's a feeling. I sure wish there was some moss on this stony ground to cushion my body. *What a sorry ass excuse for a bedroom!*

In the last vestiges of light, I journal:

"No man is an island" unless of course
   he's surrounded by a reef of loneliness.
I am an island of water in an unnamed sea
   stranded inside a reef
      that births enormous breakers
         that smash me with liquid despair
            and icy self-despication.

I am about to set a new depth record for depression. My makeshift campsite is a wicked place to unfurl the old mummy bag. As I lie dozing atop it in the sweltering summer heat, a squadron of mosquitoes tears into me. I retreat into the steam bath of my bag, zipping it up so only my mouth peaks out. I sweat the long night away – not catching another wink.

In the morning, my sleeping bag is soaked. *Damn! It feels five pounds heavier!* I wonder if when it dries, it'll be ounces heavier from the salt.

Back to hitchhiking. I stand everlastingly in the hot sun, sick of the sight my thumb. I feel beat and empty, as dead as a snail shell filled with hot sand. My brain mocks me: "On the Road!? You sure are – seems like you're homesteading on this piece of it. At this rate you'll be five years older by the time you get to France."

I finally get to Madrid and have my first redeeming Spanish experience – the incomparable Prado Art Museum. The faces of the soldiers torturing civilians in Goya's horrific anti-war paintings remind me of the nasty customs agents.

I hitch to Barcelona. The psychedelic architecture of Gaudi bejewels the city and gives me a natural aesthetic high. The breathtaking beauty of his fluid structures however cannot dispel my Spain-a-phobia. I'm sinking beneath the waves of hostile glares from the citizenry. I cannot get out of here fast enough.

It is the high heat of summer, and Europe is infested with straight tourists pointing their arsenal of cameras at the famous sights...and at me – the hirsute hippie.

I feel like I am going through my savings like a binge eater devouring a gallon of ice cream. The data in *Europe on 5 Dollars a Day* seems hopelessly out of date, but it serves well in all the toilet paper-less public bathrooms. How I relished wiping my butt with the pages of Madrid.

Finding safe places to sleep outdoors in every city is beyond challenging. I'm so sleep-deprived I'm practically hallucinating – dreaming with my eyes open. Doing Europe on the cheap is going to have to be a blitz.

I hitch on and the highlights of Paris, London, Edinburgh, and Amsterdam sometimes remedy my funk. In Paris, I am mesmerized in the Impressionist Museum for hours, and leave with Claude Monet permanently enshrined in my mind as the sultan of light and color. His pageants of flowers make me want to be a gardener.

My nostalgia for Morocco is gnawing in my gut by the time I visit the famous Amsterdam nightclubs where cannabis is legal. Repulsion floods me at the sight of rooms littered with vegetating hippies – so zonked and overdosed from smoking hash that they can barely talk or move. *How can so many hippies let their newly found vibrancy deteriorate into a hash coma?*

Scalped in the Alps

I myself am overdosed – with sightseeing. I declare a personal moratorium on tourism and hitch to the Swiss village of Saanen where an Indian Guru holds court in a gorgeous meadow of the Alps.

Krishnamurti is a Westernized Indian who was groomed by the Theosophical Society to be *The New World Teacher*. Although he eventually renounced their plans, he wrote many books about the meaning of life. My Weird Tribe friends and I were wowed by *Freedom from the Known*.

I love these passages: "It is no measure of health to be well adjusted to a profoundly sick society" and "There is no end to education. It is not that you read a book, pass an exam, and then finish your education. The whole of life from the moment you are born to the moment you die is a process of learning."

Saanen is a huge wild flower garden. I camp with twenty other hippies in a meadow exploding with color. Wandering there sparks my lifelong passion for *wild-flowering* – for combing new places in search of blooms I've not yet seen.

Living with hippies again feels like a flannel blanket on a soft couch with a warm dog and a hot fireplace. We are however, a small minority of Krishnamurti's fans. When we go to his first talk, I am shocked by the evidence of his wealth and that of his devotees. Many appear to be old world, ruling class types with upper lips so stiff you could use them to cut toast. Even their outdoor seating is elegant.

Krishnamurti arrives in a cavalcade of pristine Mercedes Benzes. When he steps out in an expensive white, three piece suit, my heart takes a nose dive. My brain swoops down like a bird to prevent it from crashing. Reassuringly it rationalizes: *These are probably necessary accoutrements of his trade. When he speaks we will be treated to the crystalline wisdom of his books.*

Would that it were so! But no, he carries himself and speaks with the postured dignity and accent of a British toffee-nosed, bowler-hatted twit. Even worse, he seems as depressed as I was on the side of the road outside Algeciras.

On and on, he drones in a somnambulistic murmur. His memorized speech is as worn out as threadbare underwear. I feel terrible sadness from and for him. He is a brilliant writer but how has it helped him? He seems to be an empty husk – unworthy of being emulated.

I try listening to him again on the second day, hoping that my mood might have made me judge him unfavorably. But it is agonizingly the same. I heard better sermons back in childhood from senile Monsignor Dillon at St. Luke's.

But all is not lost. Nearly all my new friends are equally alienated. Krishnamurti may not be heaven sent, but it feels as if we are in a heavenly place. The countryside has trails that ramble into one stunning nature vignette after another. We spend the rest of the month enjoying and exploring natural beauty and the delight of getting to know each other.

I leave Saanen with my new German friend, Rolf Kunz, who wants to accompany me to India. Rolf is a snow white blonde with a gold fish face and a soul of profound silliness. He is a zephyr of happiness – a descendant of the Muse of humor. He makes me laugh at things I usually judge as lame or immature.

Somehow Rolf convinces me to visit his parental units before we head off to Asia. I am impressed that he sells me on it, as I have been parent-phobic since I left home.

Frankfurt – leveled by bombing in World War II – is a terrible shock. What sprang up from the rubble is the ugliest ferro-concrete city I have ever seen. Devoid of decoration, design and color, it is the definition of rectilinear. I paraphrase Shakespeare to Rolf: "My kingdom for a curve."

Rolf's parents' friendliness is chilling. As with Pete Hooper's mother back in Texas, they act as if I am taking their baby away to join a satanic cult. Over the next few days however, they warm to me and buy us both a train ticket to Istanbul. I suspect they are hoping that Turkey's foreignness will shock Rolf "Off the Road."

Dave's on First

The bi-continental city of Istanbul is punctuated by the grandeur of two colossal mosques. Defying this symmetry, a sprawling *medina* swaths its undulating hills. A feast of exotic smells, colors and tastes adorns the city's bazaars, souks and open-air markets.

Hypnotic entanglements of Levantine music seem to tell us where to turn in our explorations of the city. I feel like a stranger in a strange land – a delighted stranger in a mystical land. The natives are aloof but not unfriendly. Every day we wander for hours with our new friend Dave, another hippie Vietnam Vet.

Dave sports an impressive mop of blonde hair by way of his Nordic ancestors, and like me he has a big red beard, probably from some Scotsman in his woodpile. Dave's *joie de vivre* is way more constant than mine. Mine comes and goes at the whim of a part of me I have yet to meet– a part as stingy as my parents.

Dave loves to sing and launches his melodious voice at the drop of a hat. He does great versions of Iggy Pop's "Lust for Life" and his upbeat downer: "I'm Bored...I'm the Chairman of the Board."

Dave jokes that he is an honorary member of the rock group, *The Flying Burrito Brothers*. "I'm tall and lean, and pretty hot and spicy." He does look good, wearing the nicest pair of Levis I've ever seen, and I tell him so. Instantly he pulls another pair out of his pack and says: "Here, Pete, we're virtually twins in body type. You'll look great in these, and no offense man, those pants of yours deserve a dishonorable discharge. They wouldn't even qualify for a Christian burial."

Although I'm prone to being oversensitive, I can't help but laugh. I'm so cheap I never buy anything new for myself, and can't even remember where I got these fourth-hand pants.

But I am so disbelieving of his generosity that he has to reassure me three times that he's for real. "Really! No shit, my man. My pack's way too heavy. You're doing me a favor."

I am blown out and overcome with gratitude. This is the most wonderful present I've ever been given. I'm embarrassed that I am a bit teary, but thank him as if he has just given me the Dalai Lama's secret formula for enlightenment.

—⚏—

Dave and I love discussing contemporary literature. We trade novels with each other and fellow travelers who continually replenish our reading material.

We also love to jam creatively on the ever-changing stream of new people, sights and events. Sharing an ironic, but contempt-free sense of humor – we marvel more than we judge, although we generally like the native people better than our middle-class countrymen, whose 1950's values we reject.

Dave and I become best friends. I am totally at ease with him. *I EVEN feel comfortable when we're not talking – perhaps for the first time ever!*

―ɯ―

In an Istanbul coffee shop, travelers coming from India tell us that we'd be stupid to hitchhike through Turkey or Iran. New friend Joel says: "Dudes! Two hitchhikers were robbed and killed in eastern Turkey last year. I'm not shitting you! It's lawless man. No cops, no soldiers, no protection! And in Iran, drivers stop but they charge much more than the bus."

So Dave, Rolf and I purchase a three day passage on a tramp steamer across the Black Sea to Trabzon in Northeast Turkey. I feel swaddled by the rock and sway of the sea...as I did on the cruise from New York to Morocco. Someone later tells me it is a "back to the womb thing", but I think my in utero experience was spoiled by nicotine and alcohol. The sea's comfort somehow feels more ancient and primordial to me.

From Trabzon we bus it to Tehran. We cram our tall frames into child-sized seats for over twenty-three hours – a grueling trip of dust, sweat, and butt bruises from the bus's dead shock absorbers. Bullet holes riddling several of the passing vehicles unnerve us. Somehow we manage a reasonable ebb and flow of good spirits as various body-cramps come and go.

Tiptoeing Through Tehran

It is 1970 and Tehran is scary. Nothing but bad vibes. Danger and hostility radiates everywhere. This is much worse than Spain. We are magnets for contempt – not because we are hippies, but because we look American. Poor Rolf gets glommed in with us, which is ironic because the militant Arabs hate the Jews so much that they glamorize Germans as Jew-killers.

Anti-American sentiment is seething. An angry demonstrating mob engulfs us as they pass. I feel panicky. I loudly whisper: "Shit, you guys, I hope they don't substitute us for those effigies of Uncle Sam that they're beating the shit out of." Lickety-split, we grab the next bus east.

The trip to the Afghanistan border is hours shorter but more punishing because of our already meat-tenderized hindquarters. On the ride, I meet Michael – a savvy Englishman with whom I have the best single conversation of my life. Our talk is an anthem of authenticity – no taboos, no holds barred. Everything is fair game and nothing is too heavy to talk about. We jam on our childhoods and our loves, hates, losses and most embarrassing moments – continuously riffing off of each other.

Michael says: "I'm so ambivalent about this hippie partying thing – so much reliance on alcohol and drugs. Sometimes getting high feels so spiritual. Like it connects me to something much *Bigger* and *Better*. At times I even feel like heaven is right here on earth…But then I feel so shitty when I wake up the next day."

"I hear you man," I echo. "I hate that awful feeling of waking up feeling like you've been cast out of heaven and express-trained to hell!"

"Yeah," responds Michael, "and the hellish hangovers are not even the worst of it. Because of my Catholic brainwashing, I get all swallowed up in guilt and self-judgment for days. And even worse, everyday reality just pales …everything seems like purgatory. And if I don't get high again, it takes me a week of being straight before I regain my normal appreciation of life and its little everyday wonders. "

I laugh: "I hear ya. I'm almost glad I got hepatitis in San Francisco. I haven't had a beer in over a year, and I think what you're saying is why I rarely even feel tempted to drink anymore."

Our dialog is pure fun – energizing to the same degree that listening to a narcissist is draining. The sum of our interchanges far outweighs the sum of our separate contributions.

How disappointing that Michael can't join us in our travels. He says: "I would dearly love to, but I have to get back to England, mate. You see, I'm almost broke – down to only a few quid. But my sweet lass has posted me a plane ticket, and I am off to the embassy in Delhi to pick it up. I will fly – tout suite – back to London, and bath in her affection in me old digs. If we're really lucky her parents may even support us in a manner to which I'd like to become accustomed."

With Friends Like These...

Dave, Rolf and I decide to stay in Mashhad – the last Iranian city before Afghanistan. We want to explore the remnants of the old Moghul Empire – elegant turquoise mosques highlighted and sheathed in elaborate mosaic arabesques.

We book a room in the only hotel open to foreigners. I meet lovely French Nadia, who is trying to get her boyfriend out of the local jail, where he is imprisoned for possessing hashish.

I am the moth welcomed by Nadia's flame. In the light of a candle, she shows me a topless photo of herself, and suddenly the room heats up.

She has less English than I have French, and my French is Moroccan – deemed so inferior by Parisians, that I couldn't even order a cup of coffee. But we communicate well enough via playing cards and flirting.

On the second night Nadia asks me to accompany her to score some hash from her good Iranian friend. Every cell in my body screams *do not go you idiot!* Every cell except the gonadal ones. [As I write this I flash on the male tee-shirt with the phrase: "I'M WITH STUPID" above a big arrow pointing down toward the crotch.]

We go outside and her friend is in a car with three other men. Four of the five voices in my head say: "Don't Get In!" But of course I go with the dissenter. We get in the back seat. We sit between the good friend on one flank and a guy who looks like a large Mexican wrestler on the other.

The driver takes us out of the city and when he stops the car in the middle of nowhere, my fear intensifies into nausea. I wonder if throwing up on the guys in the front seat will stop whatever horrible thing is about to go down.

Sure enough the *good* friend pulls out a five inch blade and points at her mouth and his penis, and cackles the world's sleaziest laugh. Panic implodes within me like a super-virus. I know I have to try to disarm this guy, and I know I am going to get cut.

Then something even more shocking happens. As I am I bracing myself to dive over her onto him, she suddenly bursts out laughing and coquettishly slaps him in the face: "You silly boy. You so funny!"

An instant later – an eternal instant– all four of the men join her in deep resonating laughter as if this is all a hilarious joke. The tension immediately evaporates [except in me] and I join in with the phoniest laughter I have ever heard come out of my mouth. I sound like a castrato who has just hit his personal best in a high note competition.

I think later that her defusing of the situation was the first act of real magic I have ever seen. I am also grateful and amazed that my underwear is still clean.

The driver takes us out to a small hovel that seems like it is made out of the desert itself. The friend goes in and comes out a minute later with a lima bean sized piece of hash, and presents it to her like an engagement ring. She rewards him with a kiss on the cheek that thrills him, and we are soon back at the hotel.

Restored to sanity, I decline her invitation to smoke the hash. Hash made me paranoid the few times I tried it before, and in the state I am currently in, I fear it will schitz me out. And who knows? Anyone of the guys in the car could be a narc who's about to barge in and bust us.

With painful ambivalence, I decline her invitation to spend the night.

The Stans

We pay for a ride on what looks like it might be the original truck, and cross the Afghani border to Herat. The small city looks like it has grown up organically out of the desert – like evolved stalagmites with a capacity for semi-intelligent design.

With barely a trace of modern civilization, Herat combines several clichés: older than the hills, the middle of nowhere and poorer than dirt. Its one store, remotely like a 7/11, features less than twenty different products, the most noteworthy being a row of coke bottles. For a second I think about splurging until I notice that the bottles are filled to markedly different levels. Ralf also notices and mock-shivers saying: "They probably refilled those bottles with dye and camel piss!"

Heavily bearded, turbaned and swaddled in cotton fabric, all the men in town have ancient rifles slung over their shoulders. They are gruffly and laconically friendly – yin versions of the extroverted Moroccans.

One ancient biblical looking guy invites us into a small mud brick building that contains an enormous rainbow hookah, elaborately decorated with semi-precious jewels, silken braids, colored electrical tape and filigreed metal work.

The hookah is on a small throne encircled by a narrow three inch spitting gutter. Pressed up against the walls are eight older Afghani men. We are introduced and a bowl of peppercorn-sized pieces of hash is prepared and put in the hookah.

Our host fires it up and exhales a smokescreen that hides his whole head. He coughs like a thunderclap and spits out huge gobs of mucous, colored in hues I have to look away from.

Dave is first up, and needs no encouragement to engage in this less than quaint native custom. He exhales and then appears to be coughing himself to death. The Afghanis are delighted and express further approval when he hawks up something too awful to describe.

When they finish laughing, Dave exclaims: "God I feel so paranoid, I think people are out to help me!" Ralf and I laugh, but from here on in Dave gets paranoid whenever he smokes. Like an on/off switch, hash or pot lights up his paranoia and only sleep returns him to sanity.

Rolf then reprises Dave's performance. Everyone looks at me. *How can I diplomatically abstain?*

With few common words, my awkward pantomime intensifies their goading until I use my finger to make the circular crazy sign around the temple of my head. When I add my other hand to point at my forehead, they thankfully laugh and get off my case.

The anti-climax comes with another round of deep level lung destruction, and everyone sinks back against the wall into zombie-like oblivion. Dave and Rolf are too wasted to utter a sound.

It is Amsterdam revisited, and I will see this sad scene reenacted in countless hotel rooms over the next year that I spend in the "Stans" – Afghanistan, Pakistan and Hindustan [India]. More typically however, a small pipe called a *chillum* replaces the hookah.

Rolf soon finds hash as deadening and unappealing as I do. Gratefully, we meet other travelers who do not disappear into the cannabis haze. Like us they are more intrigued with exploring the rich wonders of the East.

Herat is a blip on the trail. We re-cock our thumbs aiming for a ride to Bamiyan, our new destination in Northeast Afghanistan.

We arrive one evening to find a small village lit only with kerosene lanterns. Haunting Arabic music creates a comforting mystique in the tiny central bazaar. We drink numerous cups of tea in a local chi shop and enjoy primitive conversations with the locals.

When we awake the next morning we are greeted by huge Buddhas carved into the face of the vertical cliff behind the village. Bamiyan was the center of an ancient Buddhist society, long ago displaced by Muslims. The vertical cliffs that flank it are honeycombed with caves that formerly housed meditating monks.

The largest Buddha – the tallest in the world at one hundred and seventy five feet – is awe-inspiring. Moved by this Buddha, I immerse myself in two books I recently acquired via trade: Christmas Humphreys' *Buddhism* and Herman Hesse's legendary *Siddhartha*, the story of Buddha's life.

The former is filled with truths that I realized on LSD, and I am initiated on the spot into a lifelong love of Buddhism. Though I never become a Buddhist, the seeds have been sown for my ensuing lifelong practice of Buddhist meditation.

Dave talks us into hitching further north to Mazar Sharif. "I know you guys will dig seeing the Grand Blue Mosque, and I want to be able to tell people that I got within a pubic hair of Russia." [The Cold War is still quite hot].

When we arrive, our eyes feast on the breathtaking Mosque, until Dave points to a flock of pure white doves in the street winnowing undigested wheat kernels from steaming piles of horse manure. He quips: "Reminds me of Nixon in a white suit." Ralf laughs and purrs: "Mmm! Tasty!"

We hike north toward the Russian border. Miles up the road, menacing signs in several indecipherable languages threaten us just before the border. For once I resist my magnetic attraction to danger: "Let's just call this close enough."

Dave agrees. "Hey I got within a football field of the Russkies...Maybe that and a nickel will get me a ride on the subway."

Dave Steals Second

Back in the Mazar Sharif hotel, a whacked out hippie tells Dave: "Hindustan, man! You can sell hash there for ten times what it costs here. Shit man, that shit is easier than shit to bring in. And man...No Shit...No customs at either the Pakistani or Indian border!" Another vocabulary-depleted stoner!

Dave, regrettably, is on a smoking jag, and neither Rolf nor I can dissuade him from buying a block of hash the size of a huge chocolate bar.

We hitch to Kabul and Rolf is smart enough to fly home. I, on the other hand, join Dave on the bus trip to Pakistan through the dizzying and daunting heights of the famed Khyber Pass. Too often, the road seems too narrow for the bus's wheel base. Various bus and truck skeletons far below seem to validate this worry.

Intensely relieved, we do not get stopped at customs when we finally arrive in Peshawar. Peshawar is the capital of a frontier province in Pakistan where normal law does not apply. Guns and drugs in many sizes and potencies are available for easy purchase.

The city tingles electrically. People dart around as impatiently as New Yorkers. Maybe everyone's pissed off because it is Ramadan, the month of the year when Muslims fast all day from sunup to sunset. Hunger rarely mellows anyone out.

Lacking many civilized conventions, Peshawar writhes like a many headed beast. Human notes of raw energy scurry in and out of their anger. The notes play on a scale of discordant noise: strident voices, agitated animal cries and metal being tortured into profitable shapes. Flutes and archaic string instruments struggle vainly to rescue Peshawar's score from cacophony. Puffs of machine exhaust, foul animal odors and the rich sweet scents of delectable curries confound my sense of smell.

We stay for ten days because the place is intoxicating – especially the opium den. I visit it a few times and like it too much to ever try it again. But I think: *If I ever have to euthanize myself, opiates will definitely be the way to go.*

Dave and I become the targets – especially at night – of much unwanted sexual attention. The young Punjabi men seem to have a thing for us. Catcalls, wolf whistles and other lascivious outcries follow us everywhere.

Our anger swells as various slimeballs pinch our butts. When we snap around enraged, the group of lewdly smiling punks is always too large to confront.

One night a creep in a motorized three-wheeled rickshaw leans out and grabs Dave's ass. Dave chases the rickshaw down, leaps in the air and gives it a flying Kung Fu kick. The thing wobbles threateningly for about twenty yards and somehow regains its balance. To our great surprise and relief, the crowd around us laughs and cheers.

I have always had good female friends and my compassion for women who are taunted on the street takes a quantum leap. These experiences deepen my innate feminism, and I later lecture more than a few male acquaintances when they devolve into such obnoxious behavior.

Dave discovers another border between Peshawar and mainland Pakistan when he hitches to the American Embassy in Islamabad for a passport extension. On the way he is ignored by the border police who are seemingly there to block the smuggling of guns into central Pakistan.

On his return, Dave goes manic and buys five more kilogram-bricks of hash. They are roughly the size of a flattened burrito. Just to be on the safe side, Dave hires a tailor to sew them into a vest.

On our way out of Peshawar, Dave picks up the vest and stuffs it in his backpack. We are hitchhiking, but a rabble of school children start throwing rocks at us. I feel enraged that the adult passersby do nothing to stop them, but we are not about to get in a rock fight with a bunch of kids.

We walk fast as Dave belts out the words of the frenetic rock song "Get out of Denver," and like magic a commercial bus approaches us. We flag it down and jump aboard.

When we arrive at the province border, four armed police – one with a submachine gun – get on the bus. Dave confidently turns to me: "Don't worry, man, they're just looking for guns."

And sure enough they walk past us to the back of the bus and hassle some locals. When they come back empty-handed, one of them notices Dave's backpack bursting out from beneath his seat. Suspicion ripens across his face, and he gestures to Dave to pull it out.

The policeman opens the pack and sees a curious garment spilling out of the top. He pulls it out and laughs uproariously. The tailor has sewn the vest so that each brick is prominently outlined, making it look like some crazy giant bandoleer. To his cop's eyes it can only be filled with standard sized kilo blocks of hashish.

He motions us off the bus, fully searches our packs and has us turn out our pockets. A tongue-sized piece of hash tumbles to the ground from Dave's pocket. The cop picks it up and snidely puts it in my shirt pocket. He pantomimes surprise as he "rediscovers" it there, and waves the bus away.

My heart sinks deeper than it has ever sunk before. I flash back to Bear County Jail...and moments later, to being a child waiting for my father to come home and execute my mother's prescribed punishments.

CHAPTER 9

Tick Tock in Attock Prison

MEAN STORIES ABOUT Pakistani jail are hippie legend. Surrounded by cops, I want to cry but I do not remember how. I want to puke but we skipped breakfast in our hurry to get out of town. I wish I could have a stroke and die instantly.

I pray to the Mother Mary for the first time since I resigned from Catholicism six years ago. *Please Mary! Get me out of this.* I feel some shame for regressing like this, but I am desperate.

We are taken to Attock Prison, which looks like an old fortress with minor turrets at the corners. We move through the entrance into a small anteroom and are left unattended for an hour. All the signs are in English – a remnant of the bureaucracy established by the British when they ruled the Indian subcontinent. A large blackboard breaks down the crimes of the current prisoners. I gasp when I see that over half of the two hundred are in for murder.

Inspiringly Dave reaches down deep and pulls out some Marine Corps bravado. "Don't worry Pete! The situation is hopeless….but not serious."

Somehow this mobilizes my survival response, and I brief Dave on my Bear County Jail experience. I tell him: "It was the guys who didn't defend themselves that got raped! We should be our usual friendly selves, but if anyone gets physical, we may need to fight until we're unconscious."

He nods his head: "I hear ya man."

A large bald-headed guard with a huge hennaed-red beard comes in and fills out some forms. He is courteous and mellow which momentarily reduces our anxiety, but when he opens the thick door to the huge open-aired interior of the jail, it is do or die time. A flood of prisoners engulfs us. Voices resound and crash into each other, and I feel like we are surrounded by hungry paparazzi.

The prisoners who encircle us are a mix of Pashtuns and Punjabis. The Pashtuns seem to hold rank and are curious and cordial. The Punjabis however are snickering.

We amicably answer questions. The atmosphere warms up until a smirking Punjabi prisoner asks Dave to try on his coat – an impressive pilot's leather jacket with a lamb's wool collar.

I swallow hard. I nod to Dave and he gives it to him.

The inmate happily slips into Dave's jacket. Amused chatter splashes around us...and then the prisoner starts walking away. Tension swells up and a huge wave of fear breaks over me, but I ride it into the calm eye of the storm – a place somewhat like what athletes call the zone.

I take three long strides, grab him by the shoulders from behind, and rip the jacket off him. He does a dizzy little pirouette and collapses onto his butt. I motionlessly tuck myself in and wait for the pummeling to begin.

Instead, a sweet crescendo of approving laughter applauds my action. I laugh aloud as I silently regress and exclaim *Thank You Jesus, Mary and Joseph*! Tension drains out of me as if I am a lightning rod.

An older prisoner, Mohammed Akbar, soon takes me under his wing. When the British rule of the Indian subcontinent (the British Raj) ended in 1948, he was discharged from the army and is excited now about getting to speak English again.

Good-hearted like my best Muslim friends in Morocco, Mohammed feels like the grandfather I never had – a huge upgrade from my blood grandfathers: the paranoid schizophrenic and the in-the-gutter alcoholic.

Mohammed explains that almost all the murderers in the prison are Pashtun. "We are not really murderers, but members of a warrior society and our tribes traditionally fight each other."

The Hindu Kush Mountains, the spine of their land, is a harsh and sparse place. Like so many places in the world where population trumps resources, skirmishes often break out over resources. People get shot and killed.

Before long, I can sense that these men are not hardened criminals. They are more like the Mexican teens in Bear County Jail who through no fault of their own were born into a society ruled by gang warfare.

The contrast of these young, guileless Pashtuns and the middle-aged Punjabis is striking, as the latter are clearly career criminals – thieves, muggers, gun runners, etc.

Mohammed gets us each two blankets for our cell – one to cover us and one to shield us from the dirt floor. During the day we are free to roam the yard. Just inside the bars of the cell is a spit gutter like the one in Herat. It is a narrow trench in which we can spit, urinate, or defecate if we are unlucky enough to get caught short at night.

We notice that the bathing facilities are two outside faucets surrounded by a bevy of buckets. Prisoners douse themselves with a bucket, soap up and then rinse off.

When the last prisoners finish, we douse ourselves at the faucet and soap up until our long hair and beards support snowdrifts of lather. Imagine our dismay when we grasp that a ringing bell is an alert that the faucets have been turned off.

Our fellow prisoners enjoy the spectacle of us de-sudsing ourselves with only our hands. Dave's pissed at their laughing, but I placate him. "Dave, I know it sucks that they're cracking up, and that the Hotel Attock here doesn't have towel service. But, if they get that we can laugh at ourselves, they'll know we're not British upper class leftovers from the Raj."

Twice a day we are each dealt two barely cooked chapattis – thin, frisbee-sized discs of unleavened, indigestible bread. *Who'd have thought there could be a less desirable diet than Wonder Bread? How will we survive on this?*

Fortunately, Mohammad sees the obvious evidence of our digestive suffering in the latrine trench and from then on gives us "Care packages" every evening. Like many prisoners, his family camps outside the walls to provide him [and now us] these supplemental rations.

Three days pass and another prisoner is placed in our cell. He is a sweet, simpleminded, young Punjabi guy who compulsively shoplifted cigarettes in Peshawar's open air market.

His English is confined to the brand names of Indian cigarettes. His favorite is K-2 [named after the famous mountain peak]. He obsessively chants a looping song to connect with us: "K-2, Red and White, Woodbine, Capstan, Benson-Hedges, Gold Flake!" Soon everyone calls him K-2, and every so often, he punctuates this mantra with "K-2 accha [good] man!"

Tonight to drown out the mantra, we sing Beatle songs. Cheering and encouragement come from all the cells within ear shot – a rare pleasure for me. Too often, I've been asked not to sing because of my monotone. Sister Jean Therese once disqualified me from Christmas caroling with: "Walker, you couldn't carry a tune with three hands."

Unfortunately our duet juices up K-2's hyperactivity and he rapidly deteriorates into whirling dervish mode – singing and laughing at 78 RPM. Because he is not endowed with the balance of a dervish, we gently corral him into a safe central space to stop him from crashing into the walls. Regrettably, we have to stop singing to get him to stop spinning.

Dave drifts away from the Pashtun crowd and starts hanging out with a small circle of Punjabis. Two of them sport slick sociopathic smiles. Although neither of us understands much of their language, I am alarmed at the sexual tone in their banter – clearly at Dave's expense.

Before long, Dave is the scapegoat of this subtlely bullying group and naively laughs along with their sexual innuendos. I flash back in disgust to NYC teenagers who got their rocks off aiming their crude, sexual taunts at passing girls.

I try numerous times to enlighten Dave but he says I'm paranoid and gravitates even more toward them. Worse yet he confesses that he is now smoking dope with them, and sure enough he gets triggered into paranoia whenever he smokes. Thankfully he comes back to normal after a good sleep.

A prison official fetches us to admin. It is time to go to court…in a chain gang with ten other prisoners! Hand cuffs and leg chains interlink us with prisoners to the side, front and back of us.

Along the five blocks to the district courthouse, we see many distressed faces on the villagers. Women and children look at us in horror as if we are monsters. Who knows what the rumors are? I feel devastated. *Who knows how long the judge will give us?* Pakistani jail stories are typically demarcated in years.

Thank Allah! The judge doesn't show.

Reverend Peanut Butter

Around this time Reverend Dalton comes to our aid. He is an Evangelical Baptist minister from Incest, Missouri. On a Mission here for the last sixteen years, he has established a toenail hold in the village by creating a peanut butter factory.

Preachy, condescending and just plain weird, he interacts with us as if our souls are commodities that he could get rich off.

We tolerate this pathetic fundamentalist because he bribes us twice a week with peanut butter, which somehow makes the chapattis more digestible. But he proselytizes endlessly, promising us a parade of punishment if we do not come to Jesus. He makes the minister at the SF *Jesus Saves and Cares Mission* look like Walt Whitman.

In between visits, Dave growls: "I loathe that smarmy asshole… Reverend Fucken Peanut Butter."

I work hard to quell Dave before each visit. I get compliance out of him when I say: "Yeah I know! I hate taking Reverend PB's crap too. But man that peanut butter's way tastier than the communion we did penance for every week when we were Catholics. We gotta suck it up man. We need the protein!"

On the fifth visit, Dave rises up like Poseidon from the sea and rants away our holy communion in a sermon of his own. "Listen Reverend Peanut Butter...Yeah we've rechristened you! You sorry sack of shit! It's not that you disgust me. It's much worse than that!

"You've been here for sixteen years and have only six stinking converts! All those poor bastards are now outcastes and scapegoats. Their leader and most accomplished member, is that poor bastard Ali who you had the nerve to rename Paul. Every morning he has to clean the piss and shit trench of every cell with his fingers. Every day he drags our waste all the way across the front of the cell to the little cesspool at the end. Nice reward for converting to your church!

"You sorry ass pontificating redneck, I'm happier here in jail than you'll ever be. I wouldn't trade places with you for a second. So judge not lest ye be judged ye judgmental jerk. And fuck you if you can't take a joke."

As Dave leaves he scoffs: "Keep preaching, Your AssHolyness! Pretend I'm still here."

As pissed as I am at Dave at the time, I forgive him that afternoon when he flashes me his oxymoronic grin of contrition and self-satisfaction and says: "Sometimes you have to look a gift horse in the mouth to see how full of shit it is!"

A few days later we get more humanitarian help from our country. Two suits, from the American Embassy in New Delhi come to visit. One guy looks like the winner of the world's dorkiest suit competition.

Our Veteran status seems to count against rather than for us. Even though I sense it will be counterproductive, I cannot resist telling them I am an officer and gentleman by Act of Congress. *Well, what can I say? It helped get me out of jail in Texas.*

Less than impressed, the suits lay on the disgust and intimidation as they interrogate us. With considerable strain, we fake humility. Finally the clown-suited one hands us a bag of oranges and says as they leave: "Don't get into any more trouble! We won't help you next time!"

Not exactly overflowing with gratitude Dave whispers to me: "I wonder if those condescending pricks got the sticks up their asses from the same tree as Reverend PB."

Fling Ding in Sing Sing

The *B class prisoners* are upper class detainees who have their own walled off section inside the larger compound. They are businessmen, politicians and assorted moneyed people who got busted. We peek over their six foot wall numerous times, but nobody can shun you like an upper middle class Pakistani – a proper Englishman-wannabe.

One day we spot them playing a game called fling ding – a doubles game played with a hard rubber ring on a badminton-like court. The object is to throw the 8-inch ring across the net so that the opponents cannot catch it before it hits the ground. If it is caught, the catcher jumps in the air and flings it back – trying to make it kiss the ground and earn a point.

I challenge them to a game. Even though we have never played, we are much taller and agile than them. We probably have the edge.

They know that Americans most probably know nothing about this game. Gloating at the prospect of humiliating us, they invite us to the slaughter.

We strategize to purposely fall behind and then gradually come back to beat them. We don't want to humiliate and alienate them. The match is surprisingly fun – filled with friendly repartee – and even more surprisingly they are gracious losers.

Even better, I forge an ongoing connection with Dr. Khan who I authentically like. Twice a week he invites us to High Tea, where excellent pastries complement our enjoyable, wide-ranging conversation.

From better to best, the well-connected Dr. Khan turns out to be the deposed governor of the district. Although he cannot do anything about his sentence, he likes us so much that he decides to literally help us *out*. The next time we go chain-ganged to court, the judge is there and frees us after we pay the equivalent of a five dollar fine.

After thirty three days of being locked up, we beat feet out of Pakistan as quickly as possible. We strut out to the main road singing an old rock and roll classic at the top of our lungs: "I'm Free….I'm Freeeeee…And Freedom tastes of Reality!" When we finally tire of this, we launch tirelessly into Cream's: "I'm so Glad…I'm Glad, I'm Glad, I'm Glad."

Hitching by the side of the road, I say to Dave: "I know you hate that "spiritual shit", but Thank God, Mary, Allah, Buddha and Shiva-Shakti that that judge didn't show up the first time before we met Dr. Khan."

To myself I say: *Praise heaven for Mohammed Akbar! I love him and his people.* [Decades later I feel profoundly saddened when their offspring are indoctrinated by Muslim fundamentalists and devolve into the Taliban.]

We catch a ride with a Sikh truck driver named Anand. Ten miles outside of Rawalpindi we get stuck in traffic. In a field very near the side of the road, two turbaned men squat next to each other. Both are casually evacuating their bowels as they talk up a storm. One guy even has his hand on the knee of the other.

Dave and I laugh, but I also feel envious of their lack of shame – and then sad about all the Western taboos that surround this normal body function.

Anand takes us all the way to India – to Amritsar, the spiritual center of the Sikhs – a religious sect who never cut their hair or beards. He proudly shows us the stunning Golden Temple – *Harmandir Sahib*. "This sacred place is our spiritual heart. Please join us for dinner, and rest overnight in our dormitory."

HOMESTEADING in the CALM EYE of the STORM

After dinner I stroll around the grounds and startle when I see paintings of their two saints. One is a mounted warrior riding into battle with his severed leg raised as a club above his head; the other a bearded elder with a sword in one hand and his severed head in the other. A fountain of blood shoots up from his neck. The Sikhs are fierce warriors indeed and were much celebrated by the British Raj as elite fighters in their army.

—⁂—

We hitch south to the Old Delhi hotel we've heard about for the last thousand miles. The old world city expands my senses with a festival of mesmerizing music, fragrant foods, and joyful color.

Delhi teems with animal and human life. Monkeys roam over the rooftops of contiguous buildings. Milk white cows, festooned with flowers, exploit their god-like status and lackadaisically wander at will – trying to turn the packed streets bucolic.

A temple dedicated to the rat god is filled with plates of milk ringed by drinking rats. Naked painted saddhus are human chimneys exhaling tornado-shaped clouds of hashish smoke. One saddhu repeatedly ties and unties a knot in his penis – intermittently suspending iron weights from it and stretching it like a worm.

The markets are a paradox of wealth and poverty, of pain and pleasure. Emaciated rickshaw wallahs pull porcine high caste Brahmins everywhere.

An orchestra of sound constantly vacillates between harmony and cacophony. Hues of color that my retinas have never met bathe my vision. And look at all these bananas! How can they come in so many colors and sizes? And what are all these weird brain-teasers!? Must be some kind of fruits or vegetables I didn't know existed. I wouldn't know how to eat them unless they came with instructions.

The abject misery of the poor is impossible to digest, as they are left to wallow in their "karma". Some literally rot in it. I gag on the smell and the "spiritual" rationalization that their outcaste status is punishment for past life misdeeds.

One hard-to-look-at man is a head and half torso, pulled around by a child on a crude wagon. Time and again I feel overwhelmed by decrepit outcastes begging – often pulling on my clothing – for *baksheesh* [money]. All in the midst of markets brimming with what looks like enough food to feed the world.

Often I think that this would never happen in the USA. How shocked I am many years later at widespread American homelessness! What coldhearted nonsense that street people should pull themselves up by their own bootstraps. Pretty hard when you can't afford presentable shoes!

Never the Twain Shall Meet

During my wanderings I stop for milk tea at cafes and chat with English-speaking, middle class Indian men – hoping for spiritually uplifting conversation. They, however, only want spicy details about Western women to flesh out their fantasies about rampant free sex. How frustrating to find no common ground with these Easterners mired in Western values.

Nor do I find it with lower caste people who respond with blank looks when I address them with the vernacular I learned in jail. My naïve fantasy of finding kindred souls who share my spiritual ardor gasps for breath at my feet.

Hippies abound in my hotel. But too many devolve into vegetative states as they slip into drug addiction. Indian Pharmacies require no prescriptions. Hash, speed, opiates and tranquilizers are as easy to come by as bandaids and aspirin. Here as well as in the Western world, hard drugs are steadily destroying the Hippie Zeitgeist.

Thankfully, I enjoy enriching interactions with a few spiritually-questing, non-stoner hippies. Unfortunately Dave gravitates to the hash-heads who puddle on the roof in near paralysis. Each time he returns to our room from these sojourns he is paranoid – increasingly moving toward delusional.

One morning, restored to sanity by sleep, he says: "I get it... I really get it! Smokin' dope schitzes me out. I'm quitting for real this time." But once again, he doesn't make it to sundown before he is stoned out of his gourd again.

The Lurch That Sunk the Love Boat

A striking Australian woman checks into our hotel. Invisible magnets pull us together. Almost immediately, we lock into conversational intimacy – shades of the bus ride through Iran with Michael.

Lillian and I come here from opposite directions. Trading info about where we've been paints vignettes of our upcoming futures.

We jam on matters of the head and heart. Hinduism versus Buddhism entertains us for an hour. We both abhor the Hindu caste system, and we update each other on the gurus we've heard about who financially and sexually exploit their Western devotees.

Lillian laments about all the hippies getting lost in drugs. I share my upset about the shocking number of schizophrenic Westerners wandering the streets in an inner delusional world.

She says: "Yeah, Pete, they fit so seamlessly into this culture where the bizarre and the humdrum seem to effortlessly coexist."

"You got that right! I bet no one from the government would even think of rescuing someone from psychosis."

Lillian jokes that six months in Southern India has burnt her out on gorgeous Indian architecture. "I'll scream if I have to visit another ancient ruin – I'm templed-out!"

Reverberating whole-heartedly, I match her: "I've been gagging on splendiferous mosques. I'm templed-out here, just like I was museumed-out in Europe."

She says: "This whole aesthetic feast was great before it gave me indigestion. Hey! Maybe we could collaborate on a traveler's guide for people on the Overland Trail – title it something like *How to Enjoy Museums and Holy Places without OD'ing*. And speaking about overdosing, let's warn people that hash may be cannabis, but it's soul-crushingly heavier than weed."

"Man, you got that right! And let's do a section on the overrated attractions like The Louvre and all those boring Pommie buildings like Big Ben…and then maybe a section with all the sublime places like the Taj Mahal and Gaudi Park in Barcelona."

"Too right! And maybe we could have a culinary section for Asia. ID restaurants where you can get a great curry that isn't lethally hot."

"Yeah, how to find a curry that won't make your eyes water, your face sweat, your nose run, and your butt burn when you excrete it the next day." We fall into a great laugh together.

We talk about cooking our own curries to lighten up on the chili. Lillian's one of many hippies who fantasize about opening a restaurant someday. She says: "Who knows, Pete, maybe one day we'll meet again in Sydney and start our own Indian stir-fry restaurant?" *Oh my god. This idea excites me so much, I must be in puppy-mode wagging my tail. How embarrassing!*

We go on to commiserate over the travesty of Vietnam. Australia has been duped into joining the war, and we trade stories about the outrageous injustices of the military industrial complex.

We switch back to spirituality, especially our struggles with learning to meditate. We joke about getting lost in the quicksand of worrying, self-criticism, fantasizing and resisting the urge to scratch our itches.

I confess: "Meditating for me is like being stuck in detention with a bunch of sarcastic bullies – except the bullies are in my head." Laughter spills from her beautiful mouth like a great new song I'd like to listen to forever.

Lillian says: "I can't stop fantasizing about ice cream when I meditate, and crikey mate! You can't eat that Indian rubbish without getting hepatitis."

My flirting takes a risk. "Yes, and I can't stop fantasizing about how turned on to you I feel right now."

She's sipping her tea and laughs so hard, the tea spills. "Yeah, mate, I can't stop remembering being in bed with my old boyfriend."

Our courting is filigreed with easy laughter. Our chemistry creates volatile pheromones, and our heat and arousal climbs new peaks. Hours evaporate at warp speed. We confess that we feel like we have known each other for eons. We sidle off to the privacy of my room, where we begin to slowly and gently tease our chemical connection into an exciting new compound.

When in barges Dave, zonked and more paranoid looking than I have ever seen him. Trampling over the moment, he shouts: "I don't know if it's the drugs I've taken or the drugs I should be taking, but you guys are really bad-vibing me!"

Dave Rounds Third

Well, I cannot pretend that I am pleased to see him. For once he's not paranoid about getting bad vibes from me.

Nonetheless, I have considerable practice in "kid-gloving" him back into normality. I introduce him to gracious Lillian, and hope that after exchanging a few niceties he will grok the situation and give us some space.

Maddeningly, he is too far gone for that. He launches into a manic rave about how we wish he was dead, and how this hotel is bad vibe-ridden, and how all those guys with the elaborate designs painted on their foreheads [the saddhus] are lusting after him – and just like that my new [almost] girlfriend makes a deft exit, and apparently checks into a different hotel.

I am up half the night trying to talk Dave down. I extract a promise from him to get off the *ganja*. He swears on Jimi Hendrix's grave to get straight.

Two nights later he gets wasted again. His paranoia instantly percolates: "I figured it out man. It's you! You're making me nuts! I'm getting away from you…YOU MAN!...and don't you dare follow me."

With that he jams his belongings into his backpack and rushes off into the night, presumably looking for a new hotel.

I stay for another three days, ambivalently hoping and fearing that he will come back. I am spinning in a whirlpool of guilt, depression, and self-hate. I sleep little as my thoughts circulate around the theme: *I'm next; I'll soon be as flipped out as Dave.*

I am shipwrecked in a sea of helplessness and hopelessness. There's nothing I can do. He was irrevocably disowned by his family years ago. Moreover, when we checked into the Delhi embassy to get our mail two weeks ago, they made us sit down with the two suits who had "helped" us in jail. They reminded us: "Don't look for any help from us if you fuck up again!"

Dave couldn't resist: "Yeah man, those oranges you gave us in Pakistan really saved our asses!"

And I surely cannot turn to my parents, who have twice-banished me. Last time I went back to the poisonous well, they told me: "Go back to school, Peter, or never darken our door again." *Man, they're weird. Who says that? Never darken our door!*

Poor, Poor Dave! What will become of him? And GODDAMN! Why did bleakness leak back into my life again so quickly? Uh oh! Here comes a storm of incredibly unfriendly answers.

Goa: Lost in Paradise

My flight response eventually kicks in and rescues me from festering in my room. I hitch down to Goa, a Portuguese enclave on the tropical coast of India. Goa is legend in my mind because of the many rave reviews from travelers I've been meeting since Morocco.

I look for hope in the thought: *Maybe Dave will get it together to stop smoking and catch up with me here.* An inner voice scorns: "Yeah and maybe you'll find enlightenment wrapped in a chapatti!"

How often does something exceed your expectations? Goa is indeed a tropical paradise, but even heaven would leave me flat in my current despair.

There's a tarantula-like thought prowling around my brain: "You drove Dave crazy." It's especially disturbing to me that I intermittently get a faint picture of my mother uttering it in disgust. I am a psychological mess for a month – practically autistic and hanging onto my sanity by gossamer threads.

> De-fricken-pressed and deep pressed
>   to find a glimmer of hope.
> Desperate thinking,
>   caustic waves of introspection
>   wear away the atolls
>   of what was yester-Me.
> Oh God the devil,
>   I am nowhere to be found.

―✶―

There are two hundred hippies from all over the world living in crude bamboo and palm leaf huts around the tree line of Goa's huge beach. Ninety-five percent of the campers are naked morning, noon and night.

This is my first experience of nudism on a grand scale. My shame about being the dork too chicken to go naked soon trumps my shame about *indecent exposure*. Like many other guys, I'm afraid I'll crack a fat if I'm near a naked woman. But God is not totally cruel, and I and all the other men always seem to maintain their flaccidity.

My nudity, to my great surprise, soon feels comfortable and natural, and getting an all-over tan feels health-enhancing.

I claim an abandoned hut near the spring tide surf line. I keep to myself and lick my wounds. Reading and meditation rarely curb my perseverations about Dave.

Ironically, meditating makes my self-judgment more creative. My looping laundry list of fatal flaws grows like a blood infection.

Swimming and jogging on the beach help some. Eating succulent tropical food is also a fleeting comfort.

Proverbial time gradually begins to reduce my misery. A beachfront restaurant crowns the palm tree crescent that coifs the beach. I sit outside on a sawed off tree trunk that is still rooted in the ground. A very hairy and gregarious mountain of a man takes a seat on an adjacent trunk and introduces himself.

"Hello my friend. I am Vasilije from Jugoslavia. I am hippie. Jou look like hippie too. This is great place. Zo warm and green and nude. Everyone no clothes. Is groovy, no?"

He blathers mundanely, which I often dislike, but somehow he is refreshingly non-abstract – easy and goodhearted. He feels like a lifeline and I am happy to meet him. He is "good energy." He snaps me out of my imprisonment in self-consciousness.

We are interrupted by a quiet commotion two shacks behind us. A group of about twenty people surround a soon-to be-mother who is in the final stages of labor. She lies outside on a pile of bedding in the clearing in front of her shack.

It is clearly meant to be a public birthing. She is a lovely hippie woman who wants to share the miracle of birth with the many friends she has made in this community.

Somehow, I get that I am welcome to observe. I've never been at a birth but have heard a few people talk about the numinous energy that occurs at the moment of delivery.

And sure enough, the moment the baby comes sluicing out, there is an intense outpouring of palpable energy that feels so benevolent and elevating that I tingle all over. Happy tears well up and anoint my cheeks. People laugh and cry and ooh and aah.

Suddenly, I feel an inrush of the universal love I experienced on my redemptive San Francisco acid trip. My hopeless alienation is replaced by feeling sweetly connected to my fellow bystanders. The belief that I am a dangerous curse to others – that I should protect them from me – evaporates. A glacier of the Dave-debacle calves off of me – slides away with my transcendent tears.

Two days later I am invited to a potluck-in-progress by some of the people from the birthing. I feel flickers of warmth from the hearth of hippie tribe. Two six week old puppies bumble and tumble amongst us. *Oh Thank God! This terrible low point of my life is ending!*

One of the puppies looks like a mini-St. Bernard. I scavenge a wine cork and a piece of string, and make a necklace for him. He looks like he is carrying the archetypal, mountain-rescue keg around his neck. Everyone laughs and laughs and loves it. So simple – but my cynicism cannot get at it – and I feel worthy enough to belong.

From here on, I slowly expand into the lovely community celebrating the everyday beauty of life.

> I lick my loneliness
> As if it were a sweet
> Knowing it is I, I greet -
> And I, I'm once again
> So pleased to meet

—⚘—

A sheepish, hunched over guy calls me over: "Check out this far out restroom, man." Shaped like an iconic outhouse, its workings are strictly Indian. Inside on the center of the floor is a modest throne of three cinder blocks in a "U" shape, with the open end of the "U" flush against the back wall.

To lighten your load you squat upon the throne and evacuate your bowels between the parallel bricks. What happens next is a tremendous shock to the uninitiated. A huge pig head gruntingly intrudes into the

"U" through a small opening in the wall – and instantly gobbles up your efforts.

Because of the size of the pig, there is a stout thick stick leaning next to the entrance. If you are not quick about your business, you must smack the intruding pig on the head so that it will wait until you are done.

For Westerners who are constipated or have the runs, this is especially unpleasant as the pig has a short memory in a thick skull. It constantly re-intrudes. The longer you take, the more often you have to clobber the pig – or it will actually make contact with your buttocks.

The pig infuriates this guy – who is on the windward side of strange – and when he uses this marvelous mechanism of recycling, he poops quickly, runs around the back and urinates on the pig, cackling all the while and shouting in ironic triumph: "That'll teach you, you disgusting pig!"

Well that's a bit hypocritical, I think. I wonder if the pig reminds him of having to *eat someone else's shit*. Is that what's making him so enraged? Strangely, I flash on my father, and remember my mother once saying: "Charlie, if you'd tell your boss to lighten up maybe you wouldn't be so cranky." *Maybe Charlie was like this guy – dumping his anger on the wrong target.*

And Zen, What Do I Do?

Pleasant weeks go by while I read D.T. Suzuki's *Introduction to Zen Buddhism*. Remnants of my Catholic indoctrination still draw me to ordeal-ridden asceticism, and I am taken with these words: "When traveling is made too easy and comfortable, its spiritual meaning is lost. A certain sense of loneliness engendered by traveling leads one to reflect upon the meaning of life, for life is after all a travelling from one unknown to another unknown."

Sounds right to me! And, I'm still a bit lit up by the spiritual experience I had at the childbirth. Looks like the clock has just struck time-to-resume-my-spiritual-pilgrimage. Underwhelmed by Hinduism, I decide to check out a Buddhist country, and that spells N-E-P-A-L.

Dave is Out at Home

I leave Goa and hitch north. A benevolent Sikh truck driver takes me the thousand miles back to Delhi, and *Jesus Christ! I swear on the Koran*, within five minutes of being dropped off, I run into Dave – fully blown schizophrenic Dave. He is sashaying down the road in my direction, and looks like a kamikaze who has survived the crash.

It is three months since I last saw him, but he looks at me as if it has only been minutes. In a mad manic mumble, he spews: "Pete!... Man!...Dude!...They've just made me the Queen of Nepal. I heard it on the radio outside that chai shop back there. The radio is my guide now, man. It gives me my every move. The radio just told me to walk a hundred yards this way and turn right at the next intersection where I know as sure as shit there will be another radio telling me where to go next.

"I've been following the radio for days and it never fails to deliver me to another radio. Anyway, I'm the Queen now. The radio's been preparing me for it. Everybody wants to fuck me, but I'm not interested. I just keep on moving. So, gotta go dude. Catchya later."

"But Dave...?"

"Don't call me Dave, man! In fact don't talk to me at all. I know you're in collusion with them, and I am outta here."

And off he jauntily sways back into the crowd. I try to get my brain into gear but the clutch doesn't work. I can't find any words with which to call him back. Instead I plummet miserably down into that same profound depression that I just escaped. *If only I could cry.*

Instead, I regress instantly into my flight defense. I cannot stay in Delhi another moment, so I stick out my thumb and pull out the plum of another great Sikh ride – right to Birganj, near the Nepalese border.

Getting a ride from there is problematic. Every vehicle is filled to the hilt. Finally a Nepalese gas-truck driver offers me a spot clinging to the truck's rear ladder. It is less than one hundred miles to Katmandu, and I have been waiting for six hours, so I climb aboard.

For quite a while, the seemingly vertical journey up this Himalaya foothill is exciting, as I am still in top shape from all my combat-ready army training. Dazzling vistas of the Indian plains far below constantly shift with the hair pin turns of the switch back road. Ever-changing patterns in the patchwork quilt of fields, rice paddies, tiny villages and untamed bush are a kaleidoscope of color.

After some time, however, the temperature begins to drop. My arms and legs start to ache and the road is so windy, precipitous and slow going that the trip is flashing me back to numerous never-ending army training ordeals.

I am so cold when we get there that I can barely move. My hands are the worst. It's painful unlatching them from the rungs of the ladder, but I am so relieved to finally arrive.

Dorje, a local Tibetan, leads me up a long road to Swayambhu Stupa [a famous Buddhist shrine] where he says I can camp for free. I thank him and stumble exhausted into what feels like a holy place – until a thirty pound monkey leaps out of a tree onto the back of my pack – scaring a high-pitched girlish scream out of me.

There is no one else around so my humiliation lets me out of its headlock. My benefactor did not warn me that Swayambhu is also known as the Monkey Temple. After I ding one of the very aggressive monkeys with a rock, they all leave me alone. I bed down for a surprisingly good sleep.

I wake up in the pits. I invoke my most time-tested panacea, and try to walk it off. Before long I find a room in a hippie hotel in the heart of Kathmandu.

The next day, I visit Dorje in the Tibetan part of town. The Tibetan refugees from the Communist Chinese are the sweetest and friendliest community of people I ever meet. I naively fantasize at the time that they are all enlightened, and that this is a sign that I have finally come to the right place.

I start my preparations to do a solitary meditation retreat in an abandoned monk's hut that a guy in the hotel gave me directions to.

CHAPTER 10

Pitch Black Flight-Into-Light

NIGHT SNEAKS IN as I shop for seven days' worth of food supplies in the outdoor market. I stop at a stall that is selling yak beer, and take a long swallow – not realizing that it is made with rancid yak butter. *Argh! Yuck! How disgusting!* I leave quickly, so as not to retch and insult this sweet Tibetan man.

How disappointing! My first drink since a three dollar tattoo crushed me with hepatitis in San Francisco two years ago. I have doubled the recommended abstention from alcohol, but tonight I was hoping that a beer might get my mind off poor, poor Dave.

In the morning I hike up a mountain trail on the north side of Katmandu. Three steep miles later I find the abandoned hut. A roof is the only convenience in this crude mud brick building. There are no traces of the door. The glassless wooden window frame is almost completely rotted out.

The empty space in the wall expands the glorious mountain top view which is underscored by a pristine, flower-lined stream. The crystal clear, ice cold water refreshes me and I am happy that I won't have to hike back down every other day to refill my water bottles.

So here I am, do or die – *get enlightened or get endarkened*! I am shored up with books on Zen Buddhism, as well as Christmas Humphreys' *Concentration and Meditation*. I schedule three one hour-long meditation sessions for each morning and afternoon.

OK! Time to emulate Buddha, sitting under the Bodhi tree waiting for enlightenment. Heck, I'll settle for a ten second LSD-like peek into the other side.

Half way through my first session, I just have to look at my watch. *Damn! And I thought time dragged in the dental chair!* This is really torture, especially as I strain to approximate a lotus position. My concentration wanders incessantly from body pain to self-criticism to nodding off into nap-dom.

The price of too much napping is nighttime insomnia and misery in the mental corridors of worry and gloom. I sit up and journal by candlelight:

Snowflakes like an obsessive's thoughts
Snake and swirl in the capricious wind.
Confused by gravity
And earth's unseen spin,
Adrift and gone astray – never to alight.

And so my mind grinds away on loneliness
Each tortured thought a morbid copy
Of one that's fluttered there before
Dancing the devil's dizzy dance steps
to nowhere, no way, no how.

My melancholy feeds upon itself for three days, until I get a bad case of the trots. I learned early in my travels that fasting is the best medicine for the runs. Skipping a meal or two normally rewards me with *good solid results*. No such luck this time. I increase my fasting time but each time eating gives me the runs even more quickly than before.

Feeling desperate, I follow the stream around to the top of the mountain to investigate its source. *Oh my God there's a higher hill abutting it!* High upon its flank perches a monastery. Smoke from a cooking fire signals that it is occupied and my "pure" stream flows down from it.

Annihilated by Amoeba

I know at once I'm drinking water contaminated by the monks who are living there. Instantly, I recall the shallow river that flows through Kathmandu. There I saw people using the river simultaneously for bathing, butchering animals, and washing clothes and dishes. Even worse, I saw a four-year-old boy squatting and pooping in the river about twenty yards upstream from where a teenager was filling the family water bucket.

Inwardly I let loose a moaning prayer: *Please God tell me I don't have amoebic dysentery!* But my diarrhea is so severe now that when I drink a cup of water – boiled now – it passes through me *thirty* minutes later – and looks as clear and uncolored as when I drank it.

I have to get help. But I am too weak to hike up to the monastery – and I doubt there's much they can do anyway. I jettison most of the contents of my backpack and start stumbling back down the trail. I am almost out of gas – in danger of tumbling into a serious injury. So I sit on my rucksack and ride it ass-jarringly down the last mile of the hill. There I pass out in a heap.

I wake up groggily several days later in a semi-comatose state. For some disorienting seconds, I think I am staring into the face of the Virgin Mary. *Am I dead?* But in a shudder of confusion I see that it is Carol – Cara-Weird, and I wonder: *How can I be back in Morocco?*

Carol tells me how she and her new boyfriend, Massimo found me looking half dead on the side of the road two days ago. She says: "We're here to receive Lama Thubten Yeshe's teaching. You'd love him, Pete. He's so connected to Spirit…and so funny too. He refused to accept the *geshe* degree of Lama, because he didn't want to be known as *Geshe Yeshe*. Anyway, we've been nursing you since we found you, and I'm so happy that you've awakened."

After a considerable struggle to reorient, I reply: "Well, it's not exactly the kind of awakening I was looking for up on that mountain, Carol. I think my pilgrimage opened up my anal chakra instead of my crown chakra.

"But Carol, it's so wonderful to see you! Thank you so much for finding me…for rescuing me. I'm pretty sure I've got amoebic dysentery. Can you please get me some medicine?"

The medicine works, but it's another two weeks before I can handle solid food again. When my strength begins to return, we have lovely reminiscences of the Weird Tribe.

We also share about the rewards and frustrations of our spiritual quests. They mostly glow about the former while I mostly glower at myself for being spiritually inept.

Nonetheless, I've never had such an intense feeling of gratitude before, and never expressed it so repetitively. I could have died by the side of the road. Stories abound of travelers in India who die for want of medical care.

Carol finally says very sweetly: "C'mon Pete, that's enough!"

I am restored enough to travel again. These wonderful friends try to soothe me about the fact that I now look like an emaciated Indian monk.

I tearfully thank them once again for saving my life. "Massimo you are a bodhisattva mensch…and Carol you must be an archetype of Gaia, the earth mother. I love you so much!" Gratitude effuses from me like a Himalayan waterfall.

We share a warm farewell and I say: "The quality of your intimacy with each other is so inspiring – I hope someday I'll find such a loving match."

Death of a Quest

When I get back to Kathmandu and see myself in a mirror, I desperately want to cry. I am down to one hundred and forty pounds. I have lost forty pounds since I was in the army.

As if God is blaming and punishing me, Dave's Levis are now too big for me to wear. If there is a silver lining in this ordeal, it is as if a year of panning for gold rewarded me with a silvery gum wrapper.

> Clear as night
> Confused and dazed
> Jewels don't flash in my mind
> Old coruscations tumble into dust
> And stick sickly to the filaments
>   of my raucous despair.

I feel hopelessly lost. Inner neon announces the dead end of this search for enlightenment. The spiritual path is not for me. My spiritual quest dies "not with a bang but a whimper".

I do not know yet that permanent enlightenment – permanent transcendence of suffering – is a preposterous notion. But I still fully believe in a loving presence at the core of everything. Evidently I need to stop banging my head against a door that will never open to me. *Just another aspect of my fatal flaw, I guess.*

Decades later, during a mini-satori, I feel certain that I was kicked off the road – and most especially the *high* road, the Avenue of Flight-into-Light. Who or what did the kicking seems unknowable, but I am clear that I am meant to be more fully in the world, not om-ing my years away sequestered in a monastery. Moreover, I feel certain that my flight-into-light has been postponed until I shed this mortal coil.

As I look back at it in 2017, India was the worst year of my life – not counting my toddler years when I was too young to go outside and discover the world of friends.

I still occasionally feel angry at the pundits who seduced me into believing that enduring enlightenment is attainable. I mean what are the odds? Maybe the Buddha got there, but I have not met anyone who has experienced anything more than *satoris* – brief openings of enlightened awareness.

Over the decades I have met numerous gurus and spiritual teachers who claimed to reside permanently in Illumination. Whenever I was around them long enough, I soon saw evidence of dissociative delusion or egotistical grandiosity.

The grandiose ones were the most common. The flaws of these "Masters" leaked out commonly as less than kind superiority. Frequently, they sexually or financially exploited their followers. Even those who presented a convincing façade of loving gentleness were typically harsh to their closest devotees when no one else was around.

Refreshingly, the Dalai Lama does not claim the kind of enlightenment that is commonly sold as a transcendence of *all* suffering. I have heard him express healthy human anger at the Chinese who oppress his people. And he commonly shows his sadness and commiseration about the suffering of others.

Whither Now?

So what in Dog's name do I do now?

I despair. There is nothing else that seems worth pursuing. There's not a flicker of a calling.

Basic necessity, however, comes calling and gives me direction. I may be broken in spirit, but India is the last place on earth I want to be monetarily broke. Evaporating funds propel me to the nearest place to replenish my coffers. Western civilization beckons and the nearest port of call is Darwin in Northern Australia.

—ᨇ—

I'm travelling so light that I feel like I might as well be wearing a loin cloth. I'm down to the clothes on my back, sandals, a shoulder bag for my journal and minimum daily requirements, and a bedroll that is a sheet and plastic table cloth. The latter serves double duty as a ground cloth and rain cover here in the tropics.

I hitch to the train station, and buy a goat-and-chicken class ticket to Calcutta. Then, on to Thailand where I meet the head monk of the Buddhist monastery in Nong Kai on a ferry. He offers me four hundred baht [eighty much needed dollars] to teach English at his monastery for a month.

The monks are boys and teenagers fulfilling their spiritual obligation to be a monk for a year. They live at the temple, wear orange robes and traverse the villages with their begging bowls to get their meals. At first, I see them as sanctity personified, but am soon disappointed – and then relieved– to see them playing grab-ass in the temple while they chant.

A month passes and the head monk refuses to pay me. He says: "I see you meditate every day – you should be a true Buddhist and not covet material things."

He brushes off my cajoling...then my guilt-tripping...and then my indignation, as if they are mosquitoes. *I can't believe this hypocrite*! He strains the mosquito larvae out of his drinking water so as not to take life by swallowing them, but then he tosses them on the ground where they wriggle frantically and expire in the dust.

As I simmer about *yet another spiritual rip-off*, I suddenly flash on my father's face as he ushered me unto the bus that collected me for the army. He had the same smirk as this condescending monk.

Vengeance rises up in me like lava. I have not felt like this since I punched the windows back in college. On the way out I take his fancy umbrella, rationalizing to myself that he too should not be tainted by avarice for expensive things.

I regret it within a hundred yard of leaving. I panic that I have just committed a major crime. "Who knows?" my inner drama queen catastrophizes: "Ripping off a head monk in this country might even warrant capital punishment – or worse, torture!"

I flash to a memory of a kid in my Catholic school caught stealing from a donations basket. The priest terrorized him by telling him that he was going to be re-circumcised. At first, he had no idea what the word meant, but he could tell by the vitriol of the priest that it was going to be ghastly.

I try to soothe myself. *If they arrest me, I will tell them I have already punished myself enough. My inner priest has given me perpetual penance.*

My fear beleaguers me like an evil jack-in-the-box manically popping up and spewing scenarios of disaster. Not until I hitch my way out of Thailand and catch the ferry to Indonesia does it begins to subside.

Once I relax on the ferry, I can tell something untoward is going on in my nether regions. I find a bathroom to further investigate, but it is too putrid to enter. Instead, I climb up a metal ladder alongside a large smoke stack and squeeze through a hole in the narrow platform that encircles it.

I drop trou, sit with my back to the smoke stack and spread my legs around the hole. On closer inspection I discover that I have been pirated by crabs. Clearly they are a souvenir from the fleabag hotel I stayed in the night before.

Well, so much for feeling relieved! I ransack my pubic hairs assessing the damage. Suddenly a head pops up between my legs from the ladder below – one of the crewmen. He is either oblivious or compassionate, because he exaggerates looking sideways – overstretching left and then right – as if inspecting the small deck for anything awry. The deck, and my crabs, apparently pass muster and he quickly disappears, although the afterimage of him burns judgmentally in my brain until the farce of it all cracks me up, and I laugh my way out of being depressed.

When I arrive on the island of Sumatra, I find a crowded pharmacy but don't know the words for "crab-eradication cream." Unfortunately the proprietor's English is non-existent, so I pantomime my ailment.

Oops! How embarrassing! Everyone's looking at me as if I'm playing with myself. They are clearly disgusted by the fuss I'm making about my groin. Finally a young college student with a bit of English arrives and helps me score some crab-killing cream.

Well maybe no one else sees anything funny about all this, but it tickles my theatre-of-the-absurd funny bone. *And Hey! Crabs are butterflies compared to bedbugs. The bites barely itch and they'd be easy to get rid of if you were good at miming "crab eradication meds."*

I hitch across Indonesia toward Bali – a highly touted stop on the Hippie Trail. On the way I stay overnight in Djakarta. In the morning, a local film producer comes to my hostel in search of someone to play a Dutchman in his movie. With my recent haircut and large red beard, I apparently fit the bill. Just in time to triage my savings from bleeding out.

I am featured in three scenes as an evil Dutch commandant – the nemesis of an Indonesian revolutionary hero. [Looking now at Google I learn that the film, *The Face of a Man*, is a famous Indonesian film! Unfortunately there doesn't seem to be any way to view it.]

When my part of the filming is finished and my wallet replenished, I head to Bali, a paradisiacal island in the Indian Ocean. Everyone describes this last major stop before Australia as "must-see".

My luck vacillates back into the fortunate zone. A monumentally gracious Balinese family provides me six mellow weeks of room and board for a pittance.

What could be better! An unofficial Beach Spa for health restoration. I sunbathe, read, body surf and hang out with a mob of friendly Australians who are just beginning their overland trek to either India or England. I am instantly popular as a source of tales about what lies ahead. I informally trade hotel names and points of interest for helpful contacts in "Oz".

HOMESTEADING in the CALM EYE of the STORM

On the final night after a delicious meal of gado-gado, we sit around a table swapping stories and drinking *arak* [coconut whiskey]. The restaurateur serves it to us from a bottle with a monkey fetus in it. I tell my Aussie friends: "Thank God for Morocco and Bali. These wonderful bookends to my trip help to soften a lot of the hard knocks in between."

I buy a deck class ferry ticket for a ten day island-hopping trip through the Eastern Indonesian Archipelago. The ferry deposits me in Timor, the final island in the chain. A lead from one of the Aussies gets me free passage on a thirty-six foot ketch, sailing and working as crew down to Australia.

My shift on the tiller is 8 PM to 4 AM. The full moon invites my imagination to "trip the light fantastic" as it lays down a golden pathway across the sea. Three glorious days and nights on a mostly smooth sea cap my Afro-Euro-Asian adventure. Maybe Australia will have some answers to new questions I do not yet know how to formulate.

And, I don't know if I qualify as a good man, but you can't keep me down. I'm up for whatever's next.

CHAPTER 11

Darwin – A Taste of Evolution

ARRIVAL IN DARWIN ends my traveling for adventure. It is three years since I left the army and my *On the Road* journey is over. Unbeknownst to me *Discovery* is winding up, and *Recovery* is on the horizon.

I am not sad to be at the end of the road. If Walt Whitman counseled me from the other side he would probably say: "Your *Song of the Open Road* was a bit off key, lad…and a bit heavy on the gravel rash." I also hope he'd say: "Pretty rich, though!"

I fantasize about taking a plastic cast of my hand with the thumb extended in the hitchhiking position. Underneath I'd inscribe: *The thumb that hooked twenty thousand miles of free rides.*

So, *Praise to the Powers that Be* for Eleventh Hour Luck! – The luck that rescued me from my out-of-whack recklessness. What good fortune to have found the calm eye in most of the storms that blew through my travels!

And Praise for all the Glories that festooned The Road! I saw a lifetime's worth of beauty and significantly broadened my view of the world. And most wonderfully I met good and kind people everywhere…of every creed, skin-tone and socio-economic class. I feel like a citizen of the world now, and all kinds of men and women are my potential brothers and sisters.

3 Wells Street

Homelessness has a certain cachet these days – the Romance of the Road. Right now however, that romance feels like a bad soap opera: *Spit*

Gutters of The Road. I am bone-tired from being homeless most of the last three years.

My exhaustion salutes my decision to look for a fixed place to sleep. I've bedded down in too many different places to remember. Right now pillows, blankets and a mattress would be a great trade for all those spectacular camping sites.

In the hippie Café I heard about in Bali, I sit at the end of the breakfast bar next to a big shaggy blonde guy. I greet him with the standard Aussie greeting: "Howzit goin' mate?" and startle as I see that his left index finger is buried deep in his left nostril – almost to the knuckle that anchors it to his palm.

I freeze in awkward silence. I'm sure my eyes are gaping orbits. Finally he pulls out a finger-stump and chortles: "Good day, mate! Name's Mick Haabjoern. I'm a genuine Scandinavian-Australian – a Scando-Aussie, and I'm a walking-talking *bona fide* scandal.

"Got me finger cut off in a canning factory down Perth way, and I usually do that little trick of putting it up my nose to pick up sheilas. It's a great opening 'line', but don't worry cobber, I'm not trying to pick you up. I'm straight as a dunny door."

To which I reply: "That's the most creative come-on technique I've ever seen. The only pick up line I've ever come up with is: 'Do you have change for a quarter?'" I don't add that both times I used it, I quickly retreated into a shame attack.

After a long yarn, Mick tells me I can pull up a mattress on the living floor of his communal house at 3 Wells Street.

Oh my god, what a relief! I am so done travelling that I stay there for the next three years.

---

3 Wells Street is an eastern terminus of the Hippie Trail. Like most of the surrounding houses, it is built on stilts – an ecological accommodation to

the winter monsoons and the ubiquitous termites that have dibs on this land.

Mango and papaya trees – bursting with ripe fruit – adorn the backyard. Unbelievably, no one in the house likes mangoes, so I have a five mango glass of juice every morning.

During my stay over two hundred people stay for at least a week. I keep count by writing their names on the hallway wall. *What a wealth of people.*

In year two, our "commune" is the subject of a cover story in the local newspaper, and later we "star" on a national 20/20-type TV news program. Unfortunately I never get to see the program because Darwin is a remote, frontier town without TV.

Going Back to Basics

Well if the spiritual won't open to me, I'm not clawing at the door anymore. A new hunger finally awakens. I want pragmatic knowledge and tangible skills. I want to make things and overcome my fear of tools. So I enroll in carpentry, welding, and drawing classes.

Mick becomes an old fashioned father figure to me, bolstering and guiding me to use my hands.

My father – fixer of watches, TVs and nuclear submarines – taught me nothing, except how to fail at passing him his tools. As earnest as I was, I never passed muster at that simple task. Charlie Walker's legacy was that the sight of a tool could trigger me into fear and shame. At such times, I felt like I had a scarlet letter "K" emblazoned on my forehead. K for Klutz!

—∞—

At Wells Street, my laid back Aussie housemates teach me motorcycle mechanics. At my zenith I get four old beaters up and running. What a thrill to totally rebuild an engine and have it start up again.

Unfortunately, I come off my favorite bike four times. Despite being perfectly sensible behind the wheel of a car, I am a maniac on a motorcycle. Stitches, road rash, infections and third-degree exhaust pipe burns on my leg accumulate. I start flashing on skeletons every time I kick-start the bike. The thought that I will kill myself if I keep riding is becoming a constant companion. *I guess I haven't magically left my self-destructiveness behind.*

With great regret, I sell my bikes. *But silver lining*! I am able to transfer my ardor for mechanics to cars. I spend a year completely rebuilding a one hundred dollar junker that lasts me my remaining nine years Down Under.

To my great surprise, I soon find myself *de facto* head of the household. *Maybe I am reprising this chain of past events:* Firstborn baby-boomer on my block becomes leader of the other kids – years later is seen as officer material in the army – and then ascends to the "throne" of the Weird tribe in Morocco.

I lead by example. My instinct has always been to jump in and engage the hardest/scariest part of any necessary task. Others now and then join me.

When I move in, Wells Street is disorganization par excellence. Minor conflicts about food "disappearing" from the fridge soon push me to nudge everyone's hippie aversion for structure.

After a mellow guitar jam one night, I coax everyone to chip in five dollars for communal food. I volunteer to shop and I fill the fridge with food. Food tension evaporates and everyone soon subscribes to making this a weekly thing.

Soon, I begin cooking two communal meals every week. Meals soon evolve into mini-parties which everybody looks forward to. Before long, people buy into a cooking roster. Each person only cooks once a fortnight and we have a wholesome meal every night. The benefit of regularly prepared meals is the proof of the pudding, even if the pudding is hardly cuisine.

Gradually people look to me for guidance when things go awry. My efforts help to create a safe, harmonious and – yes – loving household. *Maybe I do have a beneficial effect on people after all.* Maybe that funny feeling in my chest is my dormant self-esteem beginning to push up and break ground.

Herbie Monroe

One morning, my housemate Bronwyn asks me for a ride to the pound to get a rescue dog. Dog-lover that I am, I come along. She chooses and pays the parole for a tiny bedraggled mutt that she eponymously names "Rat."

I'm bummed she doesn't pick the spotted cattle dog puppy with a huge head that's almost as long as her body. When the old crusty manager catches me petting her, he teases me: "That dog's no beaut, mate. She reminds me of a bloke who came into the pub with a dirty big rat on his head. Someone cried out: 'Hey mate where'd ya get that ugly looking thing!' Instantly, the rat replied: 'Well cobber it started out as a wart on my butt, and then it just kept growing'." He laughs so hard I can't tell if he's pissed himself or drooled in his lap while he was asleep in his chair.

But this half-dog, half-snout creature is on death row and she's not getting any prettier. *Damn! I really don't want to get weighed down…but this is My Dog!*

So I pay her bounty of five dollars. The attendant chuckles scornfully: "Ya gonna win a lot of dog shows with that one, Yank!" My inner detractor builds on his insult: *"You're just getting her because you think she'll distract people from noticing how bad you look!"*

For reasons beyond my ken, I christen her Herbie, resisting Bronwyn's plea: "You've got to call her Barbara Streisand; she's the spitting image!"

In an ironic nod to her handicap in the looks department, I expand her name to Herbie Monroe. Living up to her name, she waggles her butt like a sexpot whenever she's excited.

Herbie becomes my constant companion and mother substitute for the next ten years. She is the second best decision I ever make.

Working for the Aussie Dollar

I left America in late 1969 with nineteen hundred dollars, and arrived in Darwin in early 1972 with five dollars and coins from over twenty countries. Talk about the loaves and fishes!

On the day after I arrive, I go door-to-door to downtown businesses panhandling for work. At the umpteenth place I get a job as a bell hop. They like me, but because of my less than stellar appearance, they soon transfer me to be the gardener of a hotel on the outskirts of town.

Unfortunately, my intuitive skills don't bloom as gardening prowess. The crewcuts I give to the manager's favorite bushes are apparently poor pruning choices and I get the sack. But not before I've earned "a few quid". Almost a hundred dollars in fact.

I subsequently suffer short stints as a bartender, construction worker, brick cleaner and automobile detailer. With one exception, I save enough in each job to take the next month or two off. I've gotten addicted to having a lot of free time.

Brick cleaning is the worst job ever. My sole task is to clean the excess mortar off brand new brick walls. I scrub it off with a steel brush and a bucket of acid-laced water. When I landed this winner, the boss snapped: "Rubber gloves provided, but you supply your own eye protection."

I walk off the site after twenty minutes, and tell my fellow flunky: "Damn Stan, no human being should have to do this. Tell what's-his-face I quit, and no need to pay me for my time…he can keep the change! Tell him I got a better job filleting anchovies!"

I do not last long as an auto-detailer either. The job entails micro-cleaning expensive cars. I die each day working a toothbrush to clean the car's endless cracks and crannies. Finally my unconscious mind comes to the rescue and has me unknowingly reverse over the BMW's window blinds after I've taken them out for easier cleaning.

My buddy Frank, who also works there, sees this and laughs himself into incapacitation. It's minutes before he can tell me what I've done. I'm mortified but Frank's laughter is infectious, and the boss – irate that we find this funny – fires me. Frank says to the boss: "Hey mate, if you can't laugh about it, you might as well let it kill you." To which the boss replies: "You're sacked too, ya bloody wankah!"

Well this is one failure I can actually be happy about!

Warm Leatherette

Looks like I'm not going to find that thirty year job that gets me a gold watch when I retire.

My housemate Jeff teaches me the rudiments of leather work. I build work tables in the open space under the house and place a large hand lettered sign out front: LEATHER GOODS MADE TO ORDER.

People stop to check out my work. I think they mostly want to get an eyeful of The Hippie House, especially after I spray-paint letters on a sheet and hang an ironic sign from the balcony: PERRY COMO FAN CLUB.

This sign replaces the one that preceded it for three months: NO DRUGS HERE. That sign was a response to a drug raid at our house that, much to our surprise, came up empty.

The failed raid was actually a blessing. I stumbled into an entertaining repartee with the head cop, Sgt. Robinson, which led to him being a reference for me when I got my visa upgraded from tourist to migrant status. This huge boon allowed me to stay in Australia indefinitely.

Apparently my leather work is not half bad as I sell many belts, sandals, wallets, shoulder bags, and even an ornamental guitar case. I love carving designs in the leather for about a year, but when I devolve into workaholism, the joy gets tooled out of it.

Almost as if he's been sent to deliver me from the treadmill, a gregarious Texan pulls up out front in his Cadillac for a gander. He's delighted that I'm an American and recruits me to pitch for his baseball team in the local league. The Darwin Oilers are men from his oil rig in the Timor Sea – a three hour helicopter flight north.

My pitching is good enough and when the season ends he gives me a job on his rig. It's nasty work – two weeks on and one week off, with fourteen twelve hour night shifts in a row. But the wages are outstanding and my savings mushroom.

On the week off, I live on a pittance at Wells Street while the other guys binge beyond belief – partying 24/7 at expensive hotels. Booze, drugs and prostitutes help them exhaust their paychecks in record time. These guys bring "Sleep when you're dead" to a dangerous level.

When they return to the rig they look four-fifths dead, and do a zombie shuffle for the first few days. Almost all the serious accidents – typically getting mangled by machinery – happen in this time period. *How awful it is to see these young men trickling their life force away in such decadence.*

—⁂—

Darwin is losing its luster and I have *beau coup* time to think in my low focus job. Suddenly in the dead hours of the nightshift, an epiphany blares: *Go back to school!* The next time I'm on shore, I apply to Sydney University and three months later I dance around the Wells Street living room waving my acceptance letter gratefully to the gods.

Instant Family

Two months before I leave for Sydney, I watch a striking woman write graffiti on the wall of a café that welcomes the practice. In big red letters she inscribes: WAR IS MENSTRUATION ENVY.

I approach her and when I finally stop laughing, we riff on the concept. From there we venture off into a delightful three hour rave about our mutual interests: left wing politics, spirituality, alternative healing and each other. We fall immediately in love.

> Ripe in your arms
>   I roll into your mango kiss.
> Your languid heartbeat
>   lazes out my pulse.
> Your peachy ripeness floods the room
>   as we tangle in frissons
>   of passion fruit delight.

Jody is effervescent, a social whiz, and the effortless extrovert that I'd like to be. She is also a single mother, and when I meet Grayem – her two-year-old, part-Aboriginal son – I quickly grow to love him as well.

Sweet, glowing and guileless, Grayem's delight in the everyday minutiae of life is infectious. He is blessed by abundant love from Jody, her many friends, his doting grandmother and his biological father's large tribal family.

And...what a relief to get more proof that I am not like my parents! I delight in his existence!

Jody decides to accompany me to Sydney where we will make a home together. In a honeymoon-like atmosphere, She and I and Grayem spend six weeks car-camping from Darwin to Sydney. The 2,500 mile road unfolds through a landscape of exotic plants and animals – punctuated liberally with giant totemic termite mounds. Not once do I wish I was hitchhiking.

Highlighting the trip is The Great Barrier Reef – a top ten wonder of the world. Gorgeous fish defy gravity, gymnastically taking color into a fourth dimension...into ever-changing landscapes of exploding neon pigment. The fish say "No" to all the rules of combining color.

I snorkel ecstatically in this glorious new world for about an hour. When I emerge, I can't believe that I've actually been under for four hours. The daunting beauty of this "time flies" trip bolsters my faith in a magnificent Creator. *How can science so cavalierly scoff off the notion of creation? Their house of cards – of elaborate unproven hypotheses – rests on the simplistic causal notion of a Big Bang. What preceded that?*

I remember playfully telling Grayem one night: "Once there was this ginormous BIG Bang! ... and it spit out all the people and all the animals and all the things!" He laughs delightedly as if it makes good sense to him.

But I'd like to know where they think all that stuff came from...that stuff that now furnishes at least a universe. And while I am at it, for heaven's sake, couldn't evolution be the bravura event of a grand creation? Perhaps God impregnated matter with a drive to evolve towards increasing sophistication.

PART II

Recovery: Looking Inward For Answers

I see there is no prison except that which I construct to protect myself from feeling my pain.

– Sheldon Kopp

GLOSSARY

Abandonment Depression: the deadened, helpless and hopeless feeling state of being a forsaken child. Childhood trauma survivors often flashback to this state.

Abandonment Mélange: the fear and shame that frequently intermingles with the *abandonment depression*.

Complex PTSD [CPTSD]: entrenched type of Post-Traumatic Stress Disorder [PTSD]. Caused by prolonged verbal, spiritual, emotional &/or physical abuse &/or neglect in childhood or elsewhere. Key symptoms are emotional flashbacks, developmental arrests and a toxic, mind-dominating critic.

Emotional Flashbacks: regressions – short or long – to the emotionally overwhelming or deadened feeling states of being a traumatized child. These states are varying mixes of fear, shame, depression, sadness, and anger.

The Toxic Critic: Mental preoccupation with worrying and perfectionism. Thinking that only notices the negative: that which is defective or dangerous in oneself [**inner critic**] or life and others [**outer critic**].

Survivor: someone with CPTSD caused by an abusive and/or neglectful family, neighborhood, religion, and/or boarding school.

CHAPTER 12

Sanctuary Thy Name is Sydney

Done to death
With lost-in-wandering.
Ripe and ready,
I spelunk inward,
Searching for my ground,
Looking to anchor in my bedrock.

JODY, GRAYEM AND I move into a large room in a communal house near the university. Our room is so close to the adjacent house that Grayem and the kid next door reach through the windows and play pattycake. Herbie also likes our new digs and sleeps on the couch in the living room with her dog-roomie, Spunky.

Now that we are settled, I walk to the lovely inner city campus of Sydney Uni [University] to register. During the long drive down from Darwin, I had many fond memories of my Psychology 101 class at UNH, so I decide to enroll in the psychology-rich Clinical Social Work Program. What a delight to hear that I am now eligible for free counseling services!

And how synchronistic that I have just finished an inspiring article about the benefits of psychotherapy! I go straight to the counseling department and sign up for eight sessions of individual counseling and a twelve week encounter group.

I feel scared and hopeful sitting in the therapist's waiting room, mostly eager for my first session. My individual therapist, Derek Edmonds, shows me a series of drawings from the TAT – The Thematic Apperception Test. "So Pete, please free-associate and tell me what comes to mind in each drawing. And please try your best not to censor yourself."

The second sketch is a neutral-looking depiction of a young boy in the foreground looking at a 1950-ish woman with black hair standing under a clothesline. She is looking away into the distance. *Oh my god, it's making me cry! How embarrassing! He must think I'm a nutcase.*

Thankfully, his voice is reassuring: "Yes, Pete, that picture often triggers people. Can you put some words with those tears?"

Derek who I've mysteriously trusted from the get-go clearly accepts my tears. *How helpful that he calls me Pete instead of Peter!* No matter how much I emphasize that I am *Pete*, most authority figures insist on *Peter* which always makes me feel like I'm in danger.

So I open up. "The woman reminds me of my mother. Mom has black hair and wears it just like her. But I don't know why that makes me cry. My mother was practically my best friend. Maybe I'm missing her? But, I don't think so. I hardly ever think about her.

"In fact, I haven't seen her or talked to her in six years. Two years ago I had to tell her I wouldn't write anymore if she didn't stop telling me what to do in her letters. She's been fine since then.

"Now my father, there's a different story. He's an asshole of the first degree!"

Derek nods sympathetically, and following the test procedure, moves to the next picture. Not evaluating my response seems to deepen my trust and opens the spigot of a *new* voice. I talk at length about things I've forgotten, and things I've never told anyone.

This feels really good – just saying what's on my mind.

The session ends and I feel an elevating sense of relief. I feel that my tears were okay and welcome – maybe even normal. I can't remember why I was so afraid of counseling. *Only seven days 'til the next session!*

Getting Real Down Under

My individual counseling dovetails nicely with the Encounter Group. In a magenta room, I plant my butt on the plushy carpeted floor in a circle of nervous group members and large lavender pillows.

Our Afro-sporting leader, Lebanese-Australian Jo Gaha addresses us. "Our goal is to develop authentic and vulnerable communication. I believe that being your real self is what you need to feel safe and close with others. Vulnerability and intimacy are inextricably intertwined."

There are twelve of us. Everyone takes a few moments to introduce themselves, and I feel cautiously optimistic about almost everyone.

Jo continues: "Lovely to meet you all. How about we dive right into the more vulnerable work? Everyone will get a long turn to explore what's most on their mind. Who'd like to begin?"

I think about something I recently read that made me realize I'm counterphobic. "*Counterphobics* move towards fear rather than away from it." How often I've jumped into the jaws of fear just to get the fright over with as soon as possible. But curiously, Jo's scary bid doesn't compel me to dive in first like I usually do. *Perhaps I'm waiting to see what's possible... permissible. I'll see what the others do first.*

It's week six, and it's my turn today. Many group members have explored some upset of theirs that made them cry. Clearly, they felt better afterwards. I am quite impressed by their courage. In fact, I trust and like them better than those who haven't shared yet.

It seems my unconscious pain has been primed by their depth work, as I have severe diarrhea just before the group – literally scared shitless to be more real with so many witnesses.

Jo starts me off: "OK Pete, try bringing your awareness to your belly and feel the sensations there." I think: *What's she talking about! Your awareness is in your head not your belly.* Nonetheless I am suddenly overwhelmed with an image of Dave wandering around the streets of Delhi, crazy as a loon.

I try mightily to stop my tears, but I am soon crying and then weeping! In due course, I punctuate the weeping by venting about the trauma of his demise.

I angrily sob: "How Ungodly Unfair! You survived Vietnam, Dave, but I had to leave you in that hellhole with no social services. I know you must be dead by now!"

I feel like a volcano, releasing heat and pressure. When I exhaust these angry tears, I weep in guilt...and then in relief that I too survived the Vietnam debacle, despite my combat platoon leader status.

All this time, two group members are behind me softly stroking my back. *How can I be allowing this? How can it feel so comforting? And, how come I'm not even embarrassed!?*

The last time I cried around other people was when I was six – watching Alfred Saturno get beaten with stickball bats by the neighborhood bullies. *I could not have felt more mortified.* No wonder I vowed never to let anyone see me cry again. *But, Goodness Gracious! This just feels so right...so blessedly relieving.* It's almost holy – kind of like a sacrament – way, way, way better than Confession.

When I leave the room for lunch, I feel like I am lightly tripping on LSD. Colors are brighter and the air is palpably soft. I feel almost weightless – a few pounds away from walking on air. Everything has a glowing aura around it. *How wonderful it is to be alive!*

—∞—

This feeling of liberation gradually fades but the joint effect of both types of counseling translates as: *Psychology is my new passion!* I know that if I become a social worker, it will no doubt involve being a grief specialist.

Moreover, I have a life-changing epiphany. I have been looking for love my whole life with a manic, people-pleasing song and dance – yet I have never felt really loved. What a waste of energy and self-contortion! If that's all my court jester act gets me, I might as well feel unloved for being my real self. On the spot, I commit to being more authentic and vulnerable.

Dietary and Somatic Salvation Fantasies

Having discarded my spiritual quest, perfect physical health is my new El Dorado. Nothing drives me more than the quest to regain my forty pounds of lost flesh. My 140 pound self yearns for my 180 pound soldier's body.

Joined at the hip with this drive is my desperation to defeat my hated nemesis: *Tiredness*. Surely weariness does not afflict a truly healthy person.

I experiment with a series of diets and supplements. Positive results are typically short lived. No matter how I adjust my diet, my energy ebbs and falls unpredictably like a planet with too many moons.

I don't budge out of being skinny. I do not gain an ounce. My energy is like a moth's. I flail at an ever-changing candle for a salvo of energy, but always collapse singed and exhausted. There I wait until I have the strength to find a new flame – the latest miracle supplement or health-improving technique.

I try every mainstream and alternative method I can find, but my disappointments accumulate. Like a drug addict willing to shoot up almost anything, I delve into *Survival into the 21st Century* – a New Age book that some of my friends are enamored with. The author, who is so emaciated that he makes me look fat, insists that optimal health can only be reached through Breathatarianism.

Yes, Breathatarianism is what it sounds like. "First gradually let go of meat and dairy…then the starches…then the fruit and vegetable juices. Then the *prana* in the air will be enough to nourish the thoroughly cleansed and attuned organism."

My close friends and I are not fanatics and don't buy the breathing nonsense, but the book is crammed with nutritional advice that benefits some of us. Others like me and Pommie Mike experience detrimental effects when we become vegetarian. We're both as skinny as Ghandi, and giving up meat seems to be pushing us towards extinction.

We don't seem to be able to get protein out of vegetables like the book says, and we start secretly overcompensating on other sources. One day I catch him drinking tahini [sesame seed butter] from the jar. I try to soothe his guilt by confessing that I've become a closet yogurt-eater. After we stop laughing he says: "Who gives a bloody fuck about the 21st century? Care to join me on a quest for hamburgers?"

I also try every bodywork approach that is around at the time: acupuncture, chiropractic, and myriad massage techniques, including those incorporating color and energy channeling. Most are comforting, but hardly transformative.

I am a dime and two degrees short of desperate because I still have a trace of amoebic dysentery and get the trots at least once a week. Jody convinces me to try a *colonic*.

The practitioner, Connie, inserts a tube up my rump and says: "We have to cleanse the filth and toxins that cling to your colon, robbing you of your energy." She turns on the water and disappears.

Before long the incoming tide makes me feel like a water balloon about to burst. I call out "Connieee!" with increasing urgency but it takes an expletive at full volume to get her to come back and take me off the fill cycle.

I leave her office feeling worse for the wear. My digestion remains abysmal, and I add another failure to the miracle-cure rubbish heap.

Getting Schooled

The communal home in which Jody, Grayem and I live is also a *Safehouse*. As such it supports a Domestic Violence [DV] Refuge founded by house owner and visionary Anne Maclean. Most of the refugees from battering husbands stay in the refuge, but we usually house a DV victim who needs to be more safely hidden. Inspired by Anne's mission, I also do handyman work at the refuge.

Anne has a progressive tribe of friends, many of whom are social activists. Some of us refurbish a nearby derelict house and turn it into a child minding cooperative that supports fifteen families. We take shifts caring for each other's preschoolers. Their social skills and our parenting abilities develop nicely. Grayem loves it and continues to thrive.

I love being back in school. And so does Herbie. Australians disdain formality, and she is welcome in all my classes. Sometimes Herbie waggles up while I am working at my desk to remind me that it's time to drive to Uni. She loves the car as much as food and has memorized my schedule. Over time she becomes a campus celebrity, and I am happy to be her roadie.

In psychology class, my ears perk up when I hear about psychosomatic illness. *Are my weight and energy problems psychologically based? Perhaps my cure is hiding in my unconscious. I will ramp up the exploration of my psyche.*

I ask my Principles of Psychology teacher for a book that is broader than our Cognitive Behavioral Therapy [CBT] text. CBT is the weak mainspring of the Social Work Program. It ignores feelings, imagination, *the past* and anything that cannot be scientifically observed.

Shawn graciously lends me Carl Jung's autobiography: *Memories, Dreams and Reflection.*

What a book! It is funny, illuminating and *sacrilegious and spiritual* at the same time. From here on, Jung is a buoy and lane marker on my psychological voyage.

Right now, however, I'm lost at sea in my psychopathology class. Every week the lecturer bolsters my self-judgment with a new diagnosis, and I am clearly its perfect prototype. Today *Schizophrenic* has me by the short and curlies. *Of course,* I think, *just like Dave and Grandpa!*

I don't know how to defend myself from all this labeling until I think: *Wait a minute. It's statistically impossible to have every type of psychopathology!* But manic/depressive and obsessive/compulsive cling like white cotton fluff to a black sweater.

Demonizing Introversion

Finally I park these new labels out of awareness, when I conclude that *introversion* is my key psychological defect. In my mind introversion is closely allied with my despicable tiredness problem. When I am tired I feel hijacked into being internal. I feel like my jaw sets traps for my every word. But when I have energy, I can be extroverted, interesting…someone people like having around.

Unfortunately, a short-circuiting power source renders my extroversion unreliable. There's a hair-trigger trapdoor beneath my extroversion. Any second I can tumble into shameful muteness, feeling desperate to escape human contact.

In my CBT class, the instructor introduces the concept: *Inner Critic*. "It's the voice in your mind that beats you up. It says things like: 'You're not good enough,' 'You're stupid,' and 'You're a loser.'"

Well, I think, *I sure have a ginormous one of those inner critics!* But as I become aware of it over time, I notice that mine uses "I" statements as much as "You" statement. Too many times every day, I hear myself saying: "I'm so stupid" and "I'm a loser."

Damn, I'm mean to myself! I have to stop this…but that critic-sucker is so strong and stubborn. *Where the hell is the off switch? Sometimes it seems like I am nothing but my inner critic!*

I try using the CBT technique of Positive Thinking to get rid of my critic. The critic promptly decimates my every effort with insurmountable scorn. Hopeless on this front, I redirect my positive thinking towards my primary goal: eradicating introversion. I turn my obsessiveness into silently chanting this CBT mantra: "Every day in every way, I am more energetic and extroverted."

With my mother's tone and jargon, my critic counterattacks with twisted clichés like: "You can think positively until gold rusts, but you're one pig's ear that'll never turn into a silk purse!" Soon, it's: "God, I suck. I can't do anything right!" *No wonder my joking is so often at my own expense!*

Every other CBT technique seems counterproductive to my quest for *on-tap* energy and extroversion. Each failure arms my critic. "You sorry sack of shit! CBT is *scientifically proven* to be helpful. You're just too defective to benefit." I ironically die over and over into feeling more tired and shutdown.

Hunting elsewhere for relief, I try the many New Age seminars that take Sydney by storm; they have blown in, it seems, from San Francisco.

In his Creative Visualization class, Andrew Watson channels energy from Mars into our sacral chakras. As with some of my dietary explorations, I feel momentarily energized, but the trapdoor still rules.

I remain stuck in over-relying on adrenaline to kick start my extroversion. But like Icarus, I inevitably crash from adrenaline – not paraffin – failure. Over and over I drown in alienated introversion.

True Alchemy: Grief Morphing into Relief

My ruminations keep taking me back to the encounter group and how my catharsis left me feeling liberated – energetic and extroverted for weeks afterward. Unfortunately my tears elude me now. But I bet greater access to my grief is the key! *It's time to focus my efforts on liberating my tears.*

I sample all the emotional release techniques I can find. I do many workshops in Gestalt Therapy, Reichian Therapy, Rolfing and Rebirthing [Holotropic Breathwork]. I cry more often and more completely and the relief and peacefulness is wonderful.

During one face-soaking weep, my tears taste like the salty mineral water I had in France, which was reputedly life-restoring. This thought then free-associates into my thinking: *Whoa! Maybe I'm using beer like fire-water to stoke my energy and liberate my voice?*

Time for another alcohol fast to keep me focused on grieving:

No more kick starting my spirit with spirits
No more medicated mirth.
Wrapped in the burning permafrost of my aloneness
I climb into the guts of my fear.
I invite my tears to taste the salt
With which I will melt my arctic blight.

For some time I delude myself that emotional catharsis is opening up the mother lode of my extroversion – especially because I'm clearly becoming more self-expressive. But my extroversion and energy levels are only roller-coastering more rapidly. My shame-encrusted feelings of introversion – of feeling trapped inside myself – keep coming back. *As soothing as crying is, it doesn't seem to be a panacea.*

Angering is Grieving Too

*Nothing worth having comes without
some kind of a fight;
Gotta kick at the darkness 'til it bleeds daylight.*

— SONG BY BRUCE COCKBURN

One afternoon in my Gestalt group, the leader invites me to try *the two chair technique*. I sit in one chair and face an empty chair in which I imagine a hologram of my father. The leader says: "Try to get in touch with your unfinished business with your father. Tell him what you think and feel about how he treated you as a child."

I dive in. "I loved you so much. I wanted to be just like you. Mom said you loved me, but that is so not true! She said I disappointed you because I was so selfish and only thought about myself, but now I know that she was really talking about you!

"You're a Liar…A Hypocrite…A Phony "nice guy"…a workaholic pillar-of-the-community who had nothing for any of us kids!

"The look of revulsion I saw so frequently on your face was worse than all the times you slapped me in the face. Your contempt is why I feel so ashamed of myself…why I hate myself."

I feel myself getting hot. Strength percolates up in me, and suddenly I roar: "YOU'RE A SORRY-ASS EXCUSE FOR A FATHER!

"I will never again call you Dad again. You gave me nothing but scorn and the back of your hand, and if I could go back in time now, I'd kick your ass every time you got near me."

I pause again flooded with bitterness thinking about his favorite diatribe: "For crying out loud!" I yell it back at him. "For crying out loud, Charlie, if you actually cried…instead of raging and calling it crying…you wouldn't have been knocking us kids around all the time."

I tear up about this and then feel outraged that my mother mythologized him as a great father. I fume. "What a lie that you loved me! I only have two crummy memories of you being nice to me! They were such paltry gestures that I now see them as proof of your stinginess."

I fill back up with rage and spit out his favorite phrase: "You Make Me Sick…You hated me, you bully! You sorry-ass sperm donor! I hate you for the thousands of times you thought nothing of showing it, you selfish, self-righteous asshole!"

My anger peters out and morphs into what feels like a childhood's worth of tears. "How could you be so cold-hearted – so slack-ass in your fatherly duty!?"

For the first time I feel warmth in me for the scared and abandoned kid that I was! Driving home I notice that my normal idling level of anxiety has disappeared. I see – with more therapeutic tears – how often I turn my healthy anger against myself, as I had to with bullyboy, Charlie. *Oh my god, all those thousands of times I scared the crap out of myself with unrelenting self-attack!*

When I get home, I look at a photo of eight-year-old me leaning forlornly against a Dutch Elm tree in front of my neighbor's house. In the past this picture always looked ugly, yet now to my great surprise, that boy is quite good looking. I feel unqualified compassion for him, and sweet tears roll down my face.

Suddenly, in an illuminating internal flash, I see a large Tao symbol with my sad face on one side and my angry face on the other. *That's it! I tell myself. Crying and angering…the Yin and Yang of Grieving. When we're hurt, part of us is sad and part of us mad!*

Almost simultaneously I feel another big wave of anger at my father for making me so self-critical. I decide that whenever privacy permits, I will storm at Charlie to "shut up" whenever I catch the critic in the act.

Before long I am amazed at how effective this is. *Damn! I'm going to use my anger to silence the critic just like I'd yell "Shut Up!" at a bully who was raging at someone I care about.*

I do this whenever I can remember, and over time I discover that angering even works when I do it quietly but intensely in the privacy of my mind.

Angering at the critic is like emotional math. Take the anger out of annoyed self-criticism and use it to fight and silence the critic.

Man Oh Man, this grieving stuff is beyond powerful! I am going to design my own curriculum. I will privately major in grieving.

I look for books about Griefwork but find little until I discover Elizabeth Kubler-Ross. Everything I find by and about this Sage of Griefwork thrills me. Derek Gill's biography, *Quest*, is especially inspiring, and clearly Kubler-Ross sees crying and anger as essential parts of grieving. I wet many a page with delicious tears – happy tears of resonating with her wise insights.

Kubler-Ross's work further nurtures my insights that grieving is not just about physical death. Every painful loss is like a death – whether it is the "death" of a treasured relationship, job, or circumstance. When I am emotionally invested in something, it hurts to lose it, and I am growing in my ability to work through such pain by grieving.

Rajneesh

Meanwhile, there is a new guru in town – Bhagwan Rajneesh. He's actually still in India, but his presence and impact spreads rapidly through several spiritual and psychological communities in Sydney.

On his recorded lectures, he sounds like a vibrant, well-adjusted genius – the polar opposite of Krishnamurti. His approach to personal growth is cobbled from a vast knowledge of psychology and philosophy. Many of his followers are transformed in strikingly positive ways.

A few of my closest friends, including Jody, become his devotees. They clothe themselves in orange and wear a string of beads around their necks with a small oval-framed picture of him.

As cultish as this seems, they are not bound by any other rules. They are unusually free – emotionally and cognitively. They do not withdraw from society and no hierarchy protests when they forsake orange for a rainbow of reds, mauves and magentas. When this occurs, Jody goes from looking like a tangerine with human appendages to shining like a diva.

I cannot deny that the Rajneesh workshops make his followers juicily genuine and emotionally vibrant. One night while meditating, Rajneesh's beckoning visage appears in my mind. *How disturbing*! Other friends also experience this and see it as a call to join his cult. There is no way however that I will ever wear his uniform, or god forbid adorn myself with his picture. Army and parochial school uniforms and Catholic icons were the cruel accessories of my painful past.

Nonetheless, I do attend some workshops as membership is not required. I go to the ashram for the one hour Kundalini Meditation twice a week. In the first fifteen minutes we dance wildly to a thrashing beat. In the next fifteen minutes we yell the sound Hooo…Hooo…Hooo over and over, which does wonders for deepening the breath. In the third quarter, we anger and cry in whatever blend of catharses arises in us. And in the final fifteen minutes we sit in the lotus position and quietly meditate.

My insights during the sitting mediation are often mind-expanding. I typically leave feeling transformed, relieved and refreshed.

Over time, however, I hear reports of Rajneesh sexually and financially exploiting his disciples back in India. None of my friends' rationalizations sway my suspicions that his brilliance and charisma are marred with sociopathy.

Even so, I approach this Australian incarnation of his system in the spirit of the Alcoholics Anonymous maxim: "Take the best and leave the rest," and gain quite a bit in the bargain.

Jody Steps Out

Life on the home front takes a rocky turn. Jody tells me she is having an affair with the director of her massage school. *Devastated* understates my feeling state.

I am a monogamist at heart, as well as at gut. My viscera grumble with excruciating jealousy. Jealousy feels like the most painful abandonment experience of all – fear, anger, shame and despair in cruel compound. My alimentary canal symbolically abandons my digestive process, and food goes through me like a sieve.

This emotional pain is unbearable. I pack up my belongings to leave. But my humiliation turns to mortification when I cannot go. The doorway begs me to leave but my neediness short-circuits my head's command to my legs.

We have been together for over a year and I have never been so disempoweringly dependent. *No wonder this is my first long term relationship!* I must have gotten back On the Road at least a few times as an unconscious flight from the possibility of this kind of rejection.

I realize that my bond with Grayem is a large part of the invisible emotional glue of feeling hooked. He feels like my son. I surrender to staying and trying to endure my jealousy.

All week, I feel as if I have been poisoned. I barely sleep and whenever we interact, Jody and I devolve quickly into conflict.

On Friday her new boyfriend comes over for dinner. I double down on my efforts to be liberated – to accept this new trend in sexual freedom.

My anxiety feels as if lemmings are suicidally breaking out of my belly. At dinner, Jody engloves *his* hand on the table with hers, and I can bear it no longer.

I leave the room and shock the light out of myself when I impulsively punch a hole in the bedroom wall. *Oh my god what have I done? This behavior is beyond unacceptable!* This added shame is appropriate. I must move out immediately.

We are chalk and cheese,
We are chalk raked across the blackboard.
Chalk and blackboard screeching!

I find a room in a boarding house and sink into what I think Jung meant by *The Dark Night of the Soul*. It is abandonment depression to the third power.

One morning I awake after mere minutes of sleep feeling half past death. Instead of morning birdsong, I am assailed with the counter-New Age thought: *this is the first day of the rest of your never ending depression.*

Over the next six weeks – which feel like six months – I learn about how little sleep it is possible to survive on, as I average less than two hours a night.

Daily grieving sessions, however, finally rebirth me back into a modicum of hopefulness. One morning, when a popular Australian rock band comes on the radio singing their hit: "If You Leave Me, Can I Come Too", my emoting morphs into laughing instead of crying.

My humor has always been tickled by the absurd. Internally I see a turquoise light at the end of a tunnel. *Great! My favorite color! I accept the death of this relationship.*

CHAPTER 13

Working with Real Live Clients

Co-occurring with my heartbreak over Jody, my first social work internship begins at Rydalmere Psychiatric Hospital. I volunteer for it even though a fellow student warns me: "Watch out mate! It's beyond crazy out there. You can't sort out the inmates from the staff. You might wind up with a lobotomy yourself!"

This of course appeals to my counterphobia. But I also feel deeply drawn to this work. I have grown relatively comfortable around mentally ill people over the years. I've had a lot of practice over the last decade. It seems that I cannot relax on a park bench without some unhinged guy sitting down and launching into a never ending story, like the guy with the horizontal Mohawk in San Francisco.

In Amsterdam, a florid Van Goghish guy crowded me on the bench as if I were a long lost relative. He then barreled into his theory about the mess in the Middle East: "God is preparing Jerusalem for his second coming. He's got all these Arabs and Jews bombing the shit out of each other to level the city. When it becomes perfectly flat, The Lord and His Golden City will descend from space to be the hub of the new Millennium…"

Nonetheless, I'm quite intimidated on my first shift. Left unattended for an hour in the large open ward, I watch new patients in nervous breakdown-mode mingle with slow-motion, over-medicated psychotics. It's not as bad as the movies, but there's probably enough bizarre behavior for my unconscious to come up with a full-on nightmare tonight.

HOMESTEADING in the CALM EYE of the STORM

My frenetic supervisor finally greets me on the run and tells me: "Make yourself useful!" When I reply with a blank look, she elaborates walking away backwards: "Why don't you start a socialization group for those patients wasting away over there in the day room?"

I can't bear the self-consciousness of standing around like a turnip any longer, so I walk around the ward cajoling inmates to come to my group. Two psychiatric nurses befriend me in the process and add a hard sell to the mix, and *Voila!* I have a group – mostly depressives and chronic schizophrenics medicated out of their florid symptoms.

Now what? I'm not trained to run a psychiatric group. I guess I'll just wing it. I whip out an old standard and go around the circle asking members to introduce themselves. *Talk about blank looks!* Silently jibing myself, I think: *Well that went well: two names and no info!*

I then try some basic connection exercises. Nobody goes for them. In quiet desperation I pull my newspaper from my backpack, and say: "I know. I'll just read stories I think you guys might like. If they make you think of something to say, I'd love to hear it. But no pressure…you can just hang out here, and be quiet and not even pay attention…unless you feel like it."

Not much ever happens in the group, especially as I carefully avoid upsetting news items. Many members however, begin showing up without the cattle prods, and some of them exhibit mildly improved behavior. I think it is at least partly because I feel genuine compassion for them.

The hospital psychiatrists are legendarily cold-hearted, and one pompous bastard backhandedly compliments my group. "I see some of your nutters are a little less bonkers. Maybe you should write it up in The Sydney Morning Fruitcake" [bad pun for The Sydney Morning Herald newspaper].

What I wish I could say is: "Maybe you and your other psychiatrist mates wouldn't be such a disgrace to the art of psychology if you'd stop modeling yourself on the constipated, stiff upper-lipped pommies [Englishmen] that your fellow Aussies so despise."

Instead I give him a bit of Darwin Outback slang: "Fair Dinkum, Mate. Ya musta thought of that one while you were laboring in the dunny." I turn away hoping that a tinge of disdain is coming through my broad smile.

Sometimes It Is Easier To Die

One of my group members, Gertrude, is the most absent person I ever meet.

> She sits on the back porch
> Like a crumpled piece of paper.
> The wind blows her memories away
> Before she can have them.
> She is a grounded, sopping kite
> And I mourn for what I do not have to give her.

I feel disturbed looking into Gertrude's eyes. She is light years gone and yet answers simple questions calmly and rationally…almost sweetly. A nurse tells me: "She was admitted with a paralytic depression…with genuine *waxy flexibility*…so depressed her limbs would freeze in place wherever we moved them.

"Ya know Pete, I'd be like that too if I came out of a nervous breakdown and learned that I had killed my four kids with a hammer."

I gasp: "Who could ever recover from something like that? No wonder she looks so lost and empty. She must be constantly trying to avoid the memory in her eyes."

Cheryl replies: "Yeah mate, she couldn't be worse off. This morning we caught her trying to climb over the fence on the freeway overpass. When we got to her, her leg was over the railing and she said: 'Don't worry, I'm just exercising it'." We both can't help laughing at the wretched absurdity of this. But this time I feel so guilty for laughing.

When I return for my next shift, Cheryl comes up to me. "I'm really sorry, Pete. I know you really had a soft spot for Gertrude, but she made it over the railing yesterday and was instantly killed by the traffic."

I expect to feel intensely upset. I even work it up a bit by thinking about how ghastly it must have been for the drivers who ran over her.

But then I feel a potent mixture of surprise and relief. I am relieved for poor Gertrude, because there was no way she could ever come back from the horror that befell her. As I allow the relief, I then feel grief – not so much for her death – but for the tragedy of her life.

Kicking It with Sat

Another intern, Chris, and I are having falafel sandwiches for lunch at Rydalmere. "Pete" she says, "Why don't you come over for dinner and meet my husband, Sat. He's a Yank too, and an ex-Marine. He shares your irreverent sense of humor. You guys would love each other."

Sat and I hit it off like Cheech & Chong. We talk for hours about the intersections of our pasts: the military, California, sports, music and our love of tools. Sat defines laid-back. Strong and centered like the massive roots of a banyan tree, he is also funny, emotionally generous and blessed with an infectious laugh.

Before long, Chris and Sat invite me to move in: "…if you've got the carpentry skills to convert our unfinished attic into a bedroom."

The house is a simple A-frame. I nail some "found" floor boards on top of the rafters above the first floor, put in a window in the roof, and add a windowed door to the center of the "A." I hang decorative batiks on the inside sloping planes of the roof and *Whadda ya know? A fine hippie pad.* I even have a large balcony. Outside the entrance to the "A", there is a gently sloping roof covering the back room of the house.

I use a ladder to access my new digs. Herbie soon gives up trying to climb it, but it's a week before she stops barking for me to come down. Perfection is achieved when I scavenge a full length, front seat from an abandoned car and put it on the roof near the door. For $23 worth of building materials, I now have a fine penthouse…and balcony with "couch".

This afternoon, I'm on the roof-couch reading some psychology for class tomorrow when Sat comes up the ladder. We laze into a hippie news commentary on the high and low points of our days.

The sounds of Dire Straits' "Sultans of Swing" waft up from the kitchen. I rarely get stoned these days. I want to be able to retain what I'm learning at school, but when Sat lights up, I take a toke.

An especially brilliant sunset begins to unfurl with a rainbow of purples stretching from magenta rose to lavender to full-on plum. We let our freak flags flap away as our conversation warp-speeds into the effervescent, glad-to-be-alive zone.

Going Back to the Dry Well

Chris and Sat's home is my best communal experience yet. Two more couples live in the other bedrooms and we all share dinner every night. Living here feels like what family life is meant to be. Once a month, we host a potluck with other local hippie houses and bathe in a feeling of tribe.

Months go by, and with an invisible ace bandage on my sprained self-esteem, I visit Jody again. I mean *Gulamo*. That's her new *sunyasin* name, bestowed by Rajneesh himself. I sense she's embarrassed to tell me. Gulamo sounds so "gooey". I am sure she wished for something more elegant, like *Parvati* or *Tara*.

We reconnect via talking about Grayem. Spontaneous combustion reignites the old flame and something like love is back in bloom.

Jody and Grayem move into Sat's house with us. For months, every day is ripe with comfort and contentment, until Jody tells us she and

Sat's wife are having an affair. At first we think they're joking – but they disabuse us of this notion with a passionate kiss.

I briefly try to handle it, but every conversation soon deteriorates into me being painted as unliberated and uptight.

> Infidelity cannot make diamonds out of black coal words.
> Cast into the umbra of her light,
>   I cut the cord we've strung between us
>   as if it were a hanging jungle bridge…
> I free-fall into the abyss
>   with infinity soaring between us.

Jody, Grayem and Chris move out. Sat laughs sardonically: "You know, Pete, you can't always be the dog…Sometimes you're just the fire hydrant!"

He and I tumble together into the abandonment abyss. It's not as lonely down in the pits however, when a real friend accompanies you – someone you can be fully vulnerable with. We help each other release more painful feelings than a therapist's couch in an average month.

This <u>co</u>mmiseration anchors our friendship fathoms deeper. Nothing deepens trust like commiseration – an AC current of sympathy and understanding that easily morphs into humor and insight.

Our friendship grows more multi-dimensional when Sat's beloved car starts spluttering with a terminal ailment. A guy who swears the engine's good sells Sat a wrecked car of the same model.

We rig up a tripod and pulley to hoist the engine out of the car. With his feet on the bumper Sat pulls the rope and stretches out parallel to the ground. The engine rises toward the apex of the tripod. I guide it around the obstacles in the engine compartment.

Just as the engine bottom clears the body of the car, a timber of the tripod snaps. The engine crashes to the ground, and Sat lands spread-eagled on the back of his head on the road.

"Fuck Me Dead!" he screams.

In a second, my alarm morphs into terror as I see thick chartreuse fluid creeping downhill from the back of his head. If I was the fainting type, I would swoon.

Suddenly, I flash that the fluid is not leaking from his cracked skull. *Thank God! It's transmission fluid...not spinal fluid! The gearbox must have cracked when the engine smashed to the ground!*

My horror instantly morphs into hilarity as Sat calls out: "I'm ok man!" It takes a full minute before I can stop laughing to share how it all looked from my angle.

After Sat rinses the transmission fluid out of his Afro, we work for three days to finish the job. When he finally turns the ignition key, the engine sputter-farts to life, but it's almost as wounded as the one we replaced.

Sat curses: "I knew I shouldn't have believed that asshole who sold it to me. He's a speed freak and as reliable as a toilet paper umbrella."

Even so, we agree that it was a great project, notwithstanding the ordeal. There's nothing like a shared ordeal to deepen a friendship. And the fact that the car actually started is a Pyrrhic victory. We're pumped that we solved the complex puzzle of replacing an engine. It's a great emblem of the teamwork we enjoy during myriad endeavors over the next seven years.

Meditate Don't Medicate

I've tried for a decade to get somewhere in meditation – somewhere besides mushrooming self-disappointment. In my attempts to meditate, bored restlessness typically chases *centeredness* in a losing game of tag.

So I respond to an ad by a practitioner who uses biofeedback to teach meditation. He hooks me up to a machine that measures alpha waves and says: "In normal waking consciousness, beta waves are dominant in the mind, while alpha waves are more prevalent in meditative states.

"Luckily, everyone gets the occasional alpha wave. This machine rings a soft bell when your brain emits alpha. When you hear it, try to merge your awareness with that sound. With practice, the frequency of alpha will increase."

I do and it does…and so does a deepening sense of peace and relaxation. It is a state I've never experienced in unmedicated consciousness. After a few sessions I am able to replicate this via meditatively focusing on my breath.

Heavens to Murgatroyd! All those hundreds of hours of non-meditating meditation! Finally, I can meditate!

At home, I put an electric water jug in my room. When I wake up, I make and drink a cup of tea while I journal about my dreams. I then meditate for thirty minutes before coming down to the kitchen. At the end of each session, I think momentarily about the day ahead, and my ability to prioritize skyrockets. What a rich way to start the day.

Out of My Body, But in My Mind

To get in some extra meditation, I now eat lunch alone in my station wagon at the rear of the Rydalmere parking lot. To be less conspicuous, I lie down in the back and meditate for half an hour.

Today, I drop into a very deep meditative space. When my watch alarm goes off, I sit up and climb into the front seat. I look back over my shoulder and panic when I see that my body has not come with me. *Oh my God, what is happening!*

I lie back down and once again sit up – but my body does not. And then again the same cycle for a third time…a fourth, fifth.

My fear peaks as I identify with the drasticizing of my inner critic: "What's going to happen to me? Someone will find me here looking comatose. No! I can see that my eyes are open when I sit up. They'll think I've fallen into a paralytic depression. I'll be admitted as a patient. Or I'll freeze to death in the car tonight if nobody finds me before that." And so on, ad nauseam and ad infinitum.

Finally, after I loop the loop of panicked catastrophizing innumerable times, I think: *I know I'll try counting backwards from ten as if I'm ending a hypnotic trance.*

With every erg of my focusing ability, I count and pump up my intention to regain control of my body. And Battling Buddha! At the count of one, I sit up in the back reunited with my body!

And what happens then? My critic goes off: "You freakin' idiot! You've been studying psychic phenomena for years. Umpteen books and workshops, and a year of continuous letdown in that ridiculous white magic group without a speck of psychic experience. And here you are gifted with a genuine, non drug-induced, out-of-body experience, and you piss it away!"

I scrabble back to a more centered place and rebut the critic: *This is still incredible. It's a lot like the Near-Death Experiences I've been researching!*

To which my critic replies: "You really are stupid. You didn't have a near-death experience. You haven't even had a near-life experience!"

I keep looking for the silver lining, but I am mostly disappointed...and not just from wrongheaded self-judgment. How I wish I had explored being out of my body. This may be a once in a lifetime experience. I could have gone walking around invisible. Who knows maybe I could have even flown?

After a week of journaling, I work through the disappointment and finally feel elated. *I am not going to throw out this piece of burnt toast. I'll scrape off the char.* As I meditate the whole thing looks like transcendental Wonder Bread – what the Holy Eucharist should have been made of.

There's no doubt about it. This out-of-body experience was monumentally edifying. From this moment on, I feel buoyed by the knowledge that my essence is spirit. Though my body will most certainly die, I will go on.

—☽—

Weeks later at the hospital I have my eighth and final session with my patient, Margaret, who was admitted two months earlier in what looked like a sleep-walking depression. She fell into this state right after her loving husband's unexpected death.

Margaret immediately understood my psychoeducation about her need to grieve. Precociously, she jumped right into her anger and tears. In a poignant set of sessions, she grieved so effectively that she will be released after this last session.

Margaret's recovery and gratitude about our work further fortifies me to evangelize about grieving. I've been preaching so much lately that I've given up wearing black to deemphasize the fact.

My year at Rydalmere ends as does the insanity-phobia that tortured me during my psychopathology classes. I get what mental illness is now. I know that I'm sane and very unlikely to flip out. *What a tremendous reward for counterphobically taking this internship.*

From here on, I am able to reassure friends and clients, who worry needlessly, that they are not crazy. Moreover, I know how to hook up truly decompensating people with good psychiatric help. I never misdiagnose and needlessly 5150 [hospitalize] anyone.

It's also a relief that park bench emissaries of madness no longer seem to seek me out. Maybe, I've provided a quota of the kindness that I'm here to deliver, or perhaps I just finally know enough about helping people with such suffering.

Looking back at it now, I'm not surprised that psychotic people gravitated toward me, or that I felt relatively comfortable around them.

I worshipped my mother's father who lived with us when I was young. My friends and I loved him and his wildly "original" stories.

Tragically, Grandpa Stevenson spent his last ten years in a psychiatric hospital because of his unrelenting efforts to baptize my grandmother in the birdbath. He was convinced he was the Pope. My mother who hated grandma once said: "He should been trying to exorcise her."

My mother also swung in and out of paranoid schizophrenia at the end of her life. Her face continuously lapsed into a deranged evil grin as she cursed out my father and sisters – which in itself was shocking as none of us ever heard her swear before. As vitriolic as she could be, she prided herself on not having a "gutter mouth."

Interestingly, my mother became sane and lucid whenever I visited her. Once she even grieved about her childhood pain! And my socks fell down when she tearfully apologized for beating me as a toddler. "I used to smack you so hard, you'd roll across the floor and smash into the cabinets."

I also think my mother "borderlined" in and out of psychosis in my earliest years as well, as I described in the introduction.

Mercifully, I figured out how to tread delicately and *helpfully* around her when I was old enough. This occasionally mellowed her. Never for long though. I couldn't walk lightly enough to avoid all the eggshells.

So, little wonder that I followed my nose – without a trace of ambition – into training to be a mental health professional. All this early on-the-job training probably awakened my innate talent for this type of work.

How Many Times Can I Step into the Same Hole

My friend Mike insists that I get Laney – a psychological astrologer– to read my horoscope. At the reading, I am floored by how much this stranger knows about my private inner life.

There is clearly a wealth of information encoded in the esoteric symbols inscribed on my chart, and astrology immediately becomes my new passion. Laney lends me several great books that help me translate this new language, and I marathon into them – greedy for this incredibly helpful knowledge. [Stephen Arroyo's *Astrology, Psychology and The Four Elements* is most enlightening].

Months pass and Jody returns from a year in Darwin. During a visit with Grayem, I am surprised and then scared that I feel friendly toward her again.

Jody's passion for Sat's wife has long exfoliated. She flashes the high beams of her desire on me again, and somehow I forget that her affection and disregard fluctuate as often as a traffic light. When I get home I journal this:

> When I knew we'd lost our glow
> Like some rich painting now clichéd
> I cried tears that washed *us* away.
>
> And now with so much time expired
> We stray again into each other's lives.
> With our mismatched memories,
> We try to forget and fight
> The fact that we are still
> Strangers in the night

Despite my intuitive poem, I surrender to how lovely it all feels, especially now that we share an avid interest in astrology. In the past, astrology was the only thing Jody and I argued about *amicably*. I'm quite amazed at how much astrology seeped into my psyche during those debates.

So I am happy to tell her: "I'm really grateful, Jody, that you were my first astrology teacher." She glows…and together we subsequently eat, drink and inhale astrology. *Who knew cerebral discussions could be so titillating?*

What fun it is to help each other decode the hidden facts in our horoscopes. Best of all, Liz Greene's astrological classic, *Relating*, shows us that the things we often clash about are not matters of right or wrong, but normal inborn differences. We commit to learning how to *agree to disagree*.

Pleasurable months go by, but on our way to a medical astrology workshop, Jody says: "Lorraine tells me that the studly workshop leader, Paul, came onto her at the last workshop. God I hope he seduces me!"

I don't share my inner response: *God Damn, tell me this isn't happening!*

Since even more of our friends are experimenting with *open relationship*, I tell myself to chill out about her wishes. But halfway there I have to stop the car. I dart into the bush and evacuate my abandonment stress from both ends of my alimentary canal.

When I get back in I say: "Jody my body is clearly telling me this is one difference I just can't accept."

She replies: "Yeah, well that's too bad, Pete, because I can't do monogamy."

With surprising calm, I say: "Well then I guess we're well and truly done."

I drop her off at the workshop, and drive home trying to remember what I read about the need for boundaries in a relationship.

I'm not exactly sure what boundaries are, but Thank God, I wasn't stupid enough to let her move in with me again. Hmmm, maybe that was a boundary?

So our three year soap opera is officially cancelled. It's replaced by an earworm – Bob Dylan's sardonic ballad, *Don't Think Twice*:

> I ain't saying you treated me unkind
> You could'a done better but I don't mind
> You just kinda wasted my precious time.
> Don't think twice, it's alright

I incessantly sing this and other heartbreak hotel-type songs for weeks to help grieve the death of my hopes and dreams with Jody. My resolve to give her up for good is fixed. Third time lucky – I get away.

Astrology: The First Psychology

I go to Laney for a second reading. Here are some highlights from the tape recording of my session:

"People are not just their sun signs, Pete. Everyone has two or three key astrological signs in their makeup.

"You are not always the light-hearted, fun-loving Sagittarius you'd like to be, because of all this stuff up here in your Midheaven. The Moon, Venus and Jupiter were all close together in the sky in the sign of Scorpio when you were born. Scorpio is much more serious and moody than Sagittarius. These two signs couldn't be more different. If you don't make room for both of them, you may often be at war with yourself."

"Me? At war with me? I'm a peacenik!" I say, attempting irony. Then I shut up because she's totally nailed me.

She continues: "Sagittarians chase fun. They want to be constantly uplifted. They want to be free to try everything. But Scorpios are serious and intensely emotional. They are often pulled toward life-changing ordeals, especially passionate relationships – entanglements that trigger turbulent feelings.

"By turbulent feelings do you mean 'feeling like jumping off a bridge'?" I joke.

"Yes", she says: "I don't know too many Scorpios who don't occasionally wish they were dead. But let me continue. Sagittarians gravitate toward philosophy. They search for meaning outside themselves, while Scorpios find meaning through psychologically exploring their inner worlds.

"Often Scorpios discover that they have had a difficult childhood. Deeper understanding of this often triggers a yearning to revamp themselves. Facing their painful feelings often makes them feel more alive and comfortable in their own skins."

After a lengthy discussion of this topic, Laney says: "So, Pete! These conflicting signs in your chart also explain your complaint about your uneven moods and energy levels. When Sagittarius is in ascendancy, life feels cushy and exciting. But when Scorpio dominates, you may experience painful losses. When you embrace your losses, they can become symbolic deaths that lead to powerful rebirths. Pete, I think you may have many skins to shed this time around." I suddenly blush and freeze as I realize that I am nodding like a bobblehead.

"And Pete, as you get these opposite energies working together, you can evolve greatly in this lifetime. And what's more, all this Scorpio at the top of your chart indicates that your Sagittarian teacher-side could help others delve into their pain in a healing way!"

As the reading comes to an end, I say: "Well Laney, I don't know about that last part. But since I've been grieving a lot – which you say is 'ruled' by Scorpio – I feel reborn inside. And paradoxically, I'm having more Sagittarian spiritual experiences at the same time. So I guess you're saying that Scorpio and Sagittarius are the yin and yang paths of my ongoing development."

"You got it, Pete. And keep those tear ducts open!"

In the past I rejected astrology for not being scientific. But, after my second, epiphany-rich reading from Laney, I no longer believe that science is always empirical. After all, psychology would be an impoverished husk if it only consisted of CBT's experimentally proven techniques…techniques which are often "proven" by shaky statistical methods [See: *The Use and Abuse of Statistics* by W.J. Reichman].

Psychological science ignores the heart and soul because they are not observable, measurable physical entities. Sadly, this encourages more and more people to forego spiritual and emotional development. The epidemic of people treating themselves as if they are merely machines worsens, as does the incidence of correlating anxiety and depressive disorders.

Over time, I come to think of myself as an astrological oxymoron. I am a Scorpionic Sagittarian searching for freedom in commitment, for light in the dark, for life in death. Like my hero, Walt Whitman, I embrace my contradictions.

I will become more conscious of my unconscious. I will find holiness in all that is taboo. The sacrilegious ex-Catholic part of me thinks: *If God is omnipresent and everywhere, s/he must also be in the crap and the pain.*

Although I strive hard to be real, I now notice more blind spots. Apparently, I'm still too swayed by my old Sagittarian belief that people only want the good stuff – that no one likes you if you're too heavy. To broaden my ability to relate, I glom onto the maxim: "You're only as sick as your secrets." I make myself talk more about what's bothering me in the moment.

Opening up to a deeper level of vulnerability is a mixed bag at first. When I pick someone who's naturally kind, I feel comforted. But when I trust the wrong person, I get triggered into a shame attack. With practice, I get better at sensing who is safe enough.

Eventually, I find nothing-too-heavy friends who greet vulnerability as permission to talk about anything. Malcolm, Barbara and I talk as easily about painful stuff as light stuff – and often just as enjoyably. Moods and hurts are toys in the "playground" of our everyday conversations. As my fair weather friends fade into the background, we three save a lot of money on therapy.

Opening a Client to Grieving

When I complete my Social Work degree, I go into private practice as a psychological astrologer. Fortune telling and prediction are of no interest for me. My horoscope readings are about discovering inborn talents and developmental arrests. I also specialize in exploring psychological conflicts between various parts of the self, such as thinking vs. feeling and striving vs. letting go.

I am reading Alan's horoscope. His girlfriend liked my astrological reading so much that she paid for his session. Alan's chart is as loaded with Scorpio as mine. Well into the reading, I explain how Scorpios seem to have more emotional pain than other signs. He seems receptive to this, so I tell him: "Scorpios usually experience a great deal of relief when they learn how to grieve out that pain."

His face pales and tightens up. *Wow, that was quick...I've touched something that wants to be released.* Continuing on, I say: "Scorpios are particularly subject to self-hate because they feel things so much more intensely than others."

Oh, Good! He's getting teary! "Alan your tears are welcome here. I've got bulk Scorpio in my chart, and crying always makes feel better!"

He lurches into an intense release, angrily crying about what a "shit life" he's had. "Nobody's ever wanted me around...not even my mum. And I don't blame her...or them. I'm such a bummer to be around. I hate being alive." He intermittently punctuates this with bursts of angry crying.

"But I don't want you to think I like crying! It's just one more weird fucked up thing about me. Nobody likes a whinger! I'm just a big fucken crybaby!"

With suitable pause, I say: "I'm really sorry you've gotten such a raw deal. And I know it's hard to be male and cry. People can be such assholes with their teasing!"

"You've got no idea mate."

"Actually, I do mate. There aren't many people I will cry around, but I discovered that when I stopped hating my tears and letting them come, they brought me more relief than anything else...drugs, booze or sex!"

Alan seems to instantly get it. *Just like with other Scorpios I've said this to, I can see flash bulbs going off in his eyes.*

Alan says: "You know mate I did have that experience once, after me mum suicided when I was twelve. I was going to kill myself too, but I cried so hard I actually felt better...but I guess I didn't realize it was from the crying."

We talk about this a great deal, and he asks for another session to further work through his mother's death. We wind up doing six sessions, in which this emotionally precocious client severs the self-hate from his tears and begins turning his tears into self-compassion.

I have no idea at the time that this will become a signature therapy session for me.

Over the next three years, I give over a thousand psychological astrology readings. In the process, I learn a great deal about helping clients talk about their most vulnerable hopes and fears.

In the midst of this, I start teaching astrology as a self-help tool. Disturbingly, I discover a new handicap. Just when I thought I'd inventoried all my shortcomings, I now discover abominable teaching anxiety.

This feels beyond unfair. I comfortably taught so many auditorium-sized classes in the army. Yet my performance anxiety is now so intense that I have the trots once or twice before each class. Thankfully the enthusiasm of my students and a sense of calling save me from giving up on teaching.

CHAPTER 14

Onward and Inward

SAT AND I stroll the city, and the wind tricks a flier on a telephone poll into winking at me. We look closer and see that it is an ad for a live-in, ten day Vipassana Meditation retreat. Sat reads it and says: "Looks like it's free." On closer inspection, he dubiously quips: "Probably be cheap at half the price!"

I take a look and reply: "Well man, I do like the price and it looks just like something I didn't know I was looking for. How about it man? Why don't you come along?"

"No thanks, Pete. My life's already too meditative as it is." He's a pretty laid back guy, and on a certain level he's right.

I register for the retreat and when I arrive at the venue – a fenced-in Boy Scout camp on Sydney's outskirts – I get penitentiary vibes. Robed disciples of Burmese meditation master, Goenka, are stationed at the entrance and possible exits of this austere venue.

We are herded into a cold hall, and persuasively invited to take a nine day vow of silence. A customs-like examination ensures our surrender of food and other comforting objects like books, snacks, paper and pens. My butt contracts as I flashback to my last body cavity search, but we are of course not subjected to this indignity.

The senior drill sergeant-monk lays down the law. "Full participation is required in eleven fifty minute sessions of meditation every day. You may walk about the grounds between sessions, but silence will be maintained everywhere, and at all times"

Later, "Sgt. Monk" stops me from jogging during a break with the withering stare of Sister Jean Therese. "Stop!" he commands. "We ONLY move about slowly and meditatively!"

The news worsens. There will only be two meals a day – two frugal, vegetarian meals that would make "Weight Watchers" cry in their calories.

The bunks are jail-cell comfortable. Every room is furnished with at least one snorer, and sleep is hard to come by. Staying awake during sessions is dogma, but I nap and nod like a narcoleptic. Censuring nudges from the spiritual cadre keep me vertical.

Our first session starts with long, micro-managing directions from Goenka. He speaks with a heavy Burmese accent in a high-pitched, sing-song voice. There is no chance his voice will soporifically trance me out.

For three days we concentrate *exclusively* on the sensations in our nostrils [he calls them *nose-trils*] as we breathe slowly and mindfully in and out.

Then for the next seven days Goenka guides us to shift our focus to the sensations in our bodies. We begin by concentrating on the tips of our toes. Then ever so slowly, we move our focus – millimeter by millimeter – up our bodies to the crowns of our heads. From there we reverse the process down to our toes.

Over and over, our awareness crawls up and down our bodies. All the while we try to ignore distracting thoughts, feelings, images, and sensations in other body parts.

Goenka repeatedly reminds us: "Nothing to do but fully merge with the sensation at the point of your focus."

At first, my recently acquired ability to meditate makes me think this will all be worthwhile. But by the second session, gloom sets in. I've never meditated more than thirty minutes. *This is the pits! I thought I mastered tedium in the army, but this is cruel and unusual punishment!*

With no cushion and no back support, I am being abused by the concrete floor. My version of the full lotus position has half my body in pins and needles. My back is on fire with pain, but the indoctrination of my formative years silently bellows: "Quitting is not an option." My critic whips me mercilessly with a landfill of judgments. I fear Easter will be a long time coming from this inner crucifixion.

Pete Walker

Raging into Love

Hourly my negative thinking grows more cantankerous. It vacillates like ping pong between self-hate and hate for others – most especially Goenka himself. I rechristen him with Aussie slang: *Go-Wankah!*

All my anger percolates in a soup of toxic shame. *What is wrong with me! I'm a loving person. Who is this angry maniac?*

By the third day I am a fuming morass of hate and fury. *Damn, I wish I could burst out into an anger-releasing gestalt!*

Besides focusing on sensation, our only other instruction is: "Acceptance...you must accept whatever you are feeling and experiencing." Gowankah raises his whine to a trill: "Accept how your mind wanders, but gently bring it back to your nose-trils. Treat your mind kindly as if you are trying to make the puppy pee on the newspaper, not on the floor."

By the afternoon, my acceptance morphs into indulgence. I allow my angry fantasies to run rampant...fantasies of rebelling against the cadre... of calling out holier-than-thou-looking meditators.

I discover that my inner critic has an evil twin brother, who I later name the outer critic. The outer critic wants to scream: "How dare you sanctimonious assholes look so enlightened? You're faking it. You like making me look bad."

My fantasies turn so violent that it frightens me. I have never acted out in rage against another human being. But I am scared that if I do not start suppressing this ugly imagery now, I will lose control and act it out. The devil that my mother claimed to see in me so often might rise up in some awful act of violence.

Just then Go-Wankah unctuously utters: "Acceptance, acceptance. You must let yourself accept all that you find within yourself."

So I let it unfold – a frightening fantasy [thankfully bloodless] of running amok in the gym cutting off people's heads with a machete. There seems to be nowhere else to take my rage, and I surrender to the feelings and the imagery, cringing all the while at the horror of it.

And *Glory Halleluiah*! My body does not take over and scream or run amok. The hate ebbs and plays itself out. Guilt and shame replace it momentarily, but suddenly an astounding, inner vision arises.

A numinous light-enshrouded woman, effulging blue light, hovers before and above me radiating a sweet azure light of compassion. The blue light soothes every cell of my being.

Now, I am in her lap – sublimely comforted and nurtured into perfect peace. Her compassion turns me self-compassionate, and I am so completely on my side that there is not an atom of space for the critic to invade.

I know, like I know the taste of a ripe peach, that this is a reward for being brave enough to fully feeling my anger. Even better, I know that I will never have to be afraid of it again. Never hate my anger, run from it or be ashamed of it.

And of course, I will not narcissistically act it out. But I will always let the energy of it spontaneously arise to find its hidden fruit – to reap the important information that is typically encoded in its heat. In this case the message is that intense anger can be simply felt through without causing harm.

This profoundly spiritual experience culminates with me quietly and joyously crying. Many waves of relief and insight break softly on the reef of my understanding. Glaciers of past guilt about being angry melt way.

When a soft *gongggg* announces the end of the session, I feel as if I have been bathed and purified with love. My heart overflows with love for everyone – my fellow sufferers, the sanctimonious cadre and even good old Goenka.

This is a new level in my quest to become a fully feeling person, and I beam at the irony that grace came to me through a Catholic icon in a Buddhist setting.

Spiritual Chiropractic

Change is the only absolute in life. The next morning, everything is difficult again. The sparking welding torch in the middle of my back plagues me, and the critic swallows my peace of mind like a rat devouring a piece of cheese.

But it is the sixth day and my concentration is sharpening. I spotlight my focus on the ring of awareness slowly rising up and down my body. I feel massaged by a halo of soft large hands encircling my body.

I pause to fully feel the pain in my back. I reverse my instinct to move away from it. *I will plumb this pain...experience it microscopically.* I wallow in the sensations of the pain at length, and then suddenly, I feel as if lightning has struck my back.

With a mighty wrench – like a chiropractic adjustment – my back straightens, the pain evaporates and my posture perfects itself.

Holy of Holies! Two miracles in one workshop!

With my back fully relaxed, I feel serene in my body – and epiphanies begin to pour in. Goenka says to accept everything, but not in a way that encourages preferred experiences.

But that is like telling a three-year-old not to nibble on an unsupervised ice cream cake.

I cannot and will not stop this influx of understanding. An inner treasure trove of answers has opened. Question upon question arises within me. Enlightening answers are attached to each with a short cord.

I surrender to the *siddhi,* the Indian word for an opening into spiritual understanding. I am in an obsessive's paradise where worries resolve themselves and questions give birth to instant answers. Psychological conundrums that have plagued me for months instantly unravel.

Even better, a detailed outline comes through for a new class to teach – an experiential workshop about the yin/yang relationship of love and anger.

At the next break, I wander the grounds and find a pencil stub, which I secret in my sock like a POW. I even rub it on the concrete to sharpen it, like those guys in jail with the tattooing needle.

After dinner, I take several wrappers off unopened toilet paper rolls and *Voila!* I have stationary. I use the bathroom stall to make notes for this workshop.

I feel wondrously enriched. *And I don't even feel guilty about all my writing.* Some rules are made to be broken. Or, you can take the rebel out of the monk, but you can't stop the monk from rebelling.

The tenth day arrives and the vow of silence is over. The first person that I talk with is the homeless alcoholic guy, Nigel, who sat next to me the whole time. Whenever I got tired of feeling sorry for myself, I peeked over at him and my suffering paled a bit. He looked so egregiously bad that I thought I might soon be doing CPR.

Nigel tells me that he came to the retreat "…in the midst of a monstrous bender. I was just looking for a free place to get in out of the rain."

Despite his wrecked appearance, he looks amazingly good – even with his dirty hair and clothes. His face fairly glows, and his eyes are clear. His irises are dark blue corn flowers.

He smiles at me and says: "Mate, I thought I was gonna have to kill myself to get out of here. On the first night, I tried to go Walkabout…I climbed that big fence over yondah. I was up it like a rat up a drainpipe! I was almost over when these two big swami blokes hauled me back down and 'reminded' me that I had signed a commitment to do the whole retreat.

"Mate, I can't believe I didn't go bonkers, but I gotta admit – a coupla days ago I started to feel awwwlllllright! And right now I feel better than a warehouse full of beer."

—ɯ—

As I look back at this experience, I see it as the tap root of my grounding as a therapist. It was here that I realized there is nothing in me that I need to shun. I unwound many layers of my habit of hating and shaming myself for my less than "proper" feelings fantasies.

Love and Anger Couples Workshop

When I get back home, I see Sat has bought a used TV. "Pete, we can watch the World Series on it. The Dodgers are playing the Yankees and they're actually broadcasting it!" *Damn, where's the time go! This will be the first time in ten years that I live in a house with a TV.*

Sat and I bathe in sweet nostalgia as we watch the games. He is a Los Angelino and I am a New Yorker. As kids we loved our home team and hated their opponents. Yankees vs. Dodgers is a storied rivalry. Now we couch our competitive repartee in brotherhood and hilarity.

But the TV, which might have been a bargain if he didn't have to pay for it, keeps going on the fritz at crucial moments – none worse than in the final innings of the deciding game. When it's clear that another ray is never going to be emitted from its cathodes, Sat says: "This TV has to die!"

"Yeah man, let's take it outside and put it to rest!"

Our toilet is outside in a small shack attached to the back of the house. Pseudo-consecrating it, we lift the TV onto the throne – thinking that when we smash the screen, the glass will be easier to clean up.

Think again? Nah! Instead, we flip a coin to see who gets first shot at the TV.

"Tails!" I win first pitch. But instead of a baseball, I chuck a full bottle of beer. *Damn! A sinker below the strike zone.* CRASH!!! I miss the TV and shatter the toilet into a hundred pieces.

Rationally we know this is a bad thing, but we cannot stop laughing.

Sat blames this accident on the TV – which must be executed forthwith. We wrestle the Zenith out into the yard and re-enthrone it on a milk crate. Sat says: "I wonder what will happen if I chop this beast in the face with an ax."

I reply: "I don't know, Sat? Sounds pretty dangerous!"

He corrects me: "Ya know, Pete, it's so dangerous, I think it must be a good idea. But, maybe I'll stand off to the side when I chop it – ya know, just in case it explodes."

This last bit turns out to be our only smart thinking, because explode it does…with an exquisitely satisfying sound.

Miraculously neither of us gets cut, or wets his pants from laughing. The demolition feels so criminally satisfying, that we even enjoy replacing the toilet.

During the cleanup, Nick Lowe's record: "I Love the Sound of Breaking Glass" is playing on the neighbor's radio. We're both singing along and I feel so good that I flash on my Vipassana epiphany: *Releasing anger can unleash love.*

So I ask Sat to help me run a weekend *Love and Anger* workshop. Neither of us is much into the hippie it-must-be-a-sign thing…except when we are. Sat says "Yeah bro, I'm in…especially if we can break some glass!"

The working premise of the Love and Anger workshop is simple. *Appreciation for a loved one increases when withheld anger towards them is released in a harmless way.* We will use psychoeducation, creative visualizations, scripted word exchanges and safe anger-release techniques.

Ten couples sign up for the first session. Following my half hour introduction, we jump into an alternating series of anger and love exercises.

The first exercise utilizes Kubler-Ross's telephone book and hose technique. Twenty two people circle up facing outwards – each with their own hose and book. Using a guided meditation, I invite buried anger to arise for purging.

Sat and I launch in by slapping our books with a twenty inch piece of rubber hose. POW! PKOW! When struck at the right angle, the explosion of hose-on-book sounds like a gunshot…and peels off pages.

The group joins in. What an outcry! Shouting! Cursing! Strings of expletives! Pages are flying.

Hot Damn! What a responsive group! What a fine din! This is easier than coaxing five-year-olds to jump on sand castles.

The clamor provides a paradoxical shield of anonymity. Almost everyone blasts forth. Some participants exhaust their anger and a portal opens to their tears. As one person resonates with another and so on, almost a third of the group has a good cry.

When everyone's emotions are played, we shift into dyads. Each person then reads loving affirmations to their partner, like the ones in Appendix C of my first book, *The Tao of Fully Feeling*. "I love who you are." "I am always glad to see you." "You can make mistakes – they are your teachers." "I am very proud of you." Many have more tears – sweet tears. Hugging breaks out and spreads spontaneously like a healing virus.

In the go-round that completes the exercise, one guy says: "Crikey mate! Those affirmations looked pretty corny at first, but Damn! It felt good to say and hear them." *How nice it is to hear a resounding chorus of agreement.*

A woman then says: "That angering was So Fun! I just felt so freed up and unburdened that I couldn't stop laughing." More than a few nod and start laughing again in pleasurable agreement.

I end the day with a *guided visualization and bottle-breaking exercise.* "Invite any anger you have about ANY hurt or unfairness to surface into your awareness. Let it flow into the bottle that Sat has placed by your side."

After a few moments of silence, we then lead them all to an old cement bathroom downstairs. Sat throws the first bottle, people cheer, and everyone lines up like we're giving away free cruises to New Zealand. Bottles meet their doom as they interface with the wall, and people cry, anger and laugh in various combinations. Many act like they've just hit a homerun. Rich laughter peals like bells, and a few participants plea for another bottle to break.

On the next day, *exchanging back massages* follows *smacking tennis rackets against firm pillows*. Some of the love heats up so much that Sat teasingly asks several couples to get a room.

We close with another guided bottle-breaking release on the theme: "If you've ever been shamed or scapegoated, see yourself angrily giving the shame back to your abuser when you break your bottle."

Alright! This touches a nerve in almost everyone. What arms! These folks are chucking fast balls. If they were in time machines, some bullies would be going Down!

The workshop ends with a plethora of spontaneous hugs and heartfelt affections, and everyone agrees that bottle-breaking is an unparalleled release.

Later, we receive several notes and phone calls from grateful participants. One woman says: "Good on ya, mate! You brought me and boyfriend back together again. Crikey! I didn't even realize we were apart...but we were like distant roommates who never talk to each other! Now we can't shut up when we're around each other."

For months I fantasize about opening up an anger-release glass-breaking shop. For $5 throw a bottle at a wall; for $25 throw it through a piece of plate glass; and for $100 use it to take out an old TV.

Debbie

I am at a hippie commune for a weeklong outdoor astrology workshop, 300 miles north of Sydney. There I meet and promptly fall in love with gracious Debbie, a fellow social worker and an alternative healer. Debbie uses iridology for diagnosing her clients, and herbs and Bach Flower Remedies for treating them. I am immediately enamored with her warmth and intelligence.

The workshop is in Bellingen, a rare lush place in Australia. At the end of the day, Deb and I sit on the side of a hill communing for hours, watching budgerigars liberate seeds from dead flowers and listening to kookaburras screeching about something that seems darkly funny to them. Afterwards I journal:

> Twice radiant and half of blue
> Spring and summer grew from you
> You polished the tired back into new

We both have heaps of Sagittarius and Scorpio in our charts and share a passion for using astrology as a tool for spiritual and psychological growth. Unlike me she values her introverted side. "I'm a Water Violet" she says. "I love my alone time." *Hmmm, she could be a great role model!*

Hooked on self-help books, we excitedly share our discoveries with each other. What a boon – beginning a new relationship with so much shared vocabulary. We meander into a world of intimacy that feels like discovering a new continent. I am so grateful to be in my first deeply reciprocal partnership – one in which we *both* care about and contribute to each other's ongoing evolution.

And what a good person she is. She delights in seeing others do well. And she is a champion of those who are suffering. She volunteers at the Rape Crisis Center, and regularly goes out at all hours to help rape victims.

Nine months pass and Deb and I feel ready to live together. We find a huge house to rent. Clonmel [Irish for *honey vale*] is carved into the ornate door frame. Sat and Deb's best friend, heart-centered Jenny, help us find four more excellent roommates. Two of them have young children which juices up the household silliness factor.

As we move in, the great Aussie blessing, *she'll be right mate*, plays like a song in my head. We are three social workers, a hospital worker, a physician, a landscape gardener, an editor of a celebrated alternative newspaper and a full time mom. Other than "mom", we all manage to work only part-time. Her job is full time.

All of us chose each other because we are burnt out on the hippie habit of constant partying. We want to live with people who value *balancing interacting* with *having alone time*. Each of us has solitary pursuits that we prioritize.

This is my first non-begrudging nod to introversion, although the specter of perfected extroversion still haunts me. Herbie seems to be pleased that my introversion no longer requires me to disappear up onto the roof.

Life at home is lovely and mellow. We frequently gather around the kitchen table sharing a pot of tea and wide ranging conversation. We have a feast once a month, followed by a house meeting to work through hassles and to embellish living together. I often think: *These meetings are like a seminar in conflict resolution!* Talking about stuff early on sure seems to stop it from festering into something irreparable.

Over time, our Clonmel home connects with several other "freak" houses here in North Sydney and my tribal sense of belonging peaks. Never again will I have such a strong sense of belonging to a loving extended family.

Clonmel thrives for a long time after I leave, but is eventually demolished for newer housing. For many years however, "alumni" get together to remember the good old days.

Look Homeward Angel

My anger work resolves so much of my resentment toward my father that I want to visit my family! It is 1982 – twelve years since I've last seen them. My parents agree to pay half my fare, so I book a ticket.

It is an astonishing reunion. My father shocks me by looking delighted to see me. *Not a bristle in sight!* He even initiates our first hug ever! *I feel a bit faint. Okay! Never say never!*

And my sisters – all grown up now – are so delightful. I feel proud of how well they've turned out. *And, Oh my god! Look at these enchanting young creatures! A niece and nephew who seem to adore me! Someone film this, please!*

Two nights into the visit, everyone drinks a bit too much at dinner – unconsciously self-medicating for the postprandial slideshow of our childhoods. The photos trigger much barely dormant pain, and the alcohol transmutes it into group hysteria. There is way too much laughter – strangulated pain escaping through forced frivolity.

Yet much of the laughter is also the genuine bonhomie we feel at being reunited. An ambivalently good time is had by all, and actually spawns real openings with my sisters.

As the days pass, my mother's mean-spirited jibing of my father increases. I'm puzzled, as she is unsettlingly fawning with me. One night, I have a nightmare in which she verbally flays me at the kitchen table of our old New York City home.

In a lucid epiphany, the truth precipitates out of the dissociative clouds of my childhood denial. *I was often on the receiving end of her vitriol. Maybe Mom's "love" for me did not far outweigh her abuse.*

But she sure is pouring the sweetness on now, and I don't feel like thinking about this epiphany. I dissociate back into a whirlwind of fun and nurturing activities with friends and family until it's time to head back to Oz.

Well now! As Grandma Stevenson used to say: *Goodness Galoshes!* What an uplifting visit! I may be having a prodigal son salvation fantasy, but it sure seems like my family likes me…loves me! I feel so full up. Never before have my expectations been so under-blown. It's even sad to leave.

On the way back to Oz, I revisit San Francisco: *My old hippie haven!* Synchronistically, I arrive on the eve of the victory parade for the Super Bowl champion SF Forty-Niners. Although I'm scared that the crowd will make me claustrophobic, my inner anthropologist must check out this cultural phenomenon.

Six hundred thousand people line the downtown streets exuding joy and good will. Pot and alcohol is freely passed around, and I allow a gaggle of strangers to spontaneously hug me!

Though not quite tribal, the collective soul is overflowing with the heartening feelings of *esprit de corps*. I rarely wear team paraphernalia – as a fan base is too broad to elicit kinship feelings in me. But today is a thrilling exception. How soothing to momentarily belong to such a huge, welcoming group.

Even more synchronistically, I wander up the hill after the parade and spot a sign that says Antioch University. *Antioch University! The home of Will Schutz, my number one self-help guru!* His book *Profound Simplicity* is currently in my hippie shoulder bag.

Said book has been blowing my mind. In it, he brilliantly explains how authenticity and vulnerability are the key ingredients of intimacy. I've been preaching my own version of this formula for three years now – not however with Schutz' brilliance.

So I stuff a brochure about Antioch into my bag. I'll look at it later when my over-stimulated ADHD relaxes enough for me to focus on reading.

Debbie Seals the Deal

I get back to Sydney, and Debbie lets me know – with a respectful amount of regret – that she has fallen in love with someone else.

In a mostly civil conversation, she answers my protests: "I know we live together, Pete, and you're home a lot, but you're never *here!*"

I quietly fume back: "Come again! What the hell is that supposed to mean?"

"You're always so caught up in your studies and projects that you barely have time to actually relate. It's lonely being with you, Pete!"

Ouch! This rings true as it strikes a discordant note. I flash for a moment that she is right. *All too often I leave sparse time for relating on my lengthy "to do" list.*

I press the mute button on a protest that wants to get testy as it's as clear as a large smashed insect on the windshield: *Debbie's gone!*

Debbie may feel like my best relationship ever, but it's clear that this romance novel has ended. I am swallowed up in a quicksand of grief.

My main man, Sat, comes through once again. When I tell him about Deb, he says: "Relationships! Can't live with 'em; can't live without 'em!

"Let's get out of here, Pete. Let's head up the coast." He helps me grieve while we drive to our favorite camping beach. Generous beyond comprehension, he listens approvingly as I sing untold repetitions of the hard rock classic: "Love Sucks" and the Human League's poignant: "Don't You Want Me Baby."

I cannot imagine anyone else with whom I could sing this super-vulnerable breakup song. He joins in here and there reliving the death of his marriage. "Love Sucks" helps us release the anger of our grief. "Don't you want me, Baby" metabolizes our sadness. Singing and occasionally screaming the lyrics is catharsis-city.

Sat and I hang out on the beach for a week – cooking on a campfire, body surfing and verbally venting. The trip feels transformative. When we get back to Sydney, I am amazed that I don't feel compelled to move out of Clonmel. As uncomfortable as it is at first, I can handle contact with Debbie. Within weeks I am able to relate amicably with her again. *Praise Be! I have never grieved a deceased relationship so effectively.*

As time passes, the deep friendship part of our relationship breathes again.

California Here I Come

Sunbathing in the backyard, I remember the Antioch brochure. Halfway down the page I spot a heading that reads: *Master's Degree in Holistic Psychology with Professor Will Schutz.*

I know I'm California bound before I even finish reading the curriculum synopsis!

I'm staggered by the strength of this intuition. *Only "The Road" has pulled me so intensely.* This clarion call is a no-brainer from way down deep. I even have enough savings [yeah sure!] for the eighteen month degree.

I will get the degree and bring back all the California-brewed advances in psychology. This will take my teaching and therapy work to the next level.

But I'm so ambivalent. My spirit says: *Well of course!* But my soul says: *Hell No! I won't go!*

I hate it that my intuition insists that I go to Antioch University in San Francisco. But this *Knowing* is unyielding – a visitor from the Guiding Light dimension.

In another poignant grieving session about losing Deb, I also mourn the ending of my splendid life in Sydney – the only place that has ever felt like home.

> How I'll miss the warm hurricane of your love
> The effulgence of your warmth, the fig jam of your laugh
> The mocha insight percolating from your heart.
>
> You bulldozed an isthmus that connected me to my soul,
> And christened a ship that cargoed my vulnerability
> To a volcanic lake of restorative remembering.

How grateful I feel for my time in Sydney and my dear friends with whom I had so much open-hearted connection. How they deepened my ability to tolerate and increasingly enjoy intimate relating. How they aided me to search deeper within myself!

For the first time, I am not unconsciously fleeing. Ironically, I am stepping right into the jaws of my Abandonment Depression. Perhaps some wiser part of me knows that Antioch will open a navigable highway into my underworld – into my unworked through childhood trauma. Looking back, the timing was perfect.

CHAPTER 15

Home is Where the Depth Work is

I ARRIVE BACK in San Francisco in the summer of 1983, and half drown in loneliness. I know no one, and am long past finding Skid Row fascinating. I ache for the created family and tribe that I left behind in Australia.

A miserable two weeks drags by before my first class at Antioch. *What a relief to meet my exciting core group of twenty three aspiring therapists!*

Excitement turns into grace in the wink of a blink when I am rescued from my loneliness by fellow student, Hungarian/Uruguayan Lelah.

We talk for six straight hours after class, and connect multi-dimensionally at the confluence of spirituality and psychology. I am elated at finally finding someone equally addicted to introspection.

> She cats in on diamond paws – purring light
> Svelte, sleek – dancing audacious on my sight
> She's six of one -
> Aphrodite comes with the other
>
> In her daylight dress
> With its silver yes,
> Aurora Lelah pecks my lips
> And sips me from my night

The Encounter Group Maestro

The Holistic Psychology program is designed to enhance *real* connection through a daily encounter group. Will Schutz – shaved head and bullish body – could pass for a New York City tough. He jump-starts the group into vulnerability: "I'm pretty sad today. My co-leader…and now ex-partner, Judy, has just left me for someone else. We will however continue to lead the group together."

Tears roll down his unabashed face as he tells us. I love how natural and even masculine they look. I instantly know that I am in the right place…*as if Lelah hadn't already convinced me!*

Will's credentials include numerous books and a thriving private practice. His team of therapists uses Encounter as a modality to improve communications in organizations like IBM, Xerox and the Army.

His striking vitality is also an inspiring credential. Will is an exemplar of a healthy and holistic lifestyle. He's seventy but looks fifty, and later that week shuts me out in a game of handball – and I'm a decent player.

Good fortune and Will's distinction have assembled a rich international mix of people. Almost everyone dives into their emotional pain. Witnessing their vulnerability instantly endears them to me. The more I see of their pain, the more I trust and care about them.

Hundreds of hours of *Encounter* make me feel that I've known these folks for years. Wow! *Where'd all that loneliness go?*

Declaring War on the Critic

Today, Will's focusing on my self-esteem…or lack thereof. He tells me: "Pete…you pay lip service to dis-identifying from your critic…but you're always saluting it. You actually speak from its point of view as if it's your own, and you're overflowing with 'coulda, shoulda, woulda'.

"You're a passionate guy, Pete. What's it gonna take to keep you riled up about protecting yourself from its abuse." *Damn! That hit a nerve… and a couple of tear ducts!*

After an epiphany-rich angry cry, I say: "Thank you so much, Will. You just gave me what it's gonna take. I am not going to let that sucker keep lulling back into sleep!"

And war it is. I mobilize my anger for many daily skirmishes…for not letting the critic get away with anything – just like I called out Jody every time she was unfairly critical of Grayem.

The *Holism* of the program aims to promote health and balance in body, mind, soul and spirit. As such, we also have classes in Movement Therapy, Human Sexuality and Somatics [bodywork]. My favorite class next to encounter is an inspirational elective in Transpersonal [Spiritual] Psychology.

Sports psychology practicums also enhance "A sound mind in a sound body." To promote bonding through sports, we play cooperatively not competitively. In tennis and volleyball we strive to keep a rally alive as long as possible, which substantially improves my game.

One afternoon Will says: "You all take yourselves too seriously. Perfectionism has most of you hung up on this enlightenment bullshit. We need another *balancing* tool: an *Endarkenment Evening*!

"We will start tomorrow night with a monthly junk-food potluck. Bring some beer or wine, and we'll dance and shoot the shit. Discussing self-improvement will be strictly prohibited! And to paraphrase Oscar Wilde: 'everything in moderation, including excess.'"

What a feast. All the best crap I haven't eaten in ages. We're in a circle around the picnic style buffet, and Will starts a modified game of charades. "Pick a card and mime the phrase that is printed on it."

I go first, read my card, scramble up on all fours and wobble out of the room, making snorts by inhaling hard over the roof of my mouth. I look back as I scramble out the door and everyone is looking at me quizzically. Finally Leslie laughs hysterically as she shouts out "PIG OUT! Your phrase is pig-out!" "You got it," I reply, emphasizing it with a few more snorts. A few people start oinking, several soft wrestling matches break out and it all regresses into kindergarten consciousness from there.

I also enroll in a group therapy class outside the Holistic Program. With no eye toward vulnerability, it is disappointingly cerebral. Redemption comes in the last session when the teacher has us share our impressions of each other.

When I am in the hot-seat, Virginia says: "I feel attracted to you...but you're too macho to be a good match for me."

Brad, who seemingly has a crush on her, goes next. "HOW can you have a crush on him!? Can't you see he's gay! Look at that ponytail...and earrings in both ears? He's so effeminate!"

I guess I trigger his inner redneck. But how helpful to see that two people – who had the same experience of me for three months – see me so differently.

The recovery adage: "What other people think of me is none of my business" flares in my psyche, and I pledge allegiance to it. I make the critic's program of *worrying-about-other-people's-judgments* top priority for my thought-stopping work.

Bearded Nanny

I have a student-job at Antioch doing data entry in the Accounts Department. Chair-bound and focusing only on numbers, I squirm against the monotony. Dwelling on dollars and cents bankrupts me of energy. I'd quit, but I am running out of savings again.

On a whim, I answer an ad in the paper for a job as a nanny. I believe I'm qualified because of my step-parenting experiences with Frankie and Grayem, as well as my Child Minding Co-op experience in Sydney.

Somehow I camouflage my imposter syndrome during the interview with the parents, and I am hired on the spot when I hit it off like ice cream with the kids.

I take care of five-year-old Sam and two-year-old Laura nine hours a day, three days a week. The family's loving-kindness feels like a salve, and loving the kids is as easy as winning at Twister in a nursing home.

I soon love them both like I loved Frankie and Grayem. I especially love hanging out with Laura while Sam is at school. Laura is a beautiful little tree frog. She clings to my hip as I carry her about the day. While playing with the bushy red hair on my arm, she exclaims: "Pete, you have fur!" While hunting for wild creatures under the rocks in the yard, she declares: "I love, love, love pillbugs, Pete!" *My name has never sounded so good to me.*

Watching John Bradshaw's videos on inner child work takes my parenting skills to a new level. I imagine giving my inner toddler and inner kindergartner everything I give to Laura and Sam.

I regularly marvel to myself: *This is the best and most meaningful job I've ever had.* If being a therapist doesn't work out, I could be happy as a nanny. This profession feels grass roots meaningful. It's a worthwhile contribution to the Western World – a world that needs more kids who have been loved enough.

What a blessing that my nanny-hood lasts for the next three years.

Tantruming as a Healthy Developmental Stage

Tantruming is Laura's natural response to losing her infant privilege of getting instant gratification. The healthy, short-lived narcissistic entitlement of early childhood is over.

It's a painful death for every child who's lucky enough to get that sweet supply of unconditional love. Suddenly having to obey family rules hurts. Grieving out that pain will help her accept life's normal limits and disappointments.

I help Laura during her tantruming stage by using what I learned with Grayem. I sympathize with her upset when she tantrums about a family rule, like TV and refrigerator limits or boundaries with Sam's toys.

I say: "Yes you are sad! It hurts not to get what you want. It's good to cry out your sadness. And of course you're mad too! You can be mad and loud and stamp your feet. I won't let you hurt yourself or me or anything. You can yell and get your mad out now."

Occasionally she even sits on my lap while she emotionally releases. Usually it's only minutes before she accepts the painful death of on-demand satisfaction. A few angry tears and like the flip of a switch, she's happily playing with me or her toys again.

I also hope this will help her grow up – as Grayem did – without losing her grieving instincts. She'll be able to weather hard losses with a good cry and safe angry venting. Tears today may even obviate the need for future therapy.

How can Self-Esteem Exist in a Mind Poisoned Against Itself?

Homework for my Antioch Counseling Class is to pair up with another student and trade weekly therapy sessions. My co-counseling partner, Randi, and I benefit so much that we swap sessions long after the class ends.

I love working with Randi. Nothing is all-or-none with her. She speaks in percentages with word tones of gray. I see all sides of her and don't worry about the unexpressed parts that hide in so many people.

Randi and I also become great friends. For fun and for freeing up our self-expression, we enroll in the Jean Shelton Acting School. One night we practice a scene to present in class the next day. Acting the part of my long suffering wife, she gets mad at me while making my lunch – so mad that she smacks me in the face with a sour cream-smeared piece of bread.

There's way too much cream on the slice! When it thwacks me in the face, the cream explodes all over the TV and poster-covered wall behind me. Minutes of stomach-torturing laughter elapse before we can do two more sidesplitting takes. We have to get the sour cream to bread ratio right to minimize back-spray at the class performance.

Now I know why so many comedic actors reprise the cream pie in the face routine. It's a win-win situation. Being the "catcher" is even more fun than being the pitcher.

One day before our next co-counseling session, we decide to watch the movie *Mask* – the Cher and Eric Stoltz film. When the main character first appears, his birth-deformed face is so ugly, that I avert my eyes from the screen. But as the movie progresses we get to know an exceptional human being. My perception of him does a full 180. By the end of the movie he looks beautiful to me and it makes me weep.

In our ensuing session, I cry more and realize it's because I often feel ugly. We trace this back to the disgust that I saw so often on my parents' faces. Charlie and Helen drowned me in toxic shame, and I feel revolted whenever I see my reflection. How can self-esteem exist in a mind that's been so poisoned against itself?

Later that week, my jaw drops when I see Charlie's look of disgust *on my own face* snarling back at me in the mirror! From that moment on, I vow to break his legacy – to stop unconsciously snarling at myself.

It takes many seasons of grieving to be reborn out of hating my looks to genuinely appreciating them.

Mommy Dearest

Reading Alice Miller's *The Drama of the Gifted Child* rocks my foundation. Her book unfurls an inner scroll of memories of the loveless-ness of my childhood.

For weeks I frequently feel imprisoned in my crib or in my playpen. I see myself crying and reaching out to mama, hungry to be fed…to be comforted. But always, she responds with rage: "Stop crying or I'll give you something to cry about." Waves of her disgust break over me. I am swamped in shame, fear and misery. Ever alone and ever in anguish!

A month into this flashback, I pale when I realize this is how I feel in my recurring bouts with depression. This tormenting despair was deeply installed by her way back then. I guess I just can't let the past be the past. It's a giant sinkhole that keeps opening up under me.

In a co-counseling session with Randi, I tell her: "I can't believe how much I've minimized my mother's emotional abuse and neglect." She helps me grieve the death of my illusion that Helen was a loving mother. Before long, I clearly see that Helen is a Borderline – and a Narcissist. [Most of the bona fide borderlines I later meet have a narcissistic core.]

In another session with Randi, I flashback to being an older [and more entertaining] child. Helen sometimes liked me then. I was, after all, her *only* friend.

But, she was a crummy friend and entranced me like a rat in a Skinner cage with sporadic tidbits of approval. She plied me with the occasional compliment – a tiny doggie treat – as she trained me to be codependent to her narcissism. I was her hovering helper, sounding-board, approving mirror, groveling court-jester and emotional dumpster.

Pity me however when I could not elicit a laugh...or sparkle enough to be her anti-depressant. Though she herself oscillated wildly between extroversion and introversion, introversion was not an option for me. *No wonder I've been fighting it tooth and nail ever since – knotting up my insides in the process.*

As I delve deeper, I remember other abuse. She loved to surprise me with skull-rattling noogies! When I turned around upset, she maniacally cackled: "THAT'S for nothing! Do something and see what you get!"

If I dared to complain she howled: "WELL! It's better than a poke in the eye with a sharp stick!" Little wonder I now feel anxious around everyone. No wonder I startle whenever anybody comes up silently behind me.

Helen was an archetype of the Hindu goddess, Kali – feeding me with one hand while cutting off my head with the other. Praise and blame is the same for borderlines like my mother.

She was good cop/bad cop all rolled up into one. Skilled at getting me to relax into her phony kindness, she skewered me with sarcasm as soon as I let down my guard. That way her venom got in deeper.

Once she shamed me by crooning: "Your freckles are really quite becoming, Peter." After an extended pause to let me drink from the poisoned well, she chortled: "Except they make you look like Howdy Doody!"

Later: "You're actually uglier than Howdy Doody. You look like an army of flies poo-ed on your face…Ewwhh! Yuck…They did! Go wash your face! You disgust me."

And so, she tattooed ugliness on my self-image with freckles enshrined at the top of my list of fatal flaws. Try scrubbing them off!

So, is there any wonder that I'm so saturated with self-hate!? As this realization festers in me, I journal:

Why was I even Born?

Prematurely forcepted from Helen's womb
To get the doctor home for Christmas.
Like a horse leaving the gate too soon,
I was greeted with disqualification.

I couldn't read the Stop sign
So I just increased my speed,
Constantly stumbling forward
To stairs that broke my falls.

Like a box of cornflakes emptied for the prize
I was mugged by an evil wind,
And blown into a Catholic church
Where Christ himself would've been unwelcome.

Discarded in a fallow backwater
I was booked for littering;
At the hearing, the judge decried
"Who signed off on this God-awful birth?"

In yet another intense co-counseling session, I realize that my father hated me because of my *Oedipal Success* with my mother. An outside observer – seeing her in a good mood – would think she liked me better than him. I could make her laugh, while he himself never laughed – or even smiled, unless he was plastering one on to fool the camera… the outside world.

Helen's warmth flickered infrequently, briefly and manipulatively. Eventually, her warmth made me anxious. Some part of me knew it would morph into contempt…contempt with a cruel streak. Eventually, I got nervous whenever anyone radiated warmth in my direction. I should have worn a sign: "Stop being nice to me. It scares me."

> Helen smiles
> As my sisters and I squirm on the skewers of her sarcasm.
> In the flowered meadow sprinkled with landmines
> She drives her narcissistic pronouncements
> >   over little bug ears
> > >   whose deaths she never hears
> > >   whose expirations trumpet staccato
> > > >   in the chambers of her shrunken heart

I drop into deep grieving for myself and my sisters, Pat, Diane and Sharon. I feel like I got gypped out of having them as friends. There was so much painful sibling rivalry. Helen was a master of *divide and conquer*, and often had us at odds with each other – competing for her scraps.

I often felt for whichever sister was in her sites. I wish I could go back in a time machine to help them too.

Two years ago, I felt so ambivalent in my reunion with my sisters. Tremendous pleasure at seeing how lovely they'd become, but tinged with deep sadness about lost opportunities to be close when we were young. How sad we weren't allowed to build the foundation back then upon which we could now rebuild. *Damn! No way am I sending a Mother or Father's Day card this year!*

—∞—

Years, later, Pat Love's book, *The Emotional Incest Syndrome*, helps me secede more thoroughly from Helen's influence – especially when I realize how she *parentified* me and turned me into the unconditionally loving mother she never had.

Somewhat later, Christine Lawson's book *The Borderline Mother* also aids this work. And Alan Golomb's *Trapped in the Mirror* sheds more light on both my parents' narcissism.

CHAPTER 16

Flight Into Darkness

I TRY TO bottom out in my abandonment depression. I dive into more depth work and continue to grieve regularly, even though my belief in fully facing my pain feels shaky.

> I dive a thousand fathoms
> With my snorkel of belief
> Yet the depths of darkness
> Spurn my shallow attempts
> To find enough relief

What to do? I am close to graduating from Antioch but something does not feel right. *I need to take stock. Let's see?* I have made giant gains in relating more intimately. I've significantly shrunk my belief that perfection is the ticket to love. My critic – the superego run amok – is definitely losing ground, but I'm still floundering in the reality of a childhood suffocated in my mother's heartless cruelty. This *Dark Night of the Soul* has me stuck on a planet that's lost its sun.

I have to face it. There's no way I've finished my training. I have an epoch of personal work to do. I'm nowhere near ready to claim a Master's Degree in Counseling!

With painful reluctance, I decline Will's flattering offer to join his group practice upon graduation.

Instead, I transfer to JFK [John F. Kennedy University] and enroll in their Transpersonal Counseling Psychology program. It sounds like it's made for me...a sophisticated blend of psychology and spirituality. Three more years of study and personal work might make me feel competent enough to want to be a therapist.

Spiritual Bypass University

Unfortunately the transpersonal program is not as advertised.
   Most of the teachers and students are Flight-into-Light types. Blinded by the light, they "transcend" their pain by simply choosing to be happy... always.
   More than a few thinly conceal the delusion that they are enlightened, and hence permanently liberated from suffering. A precious few teachers normalize the painful existential realities of life as well as encouraging the cultivation of an uplifting spirituality.

JFK spiritual bypassers pacify themselves and others in an all-or-none way with platitudes such as: "Just choose love", "Pain is an illusion" and "Don't worry, be happy." These flimsy bandaids strand and deaden them in their dissociation.
   Our four hours of weekly group therapy are especially disappointing. Supposedly aimed at helping students to integrate their *shadows*, sessions are more like a holier-than-thou competition. [Carl Jung conceived of the *shadow* as the unconscious storehouse of pain that accumulates from social prohibitions against talking about sex, death, hurt feelings and other taboo subjects].
   Dissociating into positive thinking, leaders and group members never break through the surface tension of their pain. Superficiality renders them all pose and persona. Straining their sanctimonious faces, they channel "love" into their inauthentic smiles. Forced laughter and exaggerated loving gestures are thin veneer over the vulnerabilities they are meant to be sharing.

Fellow Vet, Scott, disturbs the pseudo-placidity of the group. He calls out the group leader: "Listen Captain Glucose, this isn't love; this is corn syrup on marshmallows…sugar in syringes! Stop trying to cover up all the shit with Shinola, Robert."

Without a blink, the spaced out leader unctuously replies: "Thank you for sharing…Now it's time for us to do a guided visualization into loving kindness." *Damn! Will Schutz is a hard act to follow.*

I find sardonic support and comfort in reading: *I'm Good Enough, I'm Smart Enough, and Doggone It, People like Me.* The book is written by Al Franken [future U.S. Senator] under the pseudonym, Stuart Smalley. His skewering of simplistic approaches to positive thinking makes me laugh aloud repeatedly.

To break the ice for the group, I model vulnerable emotional expression. Thick and impenetrable as the ice is, I keep at it, and get a lot of practice managing the shame attacks it triggers.

One day, I ask the group: "Do you think clients are going to pay for therapy just to talk about how happy they are?"

A guy who has changed his name to Serene, quickly changes the subject by saying: "I'm reading this great book about how it's never too late to have a happy childhood."

Scott replies: "Yeah well how's that gonna happen when your past is like a strip of indestructible toilet paper super-glued to your shoe?"

Here is a journal entry from that time:

Your spirits are painted
With the tundra colors
Of your underlying dearth.

Your lives are wallpapered and peeling with platitudes.
Love-on-demand is as hale as tissue
And love without substance is a sun devoid of heat.

Your rituals of safe thought and smile without surcease
Are suppurating bandages covering your lack of peace.
Your hearts without their shadows
Moan in sad silence and make-believe relief.

Drowning in aphorisms of good intention,
Suffocating in words without feelings,
Your perpetual transcendence is a false pregnancy
Laboring endlessly to give birth to nothing.

Months go by, and at last a few students start paying lip service to their shadows. Another month passes and two women precipitate out of dissociation and begin wading into their vulnerability. To me, their tears feel as soothing as the healing waters of a medicinal spring.

Nonetheless, I am only ambivalently grateful because I also feel ripped off. Why do I have to spend all my processing time defending the normality of pain? It's unfair that there's no time left for me to share about spiritual practices that enhance my psychological growth.

So much for coming home to a place with a balanced synthesis of spirituality and psychology! Silver lining? This place keeps bringing up my original abandonment stuff, and I get to practice my growing repertoire of tools for healthily releasing old pain.

Fugitive from the Law of Averages

My grieving work gets a further boost when my lover, Lelah, leaves me for a professor at Antioch. The loss of her comfort and companionship turns my Dark Night pitch black. Free-association leads me even deeper into my childhood trauma. Not exactly the two for one deal I was looking for, and I dread having to deal with a resurgence of the angry part of my grief.

It seems I am now primed to confront the group's black-and-white view that anger is unspiritual. While crying about pain has recently ascended to the status of game-winning homerun, expressing anger – no matter how responsibly – is like striking out with the bases loaded.

One afternoon, the other group leader – Ananada [formerly christened Linda] – quotes the Buddha: "You will also be burned if you pick up a hot coal and throw it." I reply: "Not if it's on my rug about to burn down my house. I can scoop it up and throw it out the window without harming myself or anyone else."

For the spiritual bypassers, anger is an unholy action that banishes one from the light. What a painful irony: Two of my most potent experiences of the *Light* came out of harmless anger releases.

I fear I am being seen as Dr. Jekyll/Mr. Hyde – no matter how mild my anger – no matter how meticulous I am about not spilling it on anyone.

My frustration waxes and wanes. I also feel sad for my transcendent "dis-associates." Flight-into-light invariably seems to be a dissociative defense against the pain of a love-starved childhood. And no one here betrays any traces of having had a happy childhood.

Like me in the past, these student-therapists banish every feeling that is not perfectly loving, hoping to attract the unconditional love they did not get as children. Matching and mirroring insincere love is rampant in the program.

And while this is somewhat understandable in the students, it seems blatantly irresponsible in the faculty.

Equally aggravating is that some teachers here have a way of turning Carl Jung into the poster child for spiritual bypassing. History is rewritten to cast him as a paragon of sweetness and light.

No one remembers his autobiographical account of a dream in which God shatters a cathedral by taking a huge dump on it. Jung himself interpreted this as a sign of being incensed about his early religious trauma.

Disappointed as I am, I feel a duty to normalize the shadow in this training program. I feel especially responsible to my colleagues' future clients.

What a boon when Nancy joins the group. Emotionally whole, she is a breath of fresh air when she lets some foul winds of truth ruffle the group's flimsy placidity.

One day, as she finishes a lovely piece of griefwork, Robert says to her: "You know you create your own reality, Nancy. Thoughts have energy. They create your world. Why do you choose to furnish yours with so much pain?"

Nancy flares with poise: "Really, Bob. I mean REALLY! You think I created my abusive parents! You think when I was two, I thought: 'Mommy and daddy please beat me with a belt.' And what about you Robert? There are a lot of nasty people in the world wrecking everyone's peace of mind, including yours...even if you believe your delusion that you are utterly tranquil. How come I always hear you complaining about Reagan in the break-room? What was it in your thinking that created him being president?"

"Come on, Nancy!" says the group leader "You know what I mean. You've heard of The Butterfly Effect…"

Nancy interrupts: "Yeah, Bob. Well I think it should be called The Fart Effect. You know…the reverberations of a single act of flatulence could change the course of history. A foul fart could cause a man to flee in repulsion, trip and fall in the street…cause a car to swerve to avoid hitting him and then run over an enlightened genius who was destined to save the world from global warming…"

Nancy and I become great co-counseling friends. We help each other vent our frustration about all this phony transcendence. We also bemoan the irony of other training situations where therapists polarize to the other extreme. Pessimistic, misanthropic and contemptuous of Humanistic Psychology, they scoff at the idea that untraumatized people are basically loving. Each of us has been branded "a spiritual bypasser" by such individuals!

Nancy and I like to contrast the air-head, flight-into-lighters with these doom-and-gloom Eeyores who see no light in anything. We use the contrast to look for the sweet spot between Stuart Smalley optimism and Samuel Beckettian cynicism.

Building an approach to psychotherapy that integrates the spiritual with the psychological is my growing edge. It feels as challenging as making bacon kosher.

Eventually the censure I feel in both camps becomes grist for the mill of working through my shame. Many years later I finally dock in the balmy harbor of the affirmation: "Disapproval is OK with me." Well, at least most of the time.

As I write now I flash on the parallels between modern Pop Culture and JFK University's "Transpersonal-*lites.*" Both are superficial and speak "… in cheap bead necklaces of words." *Gangsta* wannabes everywhere flash the peace sign and quip: "Peace out, Bro!" and "Keeping it real" in an appallingly inauthentic manner.

Disclaimer. The JFK Transpersonal Program is now defunct. JFK's clinical psychology program has an excellent reputation.

Finding Tribe in Berkeley

Walking down Market Street in San Francisco late at night, I see a fight across the street. One guy pulls a knife. The other kicks it out of his hand, breaks off a thick wooden tree support and starts beating him.

I want to run away, but my legs carry me to the scene. I won't be able to live with myself if I read in the paper that the guy on the ground was beaten to death. With some surprise, I hear these words come out of my mouth: "Man that was a great kick. You got him! But Damn man, can you hear that police siren coming down Market Street? You better split!"

Miraculously he does. For a moment I feel pride – *I'm a hero*. But my grandiosity is like one of those rapidly disappearing subatomic particles. My critic – the secret agent of my parents – typically makes short work of it.

And sure enough, I am suddenly in a terrible flashback. For the next three days, my critic frightens me over and over with variations of: "You coulda gotten beaten…killed…like that Good Samaritan in the Marina who got stabbed last week intervening in a domestic violence dispute! Don't you realize how many murderous people there are in the city? Look at that sleazy guy over there. Definitely has a big knife inside his coat!"

I'm already mega-apprehensive from living in a sub-sublet next door to a huge crime-ridden housing project on 14th Street and Valencia. After this incident, the project seems so scary that I run past it when returning from my night classes at JFK. *Please God, don't let me run into a gang*!

Back at school, a classmate tells me about a well-established communal home in Berkeley. "It's even got an indoor hot tub, man! Here's the phone number."

I am ecstatic when I am selected for the vacancy. I pack up my meager belongings, cross the Bay Bridge and head out to my new digs. I feel like a smart rat leaving a ship I wish would sink.

Floriferous Berkeley and the very together eight-person home feel like a breath of pure oxygen. Instead of sharing food, we share the four refrigerators standing at attention against the kitchen wall. I even get the top half of one of the fridges.

The next weekend, I join a pickup volley ball game in nearby Ho Chi Minh Park. Because most of the players have hippie roots, the competition is super friendly.

Gradually this weekly game expands into various social connections outside the park, and I feel like I am growing a new tribe. *Mmm…lovely memories of good old Sydney!*

Duck and Cover Jim

At the park, irreverent repartee grows into a friendship between me and Jim Buser. Jim has harvested a business out of his wit. His company, *Duck and Cover*, has sold millions of joke buttons, refrigerator magnets and bumper stickers all over the world.

Here are some of his best: "Question Reality"; "Lawyers are Politicians in Larval Form"; "This is Cruel and Unusual Employment"; "Cleverly Disguised as a Responsible Adult"; "Liberty and Justice for All: Offer not Available in Some Areas."

Over the years he pays me generously for my satirical ideas about psychology. My favorites are "Unemployed Therapist, Will Listen for Food"; "At Least I'm not in Denial that I'm in Denial"; "I'll Bill You for Your Endless Monologue at My Usual Rates"; "God Grant Me the Serenity to Know When to Change My Underpants" and "Out of Body, Back in an Hour."

In the midst of recovering from codependence I also come up with: "I Think You are Mistaking Me for Someone You Want Me to Be."

Psycho-Spiritual Sports Therapy

Jim and I meet weekly at an outdoor court to play one-on-one basketball. Our games are intense but good-natured.

Evenly matched, we each play full tilt to try for a win. Both avid defenders, there is no resting. Win or lose, it's always fun…no angry words or unconscious shoves. At the end of each game – even in winter – Jim takes off his drenched tee-shirt and wrings out a cup of sweat.

We even coach each other to improve – and that we both do over the years. What a breakthrough for me, as past coaching always felt shaming and made me play worse.

Jim and I always hang out afterwards to chat. An unintentional co-counseling! Everything's discussable. Nothing's too trivial or too heavy.

Exercise has helped me stay fit and healthy all my life. In childhood I got it mainly through sports. In my teens, most of the available sports venues were poisoned by bullying competitiveness. Coaches and narcissistic players used contempt to get a competitive edge. Contempt, that terrible cocktail of intimidation and disgust, triggered me into fear and shame.

So I avoided team sports for decades. To stay fit, I suffered *The Loneliness of the Long Distance Runner*. In Australia however, I found some mellow hippies with whom I enjoyed playing basketball.

Unfortunately, anxiety still hampered my performance. My perfectionism had me running constantly. I had no gearbox. I had only one speed: flat-out…even in practice.

I didn't need performance-enhancing drugs. I had a corner on adrenaline. I was Harry Hustle – a perpetual motion machine. My knees were permanently discolored with scrapes and bruises because I dove onto the floor for every loose ball.

All this gradually begins to shift in my games with Jim. Playing in a consistently safe milieu, I don't have to be full-on running to break free from my critic on the court.

I play from a calmer and more centered place. Gloriously, this transfers over time to the two pickup games that I now play in every week. Growing internal safety allows me to access more of my natural talent. My game steadily improves. I start getting friendly ribbing like: "What are you on Pete? You can't shoot like that!"

What wonderfully tangible proof that my critic is shrinking. My program for recovery is working. I am relaxing into my body and its intelligence is growing. I am having more fun playing than I would have ever thought possible.

And even better, basketball rescues me over and over from Cancerphobia. Cancerphobia – a common symptom of CPTSD – repeatedly crushes me in its grip. It's my critic's favorite endangerment program.

Catastrophizing like a deranged evangelist, my critic interprets the deadened feelings I experience in a flashback as cancer. It blares:

"CANCER! You've really got it his time. Your body's riddled with it!" And then it laundry-lists the things I did and didn't do to cause it.

But now, more and more, basketball is part of my recovery work. Here is a typical example. I arrive at a game feeling like a pile of cat dander – painfully deadened in an abandonment flashback. My critic rags on me in the first person: "I've never felt this bad and tired before. I won't even be able to run up the court. Something must be eating my insides. I really, really have it this time! No way in hell I'll even last five minutes."

Yet every time, I nudge myself onto the court and soon feel energized and vitally alive – and not in that old jangled, over-adrenalized way. By the end of play – every time – I know on a cellular level that there's no way I could fly around like this for two hours, and at the same time be at death's door. And even better, I've just experienced something close to joy for over two hours.

How wonderful! Of all the possibilities, basketball has become a therapeutic spiritual practice for me! Over and over it banishes the critic from my psyche, keeps my body healthy and fortifies my inner knowing that life is indeed an incredible gift.

Everything Flowers from Within

Along with basketball therapy, my growing passion for flowers also feels therapeutic. Flowers mysteriously nourish me. Last year, I jumped on a plane for a three day trip to *The Bloom of the Century*; that's what botanists called the riot of color in the Anza Borrego Desert that spring. The astounding cocktail of flowers and scents seemed to reflect the wonderful gift of hope and new life exploding in my life.

My love of flowers flourished in Australia under Debbie's tutelage. One day after work-playing in the garden with her, she said: "You know Pete, there didn't have to be color. It could have been all black and white, like the way sharks and bats see things." In tribute, I journaled this:

> Lavender hydrangeas court the sun.
> Tiny flowers petrify color into sparks,
> As silver-leafed trees steal lucratively from the earth.
>
> Mint perfumes the mauve phlox.
> Cobalt flowers bow obsequiously to the bees,
> And wild roses deal hearty flushes to the scented breeze.

I join the Sierra Club to discover more wild flowers and to participate in singles' hikes. I hope to meet a partner…and all the wild flowers that live in the vast woodlands and meadows of the San Francisco Bay Area.

I go on flower walks lead by Roy Buck, a gregarious botanist who has a local flower named after him – *trifolium buckwestorium*.

Roy knows the practical uses of many flowering species. "That buckthorn over there can liberate the most stubborn case of constipation, and the leaves of the wild tobacco next to it make great toilet paper.

"You can use the root of this soap plant to wash your hands afterwards. And whatever you do! Don't be like the guy on my last hike last who wiped his ass with these pretty poison oak leaves and soon had to rush to the hospital."

I'm part of a cohort of flower enthusiasts with whom Roy holds court. He so inflames our flower enthusiasm that Tom, Aziz, Albert and I often forget to interact with the women. Rumors are we're gay. *How funny! I'm just waiting for a woman who's also crazy about flowers.*

Whenever we hike Mt. Diablo or Mt. Tamalpais we try to identify at least a hundred species in flower. When we do, we act like we won a round in the playoffs with high fives all around. One spectacular day in

May we identify 137 different flowers and celebrate a flower-nerd's version of a Super Bowl win. Tom says: "No wonder these women think we're bent!"

Avid bird watchers keep lifetime lists of all the birds they see. Similarly, I have two lists for flowers: wild flowers and cultivars.
    Lounging in the garden, I have a visitation:

> So close to the hovering hummingbird
> I could have touched him with my tongue,
>   had the hoodlum cat not startled
>   a throng of tipsy robins,
>   noisy and drunk from
>   gobbling fermented berries.

Sometimes in my lush flower garden I imagine myself as Claude Monet who famously said: "I must have flowers, always, and always" and "I perhaps owe having become a painter to flowers." Although I am not a painter, flowers have tutored me in color, and I dabble in an art form called *Assemblage*, in which I attempt to celebrate the world of hues.

—⁂—

As a therapist, I feel like a gardener of the soul. What a privilege to see my clients bring their developmentally arrested parts into bloom. I love Galway Kinnell's poem that concludes: "Everything flowers from within, with self-blessing."

CHAPTER 17

Incubating a Therapist

IN MY LAST year at JFK, I land an internship at Unity Counseling Center [UCC]. The Center is the soul of Unity, a Unitarian-like church that welcomes all beliefs.

UCC is unfortunately top heavy with *Transpersonal Therapy-lite* counselors. Their poor clients float and flounce around with them in the superficial ethers of hysterical happiness.

At first, I feel ashamed. *Do I always have to be the misfit? Is this my core psychopathology?* But thankfully there are a few grounded souls who cast a shadow. DeeAnna, Miyoko and my JFK friend Nancy have done enough of their own work to be able to provide transformative therapy.

These allies help me shuck off my shame. As does charismatic head minister, Carol Ruth Knox, who is a key reason I'm here. An adversary of spiritual bypassing, Carol is as comfortable in the Light as in the Shadow. Her sermons poetically describe the healthy comingling of suffering and transcendence. My favorite is this one about the yin and yang of Love:

It comes and goes, doesn't it?
Sometimes related
to people and how they
treat us, and sometimes not
Sometimes related
to the moon
to personal finances
to the questions of life

HOMESTEADING in the CALM EYE of the STORM

to nothingness
to everything
to the seasons, the time
to the food we ate
to. . . .

It would appear as if the art of loving is not whether you love or not (we all do in our present way) but whether you trust that when love leaves, it has a reason and it will return again. Always.

We humans are instruments for love by design.
(So is the whole universe!)
When love blows across us,
  naturally we sing a love song.
 And when there is no love wind to blow,
  though it leaves us strange
  and willow-like,
love has gone to an empty field where it fills its
 wind sails again
 so that it might return
 and blow across our all too hungering instruments
 one more time.

What shall we do while we wait?

We shall weep of course -
 something as lovely as love
  leaves a gaping hole when gone.

We shall remember love in our hearts and wait
tenderly and compassionately

> with ourselves
> as we wander in question
> and doubt
> until we remember,
> "Love always returns."

Occasionally when I feel like I need a good uplifting cry, I re-read this masterpiece for the umpteenth time.

—⚜—

Unity also supports an Adult School for personal growth. I create and lead an eight week experiential course: *Increasing Self-Esteem through Self-Compassionate Reparenting*. Key themes are shrinking the inner critic, grieving the losses of childhood and building fierce, unconditional self-loyalty.

Over the next five years, I hold it many times – here and at Piedmont Adult School and Mandana Recovery Center. The growth I see in my students – as well as my clients – is a testimony to my approach and inspires me to start my first book.

Self-Validation Eludes Me

Within a year of being at Unity, I have what most therapists consider a full practice – twenty clients a week. Before long it zooms up to thirty.

I'm quite dumbfounded by my successfulness. Maybe it's because my travels rewarded me with feeling warmth for diverse peoples. My clients come from most classes, ethnicities and sexual orientations, and they seem to easily trust me.

Surely this means I'm a bona fide therapist? But, I often feel like an imposter. And in really bad flashbacks, I feel like a fraud. When I am more lighthearted, I feel like the therapist in the joke: "How many therapists does it take to change a light bulb? – One, but the light bulb has to want to change."

In fleeting grandiose moments, I think: *I have brought my coals to Newcastle* – Sydney coals to San Francisco, the epicenter of psychology's evolution.

In an even briefer moment of self-importance, I imagine: *I have compressed these coals into diamonds with all my dense periods of grieving.*

Marie

Seemingly unbeknownst to me for many months, I fall in love with Marie. She is a therapist and a fragile rose. As a child she had to grow a surplus of thorns to stave off being picked. Her irresponsible hippie parents often left her in harm's way. She has a good heart but getting close seems to wilt her petals.

Too often, Marie is only available when she needs me as a sounding board. I periodically feel fed up and protest. She usually responds in a black-and-white way. "If you really love me, you'll stop complaining."

One night in the latest reprisal of this struggle, I have a liberating insight. Her argument is specious *either/or* reasoning. The old *love it or leave it* with no shades of grey such as: "There's a lot I do love about you, but I do not love you when your voice gets contemptuous."

Through a score of struggles around this issue, I use "all-or-none" as a verb and confront her polarized mantra: "You never listen to me!"

"Come on, Marie. Don't *all-or-none* me. I listen more to you in a day than your parents listened to you in your entire childhood."

She rewards this truth with yet another breakup. I want to tell her: "You've ruined my life", but guess who says: "Your life's already wrecked."

Our relationship is as on again/off again as cell phone reception in the mountains. Just before our final reconciliation, I journal this:

> I cannot dine lightly with you
> You are a re*past* that defies digestion.

> Our love's balance is ephemeral
> Its scales tip like a catapult
> Shall I take this parabolic flight
> With its inevitable descending arc
>   to our demise?

It's the three year mark, and I'm fed up with her selfishness. Every time I have a complaint – no matter how fair or reasonable – she disdainfully taunts me: "Stop acting like a victim!"

How she loves the shaming power of that word. But I finally get the irony. *I AM acting like a victim –surrendering to the victimization of being used.*

I must resign from reenacting my role as mom's perfect listener, never requiring anything for myself. I tell Marie I am done as graciously as I can manage.

I leave her house thinking: *Goodbye to prickly, hours-long monologues and short shrift when it's my turn to talk.* And…more than anything…Good riddance to her demands that shift like sand dunes in a sand storm.

Now that she's gone, I see a silver lining. Marie understood the importance of grieving her childhood losses. I liked helping her to revisit and work through her painful past. I learned a great deal about helping someone else to navigate this process.

And on a more personal level, she helped me to break my nervous habit of striving to constantly interact when we were together. When she didn't need to process, she liked hanging out without talking.

Eventually, I found – for the first time with a partner – comfort in silent togetherness. *Who knew primary relationships need a balance of quiet and interaction to create relaxing cohabitation?* My mother terrorized me into being entertaining whenever I was with her and she ran out of words.

This must have been a big part of why I avoided Debbie whenever I felt introverted.

So, I feel a speck of hope now that someday I'll find a partner with whom I can be silently comfortable. But first I must surrender to another season of grieving. To launch myself I write:

> Loneliness eats like a beggar at my back door.
> Imminent tears hide in the curtains.
> There's not an echo of a whisper
> From the comfort that was you.
> Alas, I have no one to be quiet to.

Repetition Compulsion and Reenactment

My mother ambivalated between seeing me as a holy altar boy and a child with the devil in him. [*Damn! What a projection that devil bit was!*] Rapid flux between being loved and hated seemed normal. Over the years I habituated to this type of relationship.

When I was four, Michael Carmody, a five-year-old bully from across the street, made me his best friend. He took me fondly under his wing, but his wing repeatedly became a headlock with which he rode me into the ground…for almost a decade. I never thought to unfriend him. Being targeted seemed like the price of admission for inclusion.

What an illumination when I read about Freud's concept of *repetition compulsion*: the intense unconscious drive to reenact the relationships we had with our parents!

No wonder I gravitated towards people who waffled between appreciating and disdaining me. My mother normalized punishing love.

Charismatic Jody and Marie were reenactments of my mother. All three simmered much of the time and regularly boiled over. All three kept me engaged by occasionally throwing me a bone of warmth.

Mercifully, all the work I did fighting the Helen part of my inner critic paid some dividends. I learned to stand up for myself with Jodie and Marie in ways that I could not with my mother. Now I easily recognize and effectively confront verbal and emotional abuse.

Maybe I even have that lesson down now. *I don't want any more partners hooked on sparring.* Jody and Marie got off on fighting, but it always left me feeling wrecked.

No more punishing love! From now on, no more partners with camouflaged boxing gloves. I'm a lover, not a fighter. From now on, it's zero tolerance for conversational abuse.

Fawning as Reenactment

As I meditate more on these reenactments, the word "fawn" keeps flashing in my mind. I look in the dictionary and see two meanings that seem to smack me in the face: [1] "To act servilely; to cringe and flatter" and [2] "To be submissive like a dog rolling over on its belly." *Oh my god my mother forced me to respond to her bullying in this way.* Now, when people seem threatening, I fawn. I coddle and ingratiate them!

No wonder I was such a captive audience for Marie! My mother trained me to be a *listening-slave.* Afraid I'd be attacked if I wasn't attentive and appreciative enough, I fawned into hypervigilant listening.

As this sinks in, I see this same pattern in the relationships of my codependent clients. In a life-altering epiphany, I realize that fawning is a fourth instinctual response to being attacked. A fawning response is as fundamental a reaction to danger as the fight, flight and freeze responses that Psychology has already identified.

In a gush of inspiration, I write an article for my website: "Codependency and the Fawn Response". In it, I describe four types of trauma survivors whose personalities develop as elaborations of the fight, flight, freeze and fawn responses.

Survivors of traumatizing families learn to survive constant danger by [1] *Fawning* in people-pleasing ways [Codependent-like]; or by [2] *Fighting* and controlling others [Narcissistic-like]; or by [3] symbolically *Fleeing* into chronic worrying or hyperactivity [Obsessive/Compulsive-like]; or by [4] *Freezing* and spacing out, hiding in isolation or numbing out into brain fog [Dissociative-like].

Before long, I realize I am *also* an obsessive flight type who is compulsively busy.

As a kid I was always on the go. If I had to sit, I would constantly fidget and tap my feet. After all, it's harder to hit a moving target. When my hypervigilance was working well, I could dodge at the last second and Helen or Charlie's slap would clip me on the side of my head, instead of in the face.

As my hypervigilance matured, I detected my parents' mood shifts more reliably and "got out of Dodge" before they became explosive.

In my teens and twenties, I became a more hell-bent flight type because I was sure the Cold War and the deteriorating state of the world would see me dead before I was thirty. I wanted to do a lot of living in what probably wouldn't be much time.

At the same time, I was also a codependent fawn type with my mother. In fact, I was a flight-fawn type – quick to *actively* help her: take out the garbage, sweep the porch, go to the shop, help her get out of the chair that her arthritis anchored her in.

Sometimes this distracted her into remembering that I was a "good boy." It also allowed me to get out of sight and striking range until she cooled down.

Deconstructing codependency becomes a long-term plank of my recovery program. This will eventually peak with me realizing that fawning with my mother was a type of Stockholm's Syndrome…that well documented phenomenon whereby certain prisoners become enamored with their jailers.

Disarming the Homicidal Client

My Unity client, Gail, is in and out of a codependent, physically abusive relationship. During an in-phase she brings her abuser into our session – unannounced. I feel all my hair follicles standing to attention. This guy is a doppelganger of that scary creep, Moochigumba, from the Bear County Jail.

Even worse, I have zero experience working with couples at this stage. Things rapidly deteriorate into worst case scenario. She breaks up with him in the session.

He stands up in a rage, knocks over his chair and turns toward the door.

Somehow I get into the calm eye of this typhoon, and hear myself say in my most soothing voice: "Emilio, Mannnn! What's up? You seem upset. Please sit down and tell me about it?"

To my great surprise, he rights his chair and sits back down. He launches into a nasty rant about what a "sorry-ass slut" she is. As his rage subsides, he glares at her and barks: "I'm gonna get my shotgun out of the car and come back and blow both of your sorry asses away!"

How can I talk him down so that I don't have to brain him with the table lamp if he goes for the door?

"Hey Emilio, I get it. Of course you're pissed, but man you don't want to spend the rest of your life in jail. You're a talented guy. Gail tells me you're the best car mechanic in Contra Costa. You got smarts man. If you kill us, you know you're going down.

"Besides man, you're a stud. You must have a ton of women after you. You don't need her. You said so yourself. You've left her a bunch of times and didn't really give a shit. You can leave her behind man...and get on with that sweet life you're living."

Miraculously, the tide turns but I am shaken up for weeks...not to mention a bit disgusted by my fawning.

A year later, I flashback heavily to this day-mare when a client tells me she broke up with her abusive husband since our last session.

"Harvey's enraged, and I'm really sorry, but he says it's all your fault!" I am nervous for months when I lock up my office at night and walk in the dark back to my car – with my thumb on the trigger of my pepper spray.

Rosen Work

The Emilio trauma/flashback is taking forever to wane. Someone recently told me that Rosen Work can release flight response hyper-activation, so I begin this gentle-touch bodywork with Linda Landon.

Luckily for me, Linda breaks the traditional Rosen insistence on silence. She encourages me to talk about what I am experiencing. I tell her: "When you touch me, my whole body contracts. I think I'm flashing back to my childhood. The only way my parents touched me was to hit me." *Ooohh! That made me want to cry. Better hold that in until I see if she's safe.*

"Pete, that contracting is probably *armoring*. The body's musculature naturally tightens to defend against imminent attack. I've noticed that in people who were hit a lot as kids, this armoring response sometimes sets in like cement."

I soon realize that almost all touch triggers me to contract...even the "touch" of hostile words or intimidating emotions. My armoring is so triggerable that the mere presence of a stranger activates it now and again.

Linda encourages me to talk or cry about anything painful that comes up in session. When I do cry, I notice an easing in my armoring. Gradually I start opening up to the comfort of her touch.

During my nine months of weekly sessions, my experience of being perpetually armored gradually abates. The physical sense of being relaxed and fully in my body that I first experienced at the Vipassana retreat becomes more accessible.

On an equally positive note, my lover notices that my flight response-drivenness is melting. I gradually slide back into the leisurely tender kind of love-making that I experienced with Cherry Miller and Susan Schmitt on LSD.

Oh My! This is so satisfying. This must be why that psychologist, Harry Harlow, emphasizes the importance of our human *contact-comfort needs.* I am naturally reorienting toward luxuriating in maximum skin contact during sex.

How remarkable! This totally non-sexual bodywork has made me feel like sex without contact-comfort is sad and empty. As I connect more fully with my partner, sex becomes increasingly satisfying and nurturing – truly love-making. No more "wire monkey" experiences for me. [In Harlow's experiments, baby monkeys were fed by a mother made of wire. When they were frightened, however, they quickly retreated to a furry surrogate mother for comfort].

The Imposter Syndrome

At the Counseling Center, I am continuously shocked by my success as a one-to-one therapist. Self-criticism however, often has the final say. A favorite theme is: "Clients will never stick with me. I'm way too fidgety and anxious."

In the moments before most sessions, my critic bull rushes me: "Fake! Phony! Imposter!" Sometimes I can shut it down with my anger, but too often I get lost in its judgments. And, whenever clients are late, I feel sure the have quit therapy without telling me because they are sick of me.

The critic is at its worst at the beginning and ends of sessions. I find the sessions themselves – once they are under way – so engrossing and rewarding that my self-doubt largely disappears. For the bulk of the session I relax into feeling comfortably engaged with my clients. I feel like I know what I am doing and that is clearly helpful. But at the end of too many sessions, the inner cross-examiner tears at the seams of my work.

My critic-shrinking progress is gradual. In today's first session, I am teaching a new client how to meditate. She is visibly relaxing, so I close my eyes to deepen my own meditative state. Suddenly I inhale a moth. It gets in deep – Adam's apple deep. I cough like a World War I soldier in a cloud of choking gas. I cough and cough and cough to the twelfth power.

Oh Damn! I forgot to refill my cup of water after the last session. What seems like ten minutes of non-stop coughing is probably two, but I finally croak: "Well, Phyllis, that is a good example of how not to meditate."

Alarmed as she looks, she generously laughs. The session is salvaged. Phyllis subsequently dives deeply into our work together.

I am quietly ecstatic that I did not get shame-crippled by this incident. *Sweet! I AM dissolving my critic's curse on my future as a therapist. Win one for me!*

Two months later, I take two steps backwards when misfortune provides the critic with fresh ammunition.

It's my day off and I drive to a shopping center near my office. Luckily, I'm wearing a baseball cap and sunglasses. I edge out from a side street past a stop sign to merge more safely into the traffic on Mt. Diablo Blvd.

Opposite from where I am looking, an oncoming car beeps long and loud at me. I feel tired and irritable from an insomniac night – and I won't try to soft-sell it – I flip the driver off...only to instantly realize that she is one of my clients. *Oh my God! Shoot me now! What kind of therapist does that?*

And wouldn't you know it? I will not be seeing her for another six days. *My critic is going to make me pay for this.* Six whole days to persecute me!

I feel like my parents are hovering on the periphery of my sight. The critic – their proxy – mangles me in a week long flashback. I frequently rescue myself, but before long I spiral viciously back down into self-disgust, drasticizing, and perseverating for a solution.

Meditating helps some, but I cannot find the calm eye of the storm that usually reveals *right action*. So on the fateful day, I go to work hoping the calm eye will blink open when my client starts ripping me a new one.

Yet, as often happens with catastrophizing, all my worries are for naught. In the waiting room, I instantly see that she did not recognize me flipping her off. *I am home free!* There's no way this narcissistic-ish woman would let such an offense slip.

I take another paradoxical leap forward one afternoon as I greet a new client in my waiting room. With an ingratiating smile and an apology about my imperfect office décor, I back into my office glad-handing her toward the couch.

Not daring to break eye contact, I back my way towards my chair and sit down – all the way down – down-to-the-floor down. I forgot that less than a moment ago, I moved the chair to the right to remove a conspicuous cobweb from the ceiling.

Thankfully my pride suffers a greater blow than my tailbone, although in truth I wish it were the reverse. I laugh-fawn my way through my embarrassment and soon find the calm eye in the critic's violent thunderstorm.

The session goes well enough, marred only by my recurring – and thankfully invisible – worry that she will not come back.

When the session ends, I flashback to a "highlight reel" of Helen cruelly attacking me for trivial mistakes. I feel spontaneous fury. I hate her for imbuing me with perfectionism – for making me into such a fawning codependent. *Damn, she didn't damage my self-esteem...she annihilated it!*

I vividly imagine myself exorcizing her from my psyche. I vow to deprogram her lines of inner critic code. I promise my inner child I will never stop reminding him of his essential goodness and worthiness.

My approach to my inner critic subsequently morphs ito a two-step process: Intense angry repudiations of the critic followed by radiating kindness, warmth and encouragement to my inner child.

And Alright! Look at the little beauty that just sprung out of this critic-encounter: <u>Mistakes are my teachers. Every misstep is a chance to practice self-compassion!</u> I am going to wear the treads off of this mantra.

Teaching classes is the most excruciating trigger of my imposter syndrome. If courage is action in the face of fear, teaching has been continually making me braver. Parachuting out of a plane was not gutsy on my part, because it did not feel scary. But teaching! Now that is daunting. It literally scares the shit out of me. My button, *Performance Anxiety Cancelled out by Lack of Ambition*, is bravado bluff.

One day I get some potent help from my inner child while driving to a class. Terrified little Pete is scared that my parents are going to show up and heckle me. Immediately incensed, I pull over and tear into my parents for his sake: "If you sorry a-holes are stupid enough to show up, I will kick your ass from here to kingdom come because I am way stronger than you now, and so on…!" Alright! *My performance anxiety just dropped a quantum level.*

Two years later I am in a session with a client who is also in the therapy group that I lead. *Oh Damn*, I think, *I can't hold back this fart!* Well at least it's silent…Uh Oh! It's a SBD [silent but deadly].

Within ten seconds I know neither of us is going to be able to invoke denial, so I own up. "You know, Elaine, I wish we were in group right now. Then, I wouldn't have to confess to that flatulence…everyone else would be unsure who to blame it on."

We both laugh, and then I wait for the shame attack that never materializes. I, of course, have some normal embarrassment – but how different than the soul-curdling mortification I'd have suffered a few years earlier.

Instead, I flash on Little Chuckie Siletta's face – lit up with a big shit-eating grin. I am in a benign flashback to a high school basketball pickup game in which he cut the vilest fart in history. Everyone groaned and rushed to evacuate the gym.

Bruce had a cold and volunteered to peek in and test the air every few minutes. It was twenty minutes before he could stay in and declare it safe to return. But, for the rest of the week Little Chuckie strode around proudly as if he had fathered his first child. He was legend now: The man who silently and single-handedly evacuated a gym.

CHAPTER 18

Out of Abuse into Neglect

Brenda

I MEET BRENDA on a Sierra Club hike. My inner juke box plays love songs as she describes her three different Music Therapy jobs. I can feel the sweet good-heartedness she must bring to her work with the elderly, the dying and the mentally ill.

And she's no one trick pony. She worked for years as a brakeman on the railway. *Sweet, delicate and strong – a hearty flower indeed.* I bet her Id is even nice! Before we finish circling Mt. Diablo, I am enchanted by this robustly kind and beautiful woman.

I also notice that Brenda is doing most of the talking. I flash for a second on Marie, but banish the comparison because Brenda's clearly a different species. And…she's really fun to listen to.

We're in a committed relationship from the get-go.

Trying on
My name,
A melody
She made

Sky music
She played
Dealing diamonds
And purple spades

We spend every weekend together, and after a year decide to rent a house together. I feel phenomenally safe with Brenda. For the first time I experience consistent comfort in a romantic relationship.

Our romance is long blooming as we work in the garden and flower-forage the neighborhoods. The Berkeley area has the most diverse flora I have ever seen thanks to a horticulturist known as Annie the Flower Queen. She sells hundreds of flower species imported from all over the world.

I plant so many varieties of Delphiniums in the yard that I feel like we live at the Oracle of Delphi. I love to meditate in the garden surrounded by six foot high towers of pink, lavender, azure, cobalt and purple delphinium spikes – each spike smothered in multihued, fig-sized florets. The Delphinium! – The supreme diva of the flower kingdom.

We are also liberally graced by Nature's *Magnificent Decorator* during many camping trips to the Sierras and Yellowstone. My co-counseling friend, Randi, and her husband sometimes join us on these sojourns, and we are the most contented of country cow freaks.

It is early spring, and we are all together in Yosemite Valley celebrating Brenda and Pete's second anniversary. White dogwood flowers freckle the trees. Snowflakes dance around us and give the campfire a reason to be. Snow melt turns the Merced River in to a mellow rage. Yosemite Falls shoots white lace forever down the towering cliff on our left, and handsome Half Dome pulls for compliments on our right.

All's right with the world! My health has blossomed and I've put on weight – almost thirty of the forty pounds that the amoebas mugged me for in Nepal.

Licensed and Free

I love Unity, but not my supervisor and boss. With her tweezers-like mind, charismatic Hilary is cut from the same borderline cloth as my mother.

She runs the counseling center as fascistically as Helen ran our family. Like my mother, she wants me to be her henchman and tries to incite me to participate in persecuting her scapegoat-of-the-moment.

In childhood I sometimes colluded unconsciously with Helen against my sisters, but I have paid my dues in guilt, and made amends for those mistakes. There is no way I will go down that road with Hilary.

Weekly supervision with her is dreadful however, never knowing whether she will psychologically castrate me or the client I am discussing.

Before long the codependent strategy that saved me in childhood comes to my rescue. I informally turn her into my client. Sporting the narcissistic core of a true borderline, Hilary laps up my listening and eliciting, and largely leaves me and my clients alone.

Praying with Bearheart

Brenda has friends who are steeped in Native American lore by a shaman named Bearheart. They invite us to attend one of his sweat lodges.

The night before, I am revisited by a recurring dream from my childhood. I dream I am a mounted cavalry officer engaged in fierce hand-to-hand combat with ferocious Indians. I am wearing a blue uniform like the one I wore for special events when I was an army officer twenty years ago.

Suddenly a brave charges and kills me. I tumble to the ground and then instantly get up and remount a saddle-less horse...reincarnated as an Indian in the same battle!

This dream always perplexed me as a child, but now there is little wonder – and total wonder. I have been enamored with Native American wisdom for a decade.

While studying Native American hunter-gatherers in Anthropology at Sydney Uni, I romanticized their lifestyle as especially fulfilling. I so idealized it that I wept bitter-*sweet* tears at the end of the movie, *Dances with*

Wolves, when the cavalry officer joined the Indian tribe disappearing into the mountains. *Would that it were me.*

So, here I am now – a renunciant of my military experience – on the eve of being initiated in a Native American ritual.

The sweat lodge is in the redwoods thirty miles north of San Francisco. Fifteen of us scrunch into a domed structure constructed of bent tree branches and covered in many layers of canvas. Bearheart sits on the far side of the circle and guides us. He pumps up the steam in the dome by pouring water on stones that have cooked in a fire for hours.

The ritual centers on four rounds of prayer. He sings a sobering native song, and starts the first round of prayer thanking Great Spirit for all that he is grateful for. Each person in the circle then takes a turn expressing their gratitudes.

On the second round of prayer he has the *fireman* use his pitchfork to bring in two more large rocks from the fire to generate hotter steam. The heat is a nano-therm away from unbearable, and one participant flees the lodge.

In this round, soaked by rivulets of our own sweat we take turns praying for help for our loved ones. Several of the participants cry profusely while describing the ailments of their relatives and friends.

On the third round, goaded by further tweaking of the heat, we pray aloud for ourselves. People are inspiringly authentic about naming the sufferings from which they desire relief. Many faces are bathed in tears as well as sweat.

But all this pales beside the final round of praying. We pray once again in gratitude – in gratitude for our most *painful* travails. This instruction seems strange indeed – until an experienced participant leads the way.

To my amazement, a radiant woman named Tamara thanks Great Spirit for her polio-disabled legs: "My shriveled legs have brought me much grace. I've developed other strengths and received innumerable kindnesses from so many people.

"This love has healed my family's legacy of humiliation. And despite the weakness in my legs, I run with the wolves all the time." She is alluding to Clarissa Pinkola Estes' stunning book *Women Who Run with the Wolves*.

I free-associate from Tamara to an old wreck of a guy who I recently saw in the crowded YMCA showers. Buck naked, he wobbled in as if on his last legs. Somehow he had great "presence." A friend greeted him: "How's it going Joe?"...to which he jauntily replied: "Astoundingly well. Record-breakingly good! A documentary will soon be released. I'm scheduled for an award!"

He was so unabashed at the absurdity of his claim, and so happily tongue-in-cheek about it, that everyone in the normally subdued showers erupted in laughter. How envious I felt of the self-esteem radiating from this man who was surely nearing death's door.

It's my turn to share about pain that I feel grateful for. As my voice falters and cracks, I blurt out my worst pain. "I am grateful that I won the booby prize in the parenting lottery."

My tears fight each other to get out. I grasp more deeply than ever how profoundly I was abandoned. More minimization of my parents' betrayal dissolves in my weeping.

My grief ebbs and gives way to comforting flashbacks. With many happy tears, I do a play-by-play about how much human warmth I've received since I escaped Walkerville.

"So many circles of strangers have welcomed me and treated me with kindness...even in the army...even in godforsaken jail...well maybe not the first time."

I laugh/cry/laugh/hiccup: "I give thanks for all the human kindness that came my way in so many places – in so many different countries. And, thank God for Australia! I found four exceptionally loving homes to live in way Down Under."

"If it hadn't been for gross parental incompetence, I would have missed all those life-enriching interactions. So, maybe I was born into the wrong tribe, but I have found members of my real tribe all over the world. If I hadn't had to escape my parents, I might even have gotten sucked into the superficiality and conspicuous consumption of mainstream America."

When the sweat lodge ends, I feel ecstatic. I shout silently inside myself: *Eureka! Finally! A truly transformative psycho-spiritual experience with a group that embraces the marriage of Spirit and Shadow*. I bet our sweat lodge was more soaked by tears than sweat.

Singing Bird's Vision Quest

Have I mentioned that I have a thing for ordeals? The sweat lodge was so profound that I sign up for a Vision Quest with Bearheart. Three days and two nights without food or water. The vision quest is actually with me, my *selves* and I, but Bearheart allegedly "guides" from a distance.

From the base camp that supports the quest, I hike miles out into a wild hilly and wooded area of Northern California. It is easy hiking with no supplies, and nothing but what I'm wearing. Not even a secreted paper and pencil.

I find a flattish, shady hilltop and ritually "make a circle" in which I must stay for the entire time.

I'm achy and uncomfortable from sitting in this stony circle for hours. Something triggers me, and I feel very antsy. Maybe all that joking about this being bear and mountain lion country wasn't only funny. My flight response is raging but I want this inner exploration so I stay put.

My critic transmutes my flight response into obsessiveness. I fly around inside my head from one nasty thought to another. Inner mom squawks: "Don't you think you're a bit too old to play Cowboys and

Indians. Get out of this stupid circle and get some exercise!" But I side with Bearheart's firm instruction to stay inside the circle.

Fortunately I am buoyed by a second ten day Vipassana retreat that I did earlier this year. Finally I wriggle into something resembling peace of mind…until the day turncoats into pitch-black moonless night.

Lightless – but a long way from soundless! The night is pregnant with a cacophony of threatening sounds. I know I am afflicted with hypervigilance, but this hyper-audience feels even worse. Even the tiniest sound morphs into the image of something frightening.

Sleep is not available tonight, and I feel too weak to battle this endless catastrophizing.

Night
   beetle black and porridge thick
      chortles as it crouches in the hills
         gobbling up the retrograding light.
The hungry Dark,
    an ebony frog,
       swallows color like a fly
          robbing me of my sight.

The fasting part is easy. I like the monks' trick of fasting to heighten mindfulness.

Thirsting is another story, and in a mere twenty-four hours it becomes an unrelenting source of discomfort. I have a few brief helpful meditations, but mostly wallow in depression.

My thesaurus for depression builds all day: *Damn, I'm despondent, wretched, depleted, bored, dismayed, dejected, melancholic, despairing, desolate, disheartened. What's with all these "d" words? Must be "d" for death, which wouldn't be half bad right now.*

On the last night I lay awake doing a life-review. Suddenly I feel lucid and expansive. My history of recklessness unfolds before me. I realize that I occasionally brag about my near disasters as if they are a red badge of courage. I romanticize all my scrapes with danger and jokingly pathologize myself as self-destructive.

But right now my past does not look so glorious. *I'm ashamed of how much and how often I've hurt myself. I feel defective.*

What's wrong with me? Am I trying to off myself? I mean, Getting myself thrown into the wartime army…Hitching through the hippie-hating South…Winding up in that horrific Bear County Jail…Nearly drowning and then almost freezing to death in Morocco! *Dammnn! What's all that about?*

And Oh my word! Those horrible creeps in the taxi with Nadia…Jail again in Pakistan…Amoebic dysentery…Myriad motorcycle bloodlettings. And all the while relentlessly accident prone! Always sporting scrapes, cuts, burns, stitches or sprains. *Am I really unconsciously trying to kill myself?*

As all this laundry-listing winds down, my brain lights up with an epiphany. *Self-destructiveness is not the core of the matter.* I will stop adding insult to injury. I have been in such constant pain that I've just been trying to get the pain out – quite like a cutter, a person who cuts themselves to paradoxically release their pain – or like the guy in that old joke who hits himself in the head with a hammer, because it feels so good when he stops.

Well thank God I've discovered grieving! Nothing gets the pain out like a good cry! In fact, I haven't done anything really self-destructive since I've had more access to my tears.

Yet, I still seem to be enamored with ordeals! *Shit! Here I am in the midst of another one!* Well, maybe these ordeals are similar to the recklessness…but there's a vital difference. The retreats and workshops do involve pain, but it's releasing old hurt in a healthy way. I almost always come away with a sense of renewal and a boost in my self-kindness.

All this insight begins to fill me with a sense of well-being. *I am not my own worst enemy. I was* only *desperate for pain relief.*

Mapless at first, looking for relief often worsened my pain. Luckily in the last ten years I've been finding tools and techniques that help more than they harm. *I am on a healing path! And my life is truly getting better!*

It is noon of the third day and the quest is over. I return exhausted, parched and bug-bitten. I wonder if there is another vision encoded in the complex pattern of bug bites that cover my body. Maybe I'm like Queequeg in *Moby Dick* who had the meaning of life tattooed all over his body in a language no one understood.

As prearranged, I go directly to Bearheart's teepee and recount my experiences, which I top off with this poem that I composed in my head about last night's insights:

All my stupidities have made me smart.
Made wise by my foolishness,
I knit succor out of suffering,
Re-choreographing all my failures into triumphs.
I am a human oxymoron

Bearheart grunts a few native words which probably mean: "You're pretty weird, paleface!" I then wait for him to translate my quest into my new Native American animal name. This must be ninety percent of the reason that most of us suffer this awful ordeal. We get a Native American name at the end.

Like everyone else, I am hoping for a glamorous name. All of Bearheart's upper echelon cadre have the pick of the animal kingdom. There is Stolid Elk, Esa White Eagle and Water Wolverine.

I have noticed that no one among his initiates has a coyote or wolf moniker. I've been infatuated with coyotes for years. Twice I had numinous experiences running into a coyote deep in the Sierras. I take inspiration from their cunning ability to survive massive attempts to exterminate them. *Please Great Spirit, can I be a coyote?*

But the name I get instead is Singing Bird. "Singing Bird!" My inner belittler scorns: "It sounds like Stinging Turd!"

Hell! I would have been happy with anything that had a dog in it. Well maybe not "petulant poodle" which is kind of how I feel right now.

I don't mind the *bird*-part so much. I love birds. It's the *singing* part that feels too ironic. As much as I love to sing, I once made the mistake of recording my voice and was deeply troubled to hear a discordant monotone. How could this be? The singing in my head sounds perfectly melodious.

The cruelty peaks when Brenda, sporting the new name: *Lithe Lynx*, comes up to me and says: "Singing Bird! That's great. That's so you, Pete!"

I feel like cursing or spitting but my mouth's too dry. I suppress my resentment, but my outer critic silently accuses Bearheart: "You asshole! I know you have a crush on Brenda – you're trying to humiliate me in front of her." Hunger and exhaustion once again fuel the critic!

Well, I may not have gotten the sexy name, but the more accurate Vision of my "self-destructiveness" is worth innumerable flatteries. *What a soothing release from a toxic shame program I barely knew I had.*

Ameliorating Sexual Abuse

Brenda also comes from an abusive, loveless family. Having dabbled in recovery, she is passionate "...that those sociopaths won't hold me back."

When we come back from our latest trip to Yosemite, Brenda remembers being incested by her father. As sad as I feel for her, I'm honored that she can tell me, and we process his inhuman betrayal a great deal. Over and over I think: *what kind of animal does this to his own child*. Almost all human cultures have incest taboos.

At times while making love, Brenda gets triggered. We always stop and work gently with the flashback. Typically it dissolves with angering at her father and/or tears for her child-self.

One day while she is trembling in a flashback, I feel a fierce instinct to defend her. "I wish I could travel back in time and protect you. I'd do whatever it takes to stop your father from hurting you." *Wow! This really seems to help her surface up out of the flashback!*

Her father is apparently large. More than once when she is overwhelmed in fear that her father will come and abuse her again, I point out the baseball bat by the door and remind her about my weapons training in the army, where I was the pugil stick fighting champ in my platoon.

Still there is a silver lining here for both of us. As I help her grieve, I evolve in my ability to help other sexual abuse survivors. Over time Brenda is also rewarded with her first safe and relaxed sexual relationship.

Like Parent, Like Partner

I love guiding Brenda's recovery but her monologues are multiplying. Our relationship is narrowing into that of a client and a therapist. I feel more and more unheard.

At first, I think: *I'm asking too much. Her poor listening is just a painful reminder of my mother's emotional neglect. My hurt feelings must be transference from the past.*

To address this, I do a great deal of angry grieving about Helen always giving me short shrift. I even do a Buddhist "Letting Go" ritual to release me from my mother's influence. *She may be dead now, but who knows, she may still be hanging around?*

I meditate morning, noon and night for thirty days encouraging my mother to let me go – to transition into the light. At the end of this ritual however, I finally realize that my deep abandonment feelings are not just about the past. Brenda is seriously not there for me. Just like with Marie, I am once again a listening slave.

We work on this with her therapist. In a poignant session, she remembers being pinioned by her father's eyes for hours. Day after day, he made her sit at attention in a chair while he brainwashed her...indoctrinated her to be under his full control.

The therapist wonders: "Do you think you might be flashing back to your father when Pete's talking?"

Brenda says: "Yes! ...I'm sure that's it...especially as Pete has my father's green eyes and high cheek bones. I'm afraid Pete can't say much before I feel like I'm in danger. I guess that's why I keep hijacking the conversation.

"So I'm really sorry, Pete. I think this will help me to be there for you like you are for me." Right then and there Brenda commits to reciprocity, but it rarely survives longer than the life of our session with her counselor.

Deep in meditation one afternoon, this comes to me:

In groveling codependence
I beg blood from a stone.
I banish my boundaries
Sure we are letters in the same word,
While I drown in the proof
That you will always be aloof.

My gratitude for Brenda's mellowness has expired, because I feel like I'm dying to be heard. I clearly see my repetition compulsion to settle for tidbits. Even though these are the best ones yet, I can no longer be a listening slave...a perpetual audience. With tremendous sadness, I break up with her and move out.

I descend, almost immediately, into a miserable loneliness. I feel like a sheep that has tripped and fallen with its legs pointing uphill. Some sheep are so devolved that they lie there and die – too dumb to roll over and get up.

I feel like death warmed over much of the time. For a long time, I grieve the end of my five year relationship with Brenda. Tears regularly rescue me from recurring droughts of self-compassion. How awful to lose the lovely feeling of safety we shared. *So near and yet so far!*

I make a CD of songs of lost love, and never seem to tire of milking my grief with it. Grieving is such a sublime mother…the mother with the soothing breast…of tears.

There is a silver lining to this dark cloud of spent love. While grieving I realize my mother brainwashed me into taking responsibility for her problems.

Helen Walker routinely blamed me for her suffering. Once she blamed me for a hail storm that killed her tulips. She blamed me for her crippling arthritis at least a thousand times. Another time she screamed about having to get false teeth. "You mean-spirited little brat! You're the reason I had to let that dentist torture me."

Another light goes on about repetition compulsion. Because Helen routinely bludgeoned me into feeling over-responsible, I now strive too hard to fix my clients' problems. I often strain emotionally to pump up the love – to re-inflate them with soothing.

Now I see how counter-therapeutic this was. Trying too hard implicitly transmits a shaming message: "You're so flawed that emergency measures are needed."

Over-striving also seems to lock some clients into a "fix-me" stance. When I buy into being the Fixer or Healer, the client's self-care faculties remain developmentally arrested. They fail to learn how to help themselves…to be the lead in their own recovery program.

As I let go of *straining* to help, clients relax more and join me in caring about them as they are now – not waiting until they are fully healed. Often this evolves into them working on themselves outside of the session.

My Mother the Men's Group

Two years ago before our break-up, I joined a leaderless men's support group composed of lawyer Matt, free-lance writer Bill, high school teacher Phil, environmental activist John, computer programmer Brit and psychotherapist Edward.

We still meet every Monday night for two hours, taking turns hosting at our homes. Divvying up the time equally, we talk about our ups and downs in love, work, health, leisure pursuits, and so on.

I'm always amazed that no one launches into fix-it mode. I'm so grateful for the extraordinary safety of this circle. Seven out of seven guys listen non-judgmentally. *Must be some kind of world record!* They even welcome tears.

The group is in fact so supportive that members commonly ask for feedback – not something men are commonly encouraged to do. We talk about every taboo subject imaginable. Matt says one night: "I've got gas so bad, I'm gonna have to get my own canary. Can ya still buy canaries?"

Two years pass and Phil, barely forty, dies from cancer. Phil's family is so dysfunctional that no one, wife included, plans a funeral. So we hold a service for him in a beautiful park. Each of us shares a poignant memory or two. *Man, not too many dry eyes out there!*

Phil's family watches mutely and then takes off with all the flowers we provided. *Damn, what kind of awful childhood did Phil have?* Sure explains that hyper-critical wife. Maybe that's why cancer took him out so young?

As a young man, Phil had a passion for hopping freight trains. In group, when someone asked for advice about a sticky situation, he occasionally made this suggestion plausible: "Maybe you should think about hopping a freight!" So after the funeral, I say: "Maybe we should have bundled up his narcissistic wife and hopped her onto a freight."

—⚋—

The group helped me immensely during my last two years with Brenda. I always felt welcome to process my ambivalence. One night I rhetorically mused: "I know if it's not one thing, it must be my mother. But, are my issues with Brenda real or just transference from my *Mommy Dearest*?"

More than ever I finally learnt that wise choices often spring from ambivalating as long as it takes. By the time I shifted from 90% stay/10% leave to 10% stay/90% leave, I *knew* it was time to go.

Ironically, being fully heard in group finally convinced me that Brenda's listening handicap was unacceptable – no matter how good our relationship looked to everyone outside the group. For the first time, I left a partner without the unresolved ambivalence that made me repeatedly return to deceased relationships in the past.

Fast forward to a bitter-sweet day in 2005: the ending of the men's group. It is bitter because Matt has recently died – thirteen years after Phil's death.

Matt was an endangered species – a lawyer with a heart. He championed many good causes – gave free legal advice to poor seniors and was a leading light in saving the Marin Headlands from greedy developers.

A temperate *bon vivant,* he was good with his head, heart and hands, and enjoyed life in a multifaceted way. Because he was still vibrantly alive before being slain by cancer, his death at sixty-nine ironically reminds me of A.E. Housman's poignant poem: "To An Athlete Dying Young".

The ending of the group is also bitter because Edward has moved out of the area. Unable to find suitable replacements, we are too few to continue.

The ending is also sweet with the memories of how much we all grew while we belonged to each other. Especially notable is that the four long-term bachelors finally got married. Having the group as a place to fully air our hopes and fears helps explain why we all remain happily married to our partners in 2017.

The final sweetness of this grand band of brothers is that I still have these men, especially Bill O'Brien and John Barry, as close friends with whom I drop into a deep level of sharing whenever we spend time together.

I will always feel grateful for the mothering energy I received in the group week after week for fifteen years. Many are the times I drove home from an enriching group experience with tears of gratitude welling in my eyes.

CHAPTER 19

Writing the Tao of Fully Feeling

Watering my soul
   with every passing feeling
      melting from calories of emotion
         I trickle into the stream of life.

WHEN I LEAVE Brenda, I move into a small studio in the Rockridge area of Oakland and vow to finish the book I've been working on sporadically for the last four years.

I write between squalls of grieving and storms of guilt about leaving.

My writing passion grows as I witness too many therapists pathologizing their clients for not "choosing" to get over the past. My skin crawls when I hear putdowns like: "Stop feeling sorry for yourself. Stop crying over spilt milk. Stop bellyaching about something you can't change."

How can professionals declare the past irrelevant? The past is not even the past. For so many people, It is alive and dictating their present. All too often they are tortured by self-attacking mindsets which concretized in childhood.

Yet, therapists and New Age evangelists everywhere are pushing *Forgiveness* as the latest panacea. "Your parents are not to blame. You can choose to create a happier life now!" Survivors everywhere are shamed out of healthy emotional upset about unspeakable parental behavior. Many are pushed to forgive parents who are still abusing them!

I feel guilty whenever I do not challenge such client-betrayal. My silence feels like tacit approval. So I increasingly speak up in defense of my fellow survivors. I speak and write about taboo topics like Healthy Blame, Forgiveness as Denial and The Necessity of Grieving the Losses of Childhood.

A local periodical, *Recovering*, previews excerpts from my book about these ideas and publishes my piece: "Forgiveness: Begin with the Self." Subsequently *The California Therapist* publishes my related piece: "Recovering the Emotional Nature." *What a boost to my writing motivation!*

When clients are lost in self-hate during a session, I often feel like I am looking into their past…seeing their parents browbeating them into toxic shame. At such times, I feel irate at their parents. I wish I could go back in time and use my anger to protect my clients from these bullies as some relative should have done. Sharing this with them sometimes allows them to cry in compassion for their child-selves; and sometimes it awakens healthy, self-protective anger about their parents' neglect and abuse.

I start encouraging my clients and students to break contact with parents who are still abusive. Those who do not, make little progress. Those who do, finally get some traction in stopping the constant abuse of their internalized parents [aka, the toxic critic]. Their critics begin to shrink. Their self-compassion begins to grow.

My working title for the book is *The Tao of Fully Feeling*. But this continuously makes me feel uneasy. *How can it be that I understand feelings better than my colleagues?* I frequently doubt that I do. How could a male New Yorker who was taught to abhor feelings presume to know anything about emotions?

Yet evidence amasses that the growing trend in psychotherapy is to discourage the full range of human emoting. It seems that everyone is using so-called positive emotions to shame away any feelings that smack of pain. "Don't worry; Be Happy!"

One night I think: *In the land of the blind, the man with cataracts is a seer.* On a subsequent night I think: *Maybe all my sabbaticals into grieving have mined some gems about the human emotional nature.* I seem to have unearthed truths no one else is talking about. Even Daniel Goleman has little to say about the healthy side of crying and angering.

In his book, *Emotional Intelligence*, the only time he mentions "crying" is to say: "…the idea of a good cry is misleading." He completely dismisses the notion of healthy angering, and barely mentions grieving. He seems to advocate using thinking to control feeling as if were a bad dog in need of an alpha dog to keep it in line.

Damn, his book sure seems as emotionless as CBT [Cognitive Behavioral Therapy]! I have to get my book finished and out there, to help people save their souls from their brains.

I do not believe much in Divine Intervention, but sometimes I feel the presence of a Muse. My agnostic sub-personality likes the notion of a Muse: *If you have to talk about God, do it in an oblique, non-committal way.*

My Muse however never communicates from outside me. Never on-demand, s/he comes and goes subtlely and is mostly AWOL. At times finding the right word is like looking for a paper clip in a hoarder's office. At more blessed times the words are right there like low hanging fruit.

When I commit to finishing *The Tao* however, my Muse shows up big time. My supply of motivation becomes continuous and instantly available. I feel infused with a mission. For the next two years all I want to do is write.

One night in a writing frenzy I pen this in my journal: "On the corner of written, I left a few lines. I write to stop the words from bursting out of me – to prevent the oxymorons from doing internal damage. I write because I can. I write to right the wrong. I write to free Pete Walker. I write to save my life, and if you need it…I hope it helps to save yours."

Challenging Mainstream Psychology

Writing about feelings is daunting. They are such an unpopular subject in most circles. But I take strength from Jung's assertion that our feeling function is opposite to our thinking function – and *equally* important. I believe one of our most enriching challenges is to interweave the two. I have to confront this psychological imperialism that is using thinking to exterminate so many species of feeling.

Using words and logic to legitimize feelings however is like knitting with gloves on. One autumn gloaming, as I struggle to find the words, I pause to let this discordant rhythm come through:

> The flickering of falling leaves
> The world, drenched in scarlet, bleeds
> A thin rent in the light pleads
> As a moth frantically thumps and heaves
> Against my window

As a self-appointed spokesperson for the importance of feelings, I feel like a pariah among my peers. My poor colleagues are in the thrall of Cognitive Behavioral Therapy. Scientifically hamstrung CBT barely recognizes the legitimacy of feelings! They are phenomena that must be subjected to *affect regulation* via processes that can turn people into emotional eunuchs.

Oh Poor Psychotherapy! Therapists everywhere are castrated by insurance companies demanding eight week cognitive-behavioral fixes. And there are no reimbursable diagnoses for grieving the losses of childhood. More and more it is: Get better or get medicated.

Even the New Age goes CBT, and *thinking* loving and grateful thoughts is the new cure-all. Positive thinking is a wonderful tool, but insipid without emotional grounding. Without access to a full complement of emotions, human beings are like appliances without electricity. They lack the emotional power to enact the transformative intentions that they are trying to embrace.

Many days, I come home from seeing eight clients and sit down and write for three hours. In the morning, I wake up, make a cup of milk tea and tap on the keyboard for three more.

On my three day weekends I get up at dark thirty and work at least twelve hours on my lexicon of grieving. My favorite part is excavating my journals for the quotes I've inscribed over the decades. I integrate them as if I am coloring my book.

My writing and endless editing feel easy and comforting much of the time. My focus is paradoxically relaxed and expansive – not the tight focus of the Ritalin user, not my ADHD hyper-focus when I am overcompensating.

I feel blessed by this broad band focus that allows new ideas, imagery and figures of speech to manifest themselves unbidden.

As I gaze out the window, this comes to me:

> There are mysteries writhing
> > in the pattern of the leaves
> > in the faces of the plywood grain.
> Hidden forms deep inside
> > vibrate for me to name them
> > > these jewels that have
> > > > yet to meet the light
> > > > > that will open up their gleam.

Writing however, sometimes triggers an ordeal. Without warning, it heaves me from comforting solitude into painful alienation. Illustrating my book with vulnerable self-disclosures revitalizes the critic, who squawks: "How self-indulgent. Really! You're gonna put that in the book. How pathetic!"

The more I bare myself, the more I arm my critic. A list of self-disparagements lengthens and repeats in endless looping. My self-esteem repeatedly tanks into the shame of imagining what others will think when they read about my pain.

I lose match after wrestling match with humiliation, until I pause long enough to grieve it out. My most vulnerable disclosures require three or four grievings. One extra deep immersion mines the realization that toxic shame is the corpse of my slain self-esteem.

One evening, I feel into a self-disclosure that seems too raw to keep in the book. Wave after wave of angry grieving finally makes me buoyant. I float up out of the depths of my abandonment mélange with a loud: "Hell yes I'll keep it in the book. I'm not to blame. THEY ARE! I bet everybody with dysfunctional parents has longed for death many times."

This time I surface back into a much sturdier loyalty to myself. I have to publish this. The world needs to know that such toxic parents exist, especially in middle class families like mine...families that look so good from the outside.

The next morning my landlady asks me: "Are you OK? What was that yelling about last night?"

"I'm really sorry," I say. "I got a call from an abusive relative who wouldn't stop bothering me. I had to get a bit nasty to make her hang up."

I question myself about feeling so intensely called to finish this book. Is the call from my grandiosity, or from the commonweal, or from my yearning to resume my search for a life partner, or some higher entity...or some or all of the above? Gratefully my efforts mostly feel like right action.

One reference point continuously helps me. I am part of a small rebellion of therapists challenging mainstream psychology for denying that untold children are regularly emotionally traumatized by their parents.

Busyholism: "Don't Just Do Something, Stand There!"

My perpetual book-editing ends just in time. This singularity of purpose is beginning to feel unhealthy. *OH! What a joy to ship my finished manuscript off to the printers.*

I am excited to be free once again to more fully engage the world. The mere thought of it seems to release a constricted feeling in my body. I resume my diverse interests, determined not to slip back into flight mode and constant busyness.

Unfortunately, my old packed schedule has little time for sitting – outside of client sessions and meditating. I seamlessly move between many enthusiasms: running, basketball, art projects, teaching classes, gardening, home-decorating, volunteering, tea with friends, fixing stuff, flower foraging, and so forth. I manage to slow my pace, but I'm soon perpetually doing.

Now instead of running home to meditate, I walk and try not to hurry when I leave for my next activity. Nonetheless, John Bradshaw's comment about *human beings devolving into human doings* keeps popping up in my head. But surely I am progressing. I am definitely more relaxed.

Before I know it though, I feel like I am doing, doing-er, doing-est. I'm back into hurrying – a restrained kind of hurrying with one foot on the gas and one on the brake. I rationalize it's OK because my regimen is replete with worthwhile self-improvement activities. But I immediately think of several health food-freaks I know, who are putting on too much weight, rationalizing that: "It's all super-healthy food!"

Regrettably the insight is not enough to slow me down. Even worse, I start to lose weight, which always feels catastrophic to me. A friend encourages me to visit the infamous Oakland Acupuncturist, Dr. Oh, who some call Dr. Ow [rhymes with Pow] because her acupuncture is so painful.

"But she gets such great results" says my friend. Another friend jokes: "Yeah, great results because patients make themselves get better so they don't have to go back!"

In my session she inserts a needle deep into my abdominal core, twists it and with a high pitched voice exclaims: "Shock!" and *Oh, Trembling Tao!* It feels like electrocution.

Even worse, she puts me on an ascetic diet that would make a breathatarian hungry. I have to eliminate seventy-five percent of the foods I currently eat. She replaces them with Chinatown vegetables that look extraterrestrial. The weight pours off me, and before I have the sense to fire her, I am almost back to my post-amoebic dysentery weight.

My critic nastily chortles: "Nice going, Walker – what was that about evolving out of self-destructiveness?"

I feel devastated and so weak that I cannot play basketball. Soon, I have to suspend all unnecessary activity, and cancerphobia is back in spades. *Damn! One door closes and another one hits you in the ass.*

I can't stop losing weight, and more than ever before, I'm sure that I am dying. I perseverate endlessly about death because it seems a certain fact.

I even come to rest in a surprising acceptance of it. *Yes I've experienced a lot of trauma…but so much love and richness too! I've had a good enough life. I'd like to stay but I'm ready to go.*

I passed an AIDS test recently, but otherwise I rarely resort to Western medicine. Other than getting stitches or antibiotics from time to time, seeing a doctor never helps. All that I can think to do now is resume my old diet and ramp up my meditation regimen.

While meditating, I have a startling insight: *I am addicted to adrenaline. My critic has a hundred ways to scare me into pumping adrenaline to power up my flight response.*

My epiphany then devolves into a shame attack as I realize that my *On the Road* adventure was at least partially powered by an out of whack flight response. I never thought I was on the run. "Au contraire" I would bristle at anyone who dared suggest such a thing. "I am going toward…not away from."

And while the grains of truth in the first part of that protest are many, the last part contains a beach-full of self-deceits. I was not running from anyone or anything. I was fleeing myself – my unconscious – my inner critic – my swamp of painful feelings.

I think back to recently coining the term *busyholism* in my book: *Remember how you described the flight response as an obsessive/compulsive reaction to childhood trauma! No offense, but Duh! Could it be time to reread your own book, Mr. Busyholic!* I guess naming a problem is a long way from solving it.

I think about how my flight response was frequently pedal to the metal in my childhood. And now – two decades since I hitched my last ride – I am still flying down the road of constant busyness. I'm constantly moving to stay one step ahead of the *deepest* levels of my pain. Although I'm fully open to grieving, I run mentally and physically from the *abandonment mélange* – the fear and shame that mingles with my depression.

My avoidance of these deeper reaches of emotional pain is an elaborate complex of thinking [obsession] and doing [compulsion]. I am either mentally fine-tuning my to-do list or actively accomplishing its tasks. When I'm not doing, I'm thinking about doing.

I guess busyholism is essentially the same process as workaholism, but harder to spot because the *doing* is not just *working*. It can – and does for me – include quite a bit of play. I haven't seen this because my denial minimizes my compulsive productivity as a rich and healthy plan for recovery.

I am not however like Sisyphus pushing a boulder up a hill. I am more like the person in these couplets by Emily Dickenson:

> My candle burns at both ends
> It shall not last the night,
> But oh my friends and ah my foes
> It gives a lovely light.

Running on Empty

Up until this time I pay too much lip service to healthy living. The way that I treat my body is criminal. My body is just a car for my spirit to inhabit – some old beater that I crash around in and give as little maintenance as I can get away with. My body is a piece of sports equipment to launch onto the gym floor for the glory and joy of recovering a loose ball. I *must* have some dog in my genes.

I want to get at least two bits worth of results out of every minute. I am the ghost in the machine. When I am speeding on adrenaline, I drive my body as if I am in a demolition derby, and in the shower I often see bruises and scrapes that I have no memory of acquiring.

In the midst of a profound meditation, I am shocked to discover how much I hate my body. I resent it for being so thin and so prone to exhaustion. It is a third rate racing car that I attend to at warp speed – when and if I attend to it.

When I begrudgingly pull over for a pit stop, I throw a meal together and wolf it down. Because I eat healthy food – when I do feed myself – I kid myself that I am practicing good nutrition. Too often I skip the pit stops. I bypass breakfast regularly because eating makes me feel tired. So I run on fumes as long as I can. Food is all too often just something to keep me from getting too skinny.

While meditating I realize that my busyholism is merely a multidimensional form of my father's narrow workaholism. *Now there's a disappointing shock!* I have hobbies and interests up the yin-yang, but like him I am Mr. Get-Things-Done. I am an apple that rolled away from its tree to rest in a mango orchard, so I misperceive myself as a different species than him.

So I take the pruning shears to my schedule and commit to meditating three times a day...and start to really *jones* for the first time in my life. I am jonesing – yearning in every cell of my body – to get moving – to get back into action.

> Taunting clock tides
>   of too many hours
>   yet never enough time.
> Driven by a horde of needs
>   the clutch of my desire fully engaged,
>   wheels spinning in the sand.

Other than tobacco in my twenties and coffee now and again, I have never been addicted to anything that made me jones when I abstained. Certainly there were times in my life when I drank too much beer, but I easily put it aside when it became excessive. My relying too much on self-medication gradually faded in my late-thirties as grieving more effectively soothed my pain. But so far my hard core addiction to busyholism has only lost its veneer.

In another meditation, I notice that "just *one* more thing" is the favorite mantra of my denial. How often *one more thing* becomes *one thing leads to another* and busies me for hours – no matter how much I'm running on empty. I am like a gambler with "one more bet"…a food addict with "one more spoon of ice cream."

Now when I hear "just one more thing" going off in my head, I know it's a sign that I am tired and afraid of falling into my abandonment depression…afraid of the fear and shame that mingles with it. So now, I stop and fall into it. I sit in meditation trying to fully feel it. *I won't rev my engine by shooting more adrenaline.*

Occasionally I do give in, but the more I run on adrenaline, the more I lose weight. Committing to a daily nap helps. Remembering that midday napping is a custom in Southern Europe and most of the non-industrialized world helps me rebuff my critic's jamming on the word: "Lazy!"

I nap.
A lilting insurgency
Against the unfair demands
Of the Modern day

So for weeks, I grip the arms of my chair like a white-knuckling drunk stopping himself from going out for booze. But even as I block my compulsive doing, I am still obsessing about all the things I want to do. Stopping this perseveration is harder than balancing a marble on a string – harder than getting empathy out of a narcissist.

When I catch myself almost salivating to do some cleaning, I am blown out by the depth of my addiction. *Cleaning, for god's sake!* Cleaning rarely even gets on my to-do list! I even have a postcard on my bulletin board that says: "House work makes you ugly."

Behind my compulsive doing is the engine of obsession – *left-brain, flight response dissociation*. I constantly think to distract myself from my underlying anxiety – my incessant feeling of being in danger and of feeling lonely.

My favorite theme of obsessing is problem solving – constantly noticing what needs to be fixed, improved or *made safer*. I must perfect myself to protect myself from inner and outer criticism.

As a kid I was smart to use perfectionism to distract me from my underlying pain. I could have drowned in it. So perfection was a great goal. Since it is impossible, I never ran out of things to try to perfect…to distract myself with.

But now I will finally feel my way through these painful feelings of abandonment. I lengthen my periods of meditating, because once I am up, I will be like a squirrel in an almond orchard.

I forbid myself to answer my inner Siren's calls for action: "Check your e-mail…write this on the to-do list…close the cabinet door…get that cobweb out of the corner of the ceiling…What's that noise? Go look out the window…"

Cold-turkeying from relentless doing is too hard. I do not have the structure of the Vipassana retreat to support and contain me. This prolonged sitting is torture. In one session – after a mere five minutes – I give up and write this:

> Surely there's diamond dust
> In this coal black season of despair.
> I'm crushed by my rush to find it.
> My tempo yearns to crescendo
> My subpersonalities hunger for distraction
> >   in their mosh pit of frenzied search.
>
> The balance point false-promises to limbo into sight
> >   as this dancer perspires the sweat of purgatory.
> My prayers fall into
> >   the gutter-mouths of the damned
> >   who make lewd gestures with them.
> If only I could remember where I parked the ark.

Minding the Body

As my meditations deepen I focus on the physical sensations of my restlessness. There's a tension in my muscles that seems to correlate with my anxiety. I'm confused by how reluctant I am to stay present to these sensations. When I feel into them they don't feel painful, but somehow they are excruciating. I guess it's the jangled feeling that is so unpleasant. I want to run from it, like I would flee an army of yardstick-wielding nuns.

But, instead, I use what I learned in my first Vipassana retreat. I hone my focus on fully feeling the sensations of my anxiety. As my concentration sharpens, I realize that this anxiety is fear, and the epicenter seems to be this cable of tightness across my diaphragm.

With practice I merge with this tension for longer periods. One day I get a fuzzy picture of my mother's angry face.

Damn! I'm tensed up all the time as if Helen is always watching me – looking for an excuse to attack me. No wonder I always feel like I'm being watched…even when I'm alone. No wonder this perfectionistic thing is so hard to shake. I'm constantly trying to perfect myself so there won't be anything for her to punish.

I cry about this for some minutes and then return to the physical sensation in my diaphragm. *Man! It's much less tight.*

I continue to focus on this taut rope just below my ribcage. Ever so slowly, and with the aid of tears here and there, it lets go. *What a blessing!* No tension in my abdomen. No Jangling. No anxiety. What a lovely feeling of relaxation.

This peacefulness soon begins to decay as I notice tension in my thighs. I then focus there. I realize that my quads are always torqued and ready for a quick getaway. As I concentrate on this physical sensation over the next two days, my legs gradually relax.

I then shift my awareness to my jaws…and then to my eyes until all these parts of me also relax. When I hone in on my throat, I find many choice expletives straining for release. I bark them out as I remember many bullying authority figures from my past. I re-center on my throat and feel my throat relaxing. I stay present to fully feeling the sensations there until my neck completely relaxes.

Finally, I scan my whole body to find any remaining hotspots of tension. I stay focused on each until it dissolves and relaxes.

In contemplating these experiences, I realize that it is fear that underlies my busyholism. Fear gives birth to my tense muscles, my anxiety, my obsessing and my compulsive doing. All my life, I have been locked into unconsciously anticipating and reacting to the next disaster with my mother.

Fear is such a constant that I have little to contrast it with it. I'm shocked to realize that I'm almost always in some degree of fear. Unless it is flaring I rarely notice it, and being on the move typically blunts it out of my awareness.

Fear is why I run and what I run from. Fear fuels my obsessing which get me moving…which drives me to distraction. I am addicted to distracting myself from the pain of fear.

I am ambivalently jubilant about this awareness. I now know how to digest and work through my fear. And I can short-circuit my chain-reactions to it: fear tensing my muscles, then morphing into worried obsessing and then launching me into hyperactivity. *But Damn!* That fear doesn't seem to stay tamed for very long.

I practice this process over and over for many weeks. My reprieves from feeling afraid gradually grow longer. Eventually, merging with my tension feels like a subtle comforting massage that evaporates my fear as it relaxes my muscles and my whole body. Sometimes during this process, tears or anger spontaneously spill forth and enhance fear-reduction.

Ultimately this technique allows me to rest in complete body peace. The first time I fully sink into my totally relaxed body, I feel like I'm resting in the world's most comfortable easy chair. At last, I have finally done what I was supposed to be doing in those Vipassana retreats, instead of obsessively problem-solving.

I rejoice: *This is psychological bodywork.* I can use my mind to massage fear, tension and trauma out of my body. Over the years it becomes my go-to practice for releasing my hyper-activation when I get triggered into a flashback.

My withdrawal is over. I broke the bronco of my flight response. I no longer flee myself. I am now truly Pete *Walker* – not Pete *Runner* – as I was nicknamed in childhood.

As I immerse myself in the tender notes of Pachelbel's *Canon*, these words come to me:

> Hurrying and scurrying no more,
> I watch the dancing candle
>   Spill auroras of light over
>   the Brueghel snow-scape on my wall.
> George Winston's piano
>   soothes and heals my wounds of rushing.
> I lie here dreaming of thee my Lord,
>   massaged by frissons of the sweet love
>   that you as man on earth exuded.
> For precious seconds, sweet Buddha-Jesus-Krishna,
>   I bathe in thy poignant energy of heart
>   and drink in the nectar-blessing of your healing love.

And of course, this newly found emotional/somatic peace is quite fragile. But over time I get better at restoring it with a meditational tune-up.

To protect my adrenaline sobriety, I swear off multitasking...other than reading while using the facilities. In the past, multitasking often jumpstarted me into busyholism. Before I knew it, I'd be swirling in the whirlpool of three nasty merging currents: perfectionism, time urgency and compulsive productivity.

Weight gradually adheres to my slender frame. With the monkey of adrenaline off my back, I reengage the world. I gradually increase my flower foraging, both in the wild and the neighborhoods. Before long I am blessedly back out there playing hoops.

And how heartening that I quickly notice regressions into drivenness. These slips into flight-mode steadily decrease in frequency and length. My new subpersonality, *The Guardian of the Calm*, helps me with this. For reasons that only my unconscious understands, she quite resembles Wonder Woman! With stern gentleness she nudges me to cease and desist when she detects early signs of me getting re-amped.

Moreover, I soon notice the adrenaline jangle in my body when a flashback torques me into rushing past The Guardian. I notice it now because it feels so unpleasant. *I can't believe I used to love being in that state.*

Three months ago, three thousand copies of *The Tao of Fully Feeling* were delivered to my home on a flatbed truck. It took me all day to get them stored in the crawl space underneath my house. They feel like a massive clutch of eggs incubating beneath my bedroom.

Today, I am on my way to my first book reading at Diesel Books in Oakland. As I drive there, I wonder why I don't feel nervous. What happened to those pre-lecture jitters?

I enter the building and stand in front of a friendly-looking crowd of about sixty people. *Oh How Sweet*, the teaching anxiety that plagued me with the trots for so long is nowhere to be found. I am deliriously relieved!

HOMESTEADING in the CALM EYE of the STORM

The next few years are a gradual unwinding into deeper relaxation. My drivenness subsides by over ninety percent. Toxic shame is a rare visitor, and my critic seems to have lost my address.

I feel like I have withered my critic with a gastric bypass that has cut off its fear supply. Fuel-starved, the critic is weak and tiny now, and rarely triggers me into unwarranted fear.

I still feel quite lonely, but there's little shame in it. My self-kindness has bulked up via myriad meditations of soothing my inner child.

―m―

The final silver lining of this mega-ordeal is that I now value my introversion! From this point on, my genuine enjoyment of being alone increases.

Writing my book hooked me up to an IV line of inner strength. I have found places of peace and inspiration inside me that I never access in company. I hope to keep this channel open, so I prioritize making time for solitude.

Solitude gives me quality time with myself for meditating, reading, gardening, art work and listening to music. Contrary to the critic's opinion, this is not "just upgrading my addictions."

When I'm socializing too much, I now feel a craving for alone time. It's rarely the old social phobia, but rather feeling lonely for myself. I'm often pleasant to hang out with now that flashbacks are rarer and more manageable…now that the inner bully doesn't stomp around like a demented boss.

CHAPTER 20

Dating: the Dragstrip Between Abandonment and Engulfment

Poverty Consciousness Fades Away.

I PASSED MY licensing exams seven years ago and fantasized myself licensed to kill – toxic inner critics that is. I started by bidding Hilary, the boss of Unity Counseling Center, a not so fond adieu. She was the last external and nearby vestige of my critic.

How liberated I felt when I set up my own private practice, which I named The Lafayette Counseling Center. All my clients came with me and before too long I took on an associate and two interns. I also took on the right to keep all my client fees.

Now that my health is fully restored, I take stock and it finally dawns on me that I have financially returned to the middle class. I almost can't believe that I lived well below the poverty line since leaving the army. Over the last twenty years, I rarely noticed that I was living "poor".

I've had money the last seven years but I still live frugally. When I was growing up in my lower middle class family, my mother conditioned me to feel guilty about every nickel I spent. Spartan living was drilled into me from word go. Many were the starting-to-molder leftovers that I was forced to eat growing up. The turning milk was the worst.

As an adult, I unconsciously slid into asceticism. Never dollar-driven, my philosophical commitment to recycling allowed me to live quite comfortably on little.

Thrift stores afforded me a cornucopia of clothes and household goods. Communal living was room and board at a pittance, and my ancient Toyota just kept on ticking. I honestly cannot remember ever feeling deprived.

All this adds up to the fact that there is little that I want to buy with my new "riches" – despite various New Agers pathologizing me for being stuck in poverty consciousness. My savings account fattens during this time, and suddenly the unimaginable occurs. I splurge big time. Not able to bear seeing my rent go down the tubes every month, I buy my own condo in an old Berkeley house that has been divided into four units.

The French doors of my new womb-like studio open onto a small back deck that I flood with blossoming flowers. As if I am oil-painting, I arrange the potted blooms so that the plethora of hues blend harmoniously. Yesterday I imagined a Monet effect. Today, I try for Seurat, deluding myself that my penchant for small flowers like lobelias, phlox and sweet williams renders a Pointillist effect.

Almost every day I read, mediate, and daydream for at least an hour as I laze on the deck's loveseat communing with my colorific relations.

I love this place, and I have come to love a lot of solitude, but before long *"living alone sucks!"* becomes a silent chorus in my mind. I've been spoiled by communal living and living with Brenda.

One morning while meditating, I have a vivid and curious daydream. Someone is presenting me with a Woody Allen trophy – a sculpture of Woody doing a *plie* with a Roman wreath around his head. The award is for logging the most hours of self-analysis in a twenty year period.

Clearly I am taking myself too seriously, but I have no idea how to stop.

On the other hand – with all this recovery work under my belt – my odds of finding lasting love must be improving. Maybe I've worked through enough of my codependent fawning to attract the right person...and to be the right person.

And maybe if I hit the jackpot, I'll meet a single mom with a young child or two. I was as content and fulfilled as I get with Ruth and little Frankie and in the early stages with Jodie and young Grayem.

Good Enough Love

On my deck, I read famed psychoanalyst D. W. Winnicott's biography. I am awed by his concept of *good enough mothering*. Sixty thousand sessions of providing child therapy convinced him that *good enough love* [not perfect] was all a child needed to be psychologically healthy.

This fact gives birth to another momentous insight. *I unconsciously expected past partners to give me the unconditional love I never got from my parents.*

If I don't let go of this pipe dream, I will never be content with imperfect but good enough love. This insight expands as I realize *"good enough" could be an antidote to perfectionism and all-or-none thinking.*

I withdraw from the quest for perfect love. To help me get more realistic about what to look for, I read several therapist-gurus on lasting love. Dan Beaver's *Beyond the Marriage Fantasy* helps me weed out my unrealistic expectations. Susan Campbell's *Couples Journey* validates my yearning for a union that enhances personal growth in both people.

Both books normalize the inevitability of conflict in relationships. Both show how friction can be worked through in ways that deepen intimacy.

Over time, I also read everything written by John and Julie Gottman – the royalty of couples counseling. Their research-based advice about preserving intimacy in the face of normal disappointments is pure wisdom.

All this new input reminds me of Clint Eastwood in the movie, *Bridges of Madison County*. His character gives up on love forever because no one can match the "perfect" weekend experience he once had with an idealized lover. I think: *Well of course that fling felt like unconditional love. It didn't last long enough to be spoiled by normal differences.*

I realize that I too have my enshrined sarcophagi of past liaisons that never lasted long enough to taste normal disappointment. I consciously detach from them and hope and pray I can refrain from unconsciously pulling for "perfect" love.

Relational Therapy

These potent books have stirred me up: *No more blotting out my shadow in relationship with niceness!* No more stashing my complaints under the rock of my "together" personality. *I need to get back into therapy.* I want someone who'll help me practice expressing disappointment in a kind way. After all, I easily provide this for my clients, and I see how it helps them to grow.

I begin seeing Gina, a heart-centered therapist with a Relational Perspective. Her approach contrasts dramatically with traditional psychoanalysis where the therapist sits behind you and interacts minimally and antiseptically. The Relational approach is face to face and values dialog. It models *fully* authentic relating.

Early on, Gina speaks to my salvation fantasy of finding perfect trust with her. "Pete, trust can continuously grow between us, but breakdowns in feeling fully safe are inevitable. This is true in any relationship, past trauma or not. No one can be totally supportive. So please tell me about anything that comes up between us…anything that bothers you in any way."

She is remarkably open to my intermittent confessions of feeling letdown or misinterpreted. She welcomes my suspicions about what she really thinks about me, and convincingly disabuses me of my misperceptions. Over time, we gradually amass an emotional bank account of trust that keeps our "relationship" afloat – even when flashbacks temporarily destroy my faith in her; even when she actually mishears or misunderstands me.

In today's sessions, I am mired in toxic shame and self-hate. "I'm so sorry, Gina. You must be so sick of me showing up again, hopelessly stuck in yet another flashback. Who will ever put up with me sinking into this shit over and over?!"

I wrestle myself back into eye contact with her. *Oh my god! Her eyes are tearing up!* No one could fake kindness that convincingly. Gina says: "I'm so sorry that your mother taught you…demanded that you hate yourself for not always being happy! You're a good man, and it's OK to be down and alienated. Everybody is sometimes! I know I am."

She's teared up with me a few times before when I'm in pain, but this time my doubt dissolves and I really feel her sincerity. It helps that I'm often on the "giving" end of such compassion with my clients. *And Oh how comforting and reassuring it feels to be on the receiving end!*

I see Gina two to three times a week for five years. With her help, I reach a new level of authenticity and learn to voice my complaints caringly. Best of all, her consistent acceptance of the *whole* me helps me believe that someone else might.

Dating Co-Counseling

In any couple, I believe real intimacy is proportionate to the degree of *mutual self-revelation*. This strikes me as an immeasurable scientific fact. I coin the term *dialogicality* to describe a mutual and authentic exchange. Only a broad knowing of each other breeds real love. This is true no matter how ideally suited we feel and no matter how oxygenated our physical chemistry.

God help me to make this a non-negotiable!

I reenter the dating world and use my hypervigilance to notice and resist my urge to fawn. No more abandoning myself to be liked. No more backing into the corner of over-listening.

HOMESTEADING in the CALM EYE of the STORM

Sometimes on first dates I write code words on my wrist, to remind me what to talk about if fear makes me go blank. I also give short shrift to unstoppable monologists – never staying more than thirty minutes. And, if someone sounds over self-involved on the phone, I wear my button: *Codependent if You Want Me to Be*. It puts the topic on the table, and aids in narcissist-detection.

In the "Seeking Relationships" section of the newspaper [dating websites do not yet exist] I see many people declaring that they want someone with "No Baggage!" *How absurd! Who is free of worries and struggles?*

I pass over these ads with a fleeting glance. I want someone who is introspective and knows they have a shadow. For a while, I change my ad to: "Looking for Someone with Matching Baggage."

—ɯ—

I meet fellow psychotherapist, Tom, one night at a *Conscious Connections* event. This event is for singles on a spiritual *and* psychological path. Thank Tara that I live in Berkeley – good old Berkeley, where some of the best hippie values still flourish. I doubt there are many other places fielding such an event.

The button I am wearing tonight: *Dating: The Drag Strip between Abandonment and Engulfment* – launches us into a rich repartee about looking for love in all the wrong – and right – places.

Tom says: "Your button says it all. Last year I scared away a lovely woman by pulling for too much too soon; and then three months ago, the roles were reversed. I had to change my phone number after coming home five straight nights to over ten answering machine messages from the same woman."

"Thanks for sharing that, Tom. I've had similar experiences. The worst was when I repeatedly called this woman's machine because I kept messing up my message. My embarrassment grew as I couldn't get it right, and after the fifth attempt, I gave up and unsurprisingly never heard back from her. "

He laughs and responds: "Yeah, someone could make a million bucks by inventing an answering machine that lets you erase a message you're not happy with."

"I hear you man!" I half-joke: "And...how I wish I could find a relationship where my fear of rejection isn't locked in a cage fight with my fear of enmeshment."

"Yes!" he says: "Wouldn't it be great to find that sweet spot between commitment-phobic love and love that's like flypaper. I'm hoping that sooner or later...please make it sooner...I'll meet someone whose ratio of togetherness and having space is similar to mine."

We become fast friends and meet weekly for stream of consciousness repartee and informal co-counseling. One day he tells me: "I think we're both evolving towards really being relationally ready!"

I riff back: "I'd like to create a dating site for survivors to match people at similar stages of recovery. I think two people who are committed to recovery have greater potential for real intimacy than people untraumatized in childhood. I mean: "normal" society's ignorance about real intimacy leaves people clueless. Real love's got to be more than long walks on the beach, pina coladas, and never having to say you're sorry."

Learning What To Want

As a first date topic, I raise the question of what we're both looking for in a relationship. No more mindlessly cruising in the vague flow and glow of physical chemistry without discovering that we have a lot in common.

New research confirms that *opposites* do attract, but being more alike increases the chances of a harmonious, lasting relationship. I resuscitate the cliché "friends first" and enshrine it as wisdom. Multidimensional friendship has to be the secret passage to lasting love.

My critic however, rags on me about this: "A romantic partner who's also a best friend! How pathetically naïve! You'll have to build an android." But I'm all over that that like a cop on a terrorist.

In a new personal ad, I list my values and interests, and write: "Hoping to connect with someone who shares many of these…especially an interest in personal growth." Almost immediately, respondents are more in the ballpark. The wheat is separated from the chaff – the fruit from the fruit loops.

One night, I meet a woman at a dance who pulls up her nose and says: "ewwhh" when I mention personal growth. I feel equally repelled, and only a photo finish could have shown which one of us retreated faster.

Nonetheless, dating is often difficult and triggering. Every hopeful connection quickly withers. I flash on all the water mirages I saw in the Sahara.

I rarely collapse into toxic shame anymore, but at times I feel drowned in loneliness. After licking my wounds with a squall of grief, I crumple into nostalgia for Brenda:

> Our love that's long expired,
> Though gone is still in place.
>
> The plural of purple
> Fills the pluperfect shadows
> Of your remembered face.
>
> Half past green are your eyes
> Penetrating the dream
> That assails my sleep.
>
> Would that your ruby onyx gleam
> Could wash upon me
> And flush away this awful night

CHAPTER 21

Volunteer Work

THROUGHOUT THE 1990'S, I feel called to volunteerism. I supervise intern counselors for two years at the Berkeley Free Clinic, and for three years at Crisis Support Services [formerly Suicide Prevention Hotline].

Following this I work half-time supervising the crisis lines at Parental Stress Services [PSS]. My own reparenting work informs me about children's needs, which enriches my training of the phone counselors. The pay is so low compared to my private practice that I view it as semi-volunteering.

I also volunteer as a psychological paramedic at John Bradshaw's weekend symposium: *Reclaiming the Inner Child*. Bradshaw is a genius at stimulating self-compassion. Hundreds cry in empathy for the traumatized children that they were during his guided visualizations to the past.

All this compassion blends and swells over us all as numinous waves of unconditional love. I am especially moved that so many of the weepers are men – way more than all the men I have previously seen cry. This group makes me feel proud to be human.

Throughout this time, I also provide pro bono staff trainings at various non-profit clinics that work with trauma victims. Mandana House in Oakland, home of myriad AA-like programs, is my favorite place to teach.

These twelve step spinoffs provide crucial help to codependents, incest survivors, drug addicts, workaholics, sex and love addicts, and adult children of alcoholics. There's even a Beauty's Anonymous, but Lord knows what that's about or who has enough chutzpa to attend.

I love volunteering. I meet so many people who help simply out of the goodness of their hearts. Over time, my inner child feels safer from meeting all these kind people…less quick to project danger on people he doesn't know.

Zen and Laguna Honda Hospice

In the late 90's I train to become a non-professional volunteer at the Zen Hospice Program.

The "Zen" part of the title scares me at first. I felt burned by earlier dabbling in Zen. Back then, I was taken with the ritualized discipline portrayed in Eugene Herrigel's Zen *in the Art of Archery*. Monks on that path spent five years in intense meditative practice before they ever shot an arrow.

The first year was merely contemplating the bow and arrow, the second handling the bow, the third holding it with an arrow slotted in the bow string, the fourth pulling the string back, the fifth aiming and the sixth finally letting it fly.

I liked ordeals, but was not that fanatic. Instead I did other Zen workshops, many of which were rigidly strict. In one weekend retreat, three monks stared so long and hard at a wall that I was tempted to check afterwards to see if their gaze had melted the concrete.

Zen dovetailed with my Catholic indoctrination. Back then I strived to be the flawless altar boy who would be deemed worthy of the priesthood. Both creeds rewarded bad posture with a smack to the back of the head. Together they made me even harder on myself.

Thankfully Zen Hospice is nothing like that. It is soft and sweet with true Buddhist compassion – compassion that radiates inward towards the self, as well as outward toward all sentient beings.

The hospice caters to the poor in a ward of about thirty beds. Many patients are from the streets and are grateful for having finally landed in a safe place. Many are remarkably dialogical and are put off by pity. They prefer the volunteers who share about their own lives – especially their everyday ups and downs.

Retreating into the condescending position of I-won't-complain-because-you-have-it-so-much-worse-than-me is clearly a compassion-lite move.

A terminal prognosis of less than six months is required for admission to the hospice. Patients sign a form acknowledging that they are dying and that no *extraordinary measures* will be taken be keep them alive. This does not stop many of them from imagining and rhapsodizing about some non-existent day when they be released. In the court of death, denial is king. And of course we respect their delusions.

Betty not-Boop

My five hour shift at the Zen Hospice in San Francisco is often my weekly highlight. I feel calm around death and dying...maybe because I flirted with it so often in my travels...*and, maybe because I yearned for it during many emotional flashbacks.*

My favorite patient is ancient doughy-faced Betty. She reminds me of the old babushka-ed Russian widows who lived in my childhood neighborhood. Within a year, she seems to subtlely morph into a likeness of my grandmother.

My mother's mother lived with us for much of the first seven years of my life. Back then, I felt warmth from Grandma Stevenson – like she loved *and* liked me. I believed my parents loved me, but there was little *like* in it.

In retrospect I believe grandma's love tempered the severity of my CPTSD. Now however, my love for her is tinged with ambivalence. Her long-term nastiness to my mother made her the pill that she was. Even worse, when grandma sparkled at my presence, Helen boiled in jealous resentment, and punishments came in swarms.

Still, had it not been for grandma, I would have been without affection or contact-comfort. My mother confessed to me on her death bed: "I didn't touch you for the first two weeks of your life. And if it wasn't for your grandmother, you never would have been picked up at all."

So the sum of all this is that I really like Betty, which saves her from isolation. The other volunteers play hit and run in their visits to her bedside because of her volcanic bursts of angry fear.

Betty is pretty far gone – barely contactable in her dementia. Nonetheless she tolerates my presence – and I'm certain that her eruptions are not about me. They seem to be about old emotional pain that her meds cannot anaesthetize. As with my clients – whose anger mostly comes from flashbacks and parental transference – I don't take it personally.

Early on, I start humming and singing softly to her when no one else is around. Remarkably, her body visibly relaxes. She seems to have regressed to infancy. Perhaps I supply an unmet developmental need – the soothing of the lullaby.

About six months in, I come to hospice in a howling winter storm that has emptied the roads. We are understaffed and volunteer-less except for me. The attendants finish administering breakfast and diaper changes, and disappear for other duties.

I make the rounds, briefly interacting with conscious patients, and silently dispensing blessings to those who are checked out or comatose. I then settle at Betty's bedside. She releases a shuddering breath and becomes still.

I look closely for evidence of breathing. I occasionally think I see her open eyes shimmer. But then my certainty grows that she has passed. I alternate between humming and meditating for the next hour, and finally lay my palm on her forehead and feel a chill settling into her dead body.

My subsequent reaction astounds me. Instead of grief, I feel a great sense of relief. All quality of life ceased long ago for her. She has transitioned.

Her death is profoundly peaceful – subtlely numinous – not unlike what I felt at the birth I witnessed in Goa.

I feel that although her body is dead, she is not. She is still here – at perfect peace with herself. I feel great comfort – as if I have climbed another rung on the ladder of accepting my own eventual death. I am far enough up that ladder that I can "see" that I have nothing to fear.

As I write about this mini-satori now, the nun subpersonality of my critic interjects: "Jesus, Mary and Joseph – you wretched urchin! Why would you curse your own death by writing such presumptuous tomfoolery?" But I've built up so much Teflon against my critic, that I merely laugh at it and watch it disappear.

Later, when I process Betty's death with Eileen, the wise volunteer coordinator, she says: "You know, Pete, the Buddhists say: 'A new baby cries when it comes into the world, but everyone else laughs in delight. But everyone cries when a person dies…except that person, who instead laughs in joy at returning home.'"

"I've got to tell you, Pete, I've been doing this work for a long time, and every time I'm at a deathbed, I feel mildly envious of the person who has just passed."

How I know what she means. I fantasize that when and if I see my grandmothers when I die, I will also get to see Betty and know more about my strong connection with her.

In response to my dialog with Eileen, my theist subpersonality trumps the agnostic one and I write:

Each infant
A tear
Cried by God
Saddened

At the lengthy release of one of Her own
Into the wobbly adventure
Of human life

Therapist Heal Thyself

Five volunteers work each shift and we minister to patients in the ways that come most natural to us. Most of the volunteers are psychologically and spiritually balanced people. The contrast between these volunteers and the many untherapized therapists that I meet is often glaring.

So many therapists pay lip service to working deeply on their own issues, but never seem to take a step below sea level. The best therapists are those who spend significant time being a client in psychotherapy.

Therapists of clients who are drowning in their childhood pain are lousy lifeguards if they have not gone under a few times themselves. Shockingly few training programs require therapists to do their own therapy.

So, I write an article for my website entitled: "Therapist Heal Thyself", and advise CPTSD survivors to ask prospective therapists if they have worked on their own family of origin issues. I emphasize this because most of the therapists I know were first drawn to this work by their own as yet, unresolved childhood trauma. *Just like me!*

Roy Bleeds Out

Eric Poche is the supervisor of the volunteers at Laguna Honda. He often encourages us to be as compassionate with ourselves and each other as we are with the patients. Early on, he gave us the mantra: "All that I give, I give to myself."

We meet in a small circle with Eric for twenty minutes before and after every shift. He creates a subtle form of group therapy to help us deal with the challenges of working with the dying.

Today before going onto the ward, Rene tells us about the extra shift she did last night with hospital favorite, Roy. We all love bright and gregarious Roy, and know that he has cancer of the throat…from which he will probably bleed out. Cancer causes this when it destroys a blood vessel and the person bleeds to death internally – or externally if the artery is near an orifice.

Rene tells us: "I was having a lovely chat with him in the sun room when he suddenly raised his hands up and softly said: 'Have to lie down,' which he did right there on the floor. A stream of blood then began to flow from his mouth."

Trying to sooth us from vicarious trauma, she says: "I feel like you're all worried about me, and I hope you'll believe me: it was okay. I'm not sure why. I guess it's because it was okay with him. Roy just looked so peaceful, so accepting of what was happening. It was quite amazing…his death didn't even seem violent. I guess he knew what was coming and somehow let go without a trace of struggle or pain. His life force just kind of gently faded away."

Rene's serene account proves the peacefulness of Roy's death, especially as we all previously heard her pray: "Please don't let Roy die on my shift."

How *I love Rene in this moment!* Clearly, she was able to midwife his death with tranquility. We all cry together in one of those oft demeaned group hugs, *but oh, it is comforting.*

Our tears are ambivalent – mostly relief. But Roy was such a sweet person that we grieve that we will never see him again. And of course, entwined in there in varying degrees, are everyone's tears for departed loved ones…and for the inconceivable fact that we too will inevitably die.

After this experience, seeing Grace smoke through her tracheotomy hole is child's play. As is Belinda's eccentric habit of flashing her cancerous breast ubiquitously around the ward. She is only thirty-two and has judged herself ugly her whole life, and suddenly this horrible cancer has expanded her left breast into an archetypically alluring breast, which she delights in "accidentally" exposing.

Deafening Silence

During this time I fall in love with Lynn – a volunteer on my hospice shift who is also a therapist. Lynn exudes sweetness and comfort. Patients open up to her like flowers do to humming birds. She shepherds them into their grieving more easily than any of us.

An electricity flows between us that only the comatose patients don't notice. On the ward, we resist the magnetic pull that makes it hard to keep our hands off each other. But our attempts to hide our liaison are pitiable and we soon abandon them. The women patients love our romance and paint an aura of fairy tale around it. How it enhances the fable I am constructing in my own mind.

We graciously accept the patients' blessings but refrain from PDAs. When we are alone however, it is pretty torrid stuff. I mindlessly slide into denial about how much of our relationship is taking place horizontally.

As lovely as Lynn is, she has little to say for herself. I'm good at eliciting, but she is a master of the monosyllabic. As a recovering codependent I don't like being the only one with something to say.

Three months in, we spend the whole day in bed, and then adjourn to a nearby café where she kills a fledgling conversation by panting: "Shut up and kiss me!" She can't or won't understand why this upsets me.

I grow increasingly uneasy – feeling like I am not getting to know her. "I'm just very introverted, Pete" becomes less and less reassuring. I feel lonely with her when we're not making love.

At the six month mark, she finally opens up about her ghastly childhood. Among other horrors, her schizophrenic mother pathologized every word out of her mouth.

I feel deep knowing commiseration, grief for her and relief for us. I think her vulnerability means we are finally moving toward conversational intimacy. I share that I often felt verbally flayed by my crazy mother.

Lynn appreciates our interchange. "It was really good to get that out, Pete. I really do want to open up more to you." But her attempts are sporadic and progress is glacial.

When I express ambivalence about our future, she says: "I'm tired of being shut down. I'll call this therapist who I heard good things about."

But weeks become months, excuses pile up like dirty laundry and I am not willing to campaign about this.

Finally Lynn makes a suggestion. "I think living together will help me open up more." On the eve of me moving in, she postpones the move for reasons that are "…beyond words."

I feel devastated for weeks. She's so generous with saying "I love you", but her love increasingly feels like frosting, and who knows what's in the cake.

I am increasingly triggered into my abandonment depression – too often feeling that it is about the present. Beneath the surface of our placid lake, there are only shallows. I am almost fifty-two and I want a life-partner. *I must be mistaking lust for love.*

My body may want to continue basking in Lynn's sensual comfort, but my intuitions insist: *I bring a lot to the table; I want a lot in return.* The mother side of my critic counters: "You bring dog food and should be happy someone will even sit with you!"

But my critic is a private in my platoon now. Lieutenant Me is in charge and decides that I must face the pain of withdrawal and cut my losses. I feel almost as guilty as when I left Brenda, but I keep working the mantra: *Feeling guilty does not mean I am guilty.* I was brainwashed to feel guilty whenever I put my needs first!

—∞—

My sexually dissociative romance with Lynn has a tarnished silver lining. I realize she is the reverse of Brenda. Not hearing from Lynn was as painful as not being heard by Brenda. Maybe now that I've experienced the yin and yang of illusory connection, I'll figure out how to find the contactful middle ground.

So, I will never again settle for a partnership without mutual deep self-disclosure. "Yeah sure! I've heard that before" quips my critic rather accurately. But grieving helps me forgive myself for falling into the same hole…on a different street.

I take some comfort in the fact that people are often blinded by the glare of romance. Many of us need repeated hard knocks to cure romantic astigmatism. From now on it will be: *You show me yours and I'll show you mine.*

I lie low for months and stay open to gusts of grief about my deceased hopes with Lynn. On an especially lonely Thanksgiving Day, I record this experience of reemergence.

> I choose to be a castaway from the Thanksgiving gorge,
>   until a deluge of grief
>   washes me off the rack of my loneliness.
> Resurgent, I shed the house
>   and walk the deserted streets.
> Trees weep their teardrop leaves.
> Rain pastes them umber and vermillion to the pavement.
> Plumped by the sidewalks' deliquescence,
>   leaf corpses summon happier remembrances
>   and applaud my resurrection.
> Pain sipped and swallowed,
>   toasts my metabolism of loss
>   clearing my pallet for a feast of new beginnings.

A Clarion Call for Euthanasia

Once again I counterphobically gravitate to a new patient on the ward. Twenty-five-year-old Edmund is hard to look at. A ghastly carcinoma covers one fifth of his forehead. It recently crept down between his eyes, devastating the bridge of his nose. Inoperable, the cancer is eating rapidly through his face toward his brain.

Something about him reminds me of my twenty-two-year-old San Francisco self. He is Celtic, hippieish and self-doctoring. A year ago, Edmund was sure he could cure a small growth that appeared on his forehead with herbal poultices. By the time he realized he needed help, the normally easy-to-excise cancer was too entrenched to remove.

As hard as Edmund is to look at, being with him in his pain is even harder. He is the only patient I ever see whose pain cannot be adequately controlled.

God, I hate this! Before this, death seemed so painless. The doctors are so skilled with the meds.

Edmund's morphine drip seems useless. This morning he is writhing in pain. No one else is around. I begin pushing the button on his IV mechanism for increasing the dose. When I see no visible relief, I push it more often, almost frantically – hoping to give him a lethal dose and end his pointless misery. *Arggghhh! It's not working.* Tearing up in dismay, I give up and leave.

When I show up for my next shift, I thank God that Edmund has made his transition. Yet I am still quite upset. I go to the coordinator, Eileen, and guiltily tell her what I did.

In her singularly comforting way, she says: "It's OK, Pete. You didn't kill him. The machine that controls the drip overrides the button when the dose is too high. But I sure know how you felt. There's been more than one occasion when I wished we had the right...the wisdom...the means to euthanize a patient whose suffering we could not alleviate."

Eileen's words help greatly, and from that day on I keep abreast of the *Assisted Suicide* and *The Right to Die Movements*. I am grateful to Dr. Kevorkian. I honor him as a hero despite his mistakes.

I hope the *right to die* will eventually reach Bill of Rights status. Everyone should have the option to choose euthanasia when their suffering becomes too great.

Because I hold these beliefs, I join the grass roots *Death Café Movement*. Anyone can attend a Death Café meeting, where all thoughts and feelings about death are welcomed for airing and discussion [www.deathcafe.com].

Three years have passed, and it's time to leave hospice. Rosa, my favorite patient, has been here all that time defying the odds of her diagnosis. She is a splendid presence – the "mother" of the back ward.

Rare exceptions have been made for her, and she is allowed to enshroud her corner bed with layers of brilliantly colored fabrics. She's created dignified privacy in a flamboyant pavilion.

There is wisdom in Rosa's great unschooled intelligence. I love to witness her holding court. She runs rich repartees, tells risqué jokes, dispenses informal blessings and helps others grieve the death of fellow patients. And best of all, she is still alive when I finish my final shift.

CHAPTER 22

A Marriage and Family Therapist Gets a Marriage and Family

I HAVE BEEN searching for a partner for twenty five years. I've gone down with the ships of too many failed relationships. Will I ever solve the puzzle of the mating game? Maybe I am getting closer. Each failure was an upgrade of sorts. Each was a lesser reenactment of my relationships with my parents

I get back to prioritizing my search and my acquaintances call me fussy, naïve, masochistic, etc. But I keep on roller-coastering between hope and despair. I give up many times, but invariably buy another ticket…take another ride. What could possibly add more to my almost good enough life?

And besides, all my dashed hopes have not been in vain. I've gotten my baggage down to a carry-on. And on a more tangible level, two sweet women who did not work out as partners are now good friends. We meet regularly and chat and commiserate about anything and everything.

I am at an afternoon potluck critiquing "normality" with a small circle of people: "It is virtually unpatriotic to be unhappy…treasonous to express sorrow about your difficulties. Admitting depression – no matter how fleeting– invites instant shunning."

I see *her* overhearing me from another nearby circle. When she gives me an opalescent smile, I almost forget what I am saying. She – Sara – joins my circle and weighs in about the epidemic of conversational surface skating. When she smiles at me again, I feel like I am deliquescing.

Soon we are chatting by ourselves. As we relax into each other's eyes, the chemistry is organic, electro-magnetic and radioactive.

On our first date, we meet at the Oakland Museum to commune with the live exhibit of California wild flowers. Radiant, Sara walks up, even more gorgeous than I remember. I whisper *luminous* to myself.

My critic of course has to chip in. "I know you feel like you are in a movie right now – and maybe you are, but you don't belong in it." I dismiss it easily with a silent *Piss off Helen and Charlie*, and dive into to the immediate warmth of our connection.

We fluoresce with the flowers and then spend every minute of the next two days together. I'm joyous, but my fear is amping up because my excitement has trumped my caution, and I've given up control. *Well there goes the take-it slow-rule*.! It just looks and feels so right…so destined… so capital WE.

We light-speed bond in a minuet of conversationality. Sara brings up the idea of psychological androgyny. *Screw caution*, I think. "Sara, I feel like a lesbian trapped in a man's body." She folds over laughing and I feel potential deeper than the Mariana Trench.

> At the yin of heart-stopping
> And the yang of heart-racing speed
> Our hearts storm, barns burn
> And past hindrances vaporize away.

Sara is an exotic raven, plumed with both emotional and cognitive intelligence. She laughs easily and authentically, yet also expresses herself with a full emotional palette.

Drinking tea in my back garden, we converse about psychology and spirituality all morning. We are both long term explorers of our inner worlds.

I say: "It's so hard to be passionate about esoteric and introspective concerns in this culture." She adds: "YES! Everything is so dominated by scientific and materialistic values."

We oscillate between poignancy and laughter, as we riff and commiserate about being round pegs in a square world. I opine: "Science IS the blind men examining the elephant. So many scientists over-focus on minute details that they're clueless about the big picture."

"Yes! It's disgraceful! Most modern doctors are so overspecialized that they have no idea about how the *whole* organism contributes to illness or health. Diet and exercise rarely even make it into the treatment plan."

Sweet! Talk about being in the ball park. She's standing on home plate!

Sara is an acupuncturist who also has a deep grasp of psychodynamics. We are both enamored with the unconscious mind and everything taboo relegated to it by the *Normies*. We frolic in the unmentionables and share a passion for finding the light in the dark.

We also both love volunteer work. While my volunteer work was at hospice and suicide prevention, hers was at the S.F. County Jail and at Charlotte Maxwell, a free health clinic for cancer patients. She is currently employed at SAGE – a holistic treatment center in San Francisco for survivors of commercial sexual exploitation.

We eventually make love. We glide in the surf of midday sex. When the last tremors of our orgasm dissipate through our bodies, I feel a gentle release of tears – tears of relief and happiness at the profundity of our connection. *Break out the clichés, it is holy.*

I've fallen in love and thought I'd found a soulmate more than a few times. But this time, much to my amazement, I discard the soulmate notion. This time I am filled with certainty that I have met my wife.

Wife! I never wanted a wife – even though I have searched doggedly for a life partner. Hippie iconoclast that I am, I never desired marriage. But there it is, emblazoned on my inner sight screen: *I am going to marry Sara.*

In my next therapy session, I tell Gina: "I know what you're gonna say, but I just met my wife!" I have been working with Gina for four years now. She seems to intuitively get it, because she does not pull out the standard don't-go-too-fast advice.

Maybe she thinks that at fifty-four, this old codger doesn't have time to go slow. But when I ask her if that's what she thinks, she shakes her head laughing: "Of course not! Something wonderful has happened to you. You're radiating. Tell me more about her."

Sara Cheech & Chongs Her Way into My Heart

The thrill of discovering how much we have in common just keeps on coming. Perhaps our greatest similarity is that we are both psychologically androgynous. Each of us has considerable access to both our male and female selves.

Sara is an assertive, powerful woman who has not ditched her kindheartedness to have a successful career. And I can be as tender as the night or as fierce as I need to be in the service of Right Action.

In the midst of another long conversational free-for-all, Sara tells me a Cheech and Chong joke that's new to me.

"Two Neanderthals are walking down the trail. The first spots a brown tootsie roll on the ground and says to his friend: 'I see shit. Is that shit? You bend down and check it.'

The second caveman complies and says: 'Looks like shit.'

The first guy then says: 'You smell it.'

He bends down, sniffs and says: 'Smells like shit.'

The first continues: 'You taste it.'

The second pokes his finger in it, tastes it and says: 'Tastes like shit.'

With great relief, the first caveman exclaims: 'Good thing we no step in it.'

'Yeah, Good thing!' echoes the second!"

I laugh so hard that the V-8 juice that I'm drinking leaks out of my nose. When I recover from the tears of laughter and the tears of the juice-burn, I say: "I have never had a girlfriend with a crude sense of humor. This must be sign number twenty-seven. You are an absolute keeper, Sara!"

Sara and I go camping in the Eastern Sierras at a remote hot springs. We dive into pitching the tent together. Wordlessly, we uncannily sense how to support each other. The tent is up in mere minutes. *How cool! Psychic teamwork!* This simple dance presages an opus of easy cooperation in our future endeavors.

After our trip, Sara writes this to me on a Susan Boulet greeting card:

> A portrait of you in deep thought surrounded by rocks and stream –
> All meditating as one on the pulse and heartbeat of the earth.
> My heart embraces you even in your silence.
> I love it when your body flows against me
> Like water filling all the empty spaces between us.

I reply in a Claude Monet card:

> With the mead that we daily distill,
> I toast the honeycomb of our new love:
> Relishing the moments with you
> As we amble through the minutes,

I pledge to meet you
Body and soul, heart and mind.

On the anniversary of our first meeting, Sara and I become engaged. I grow a festival of flowers in my friend John's backyard to backdrop our wedding.

Days before the ceremony, a new love song on the radio sweeps me away. The singer croons and exults as he sings this chorus over and over: "This woman....she loves me!" Clearly delighted and astonished he belts it out as if the notion had previously been unimaginable – the notion, that is, that someone could so totally love him.

His tone smacks of an earth-shattering revelation – one that I feel so poignantly right now that my heart feels too big for my chest.

On Bastille Day of 2002, we marry each other to the accompaniment of a CD of love songs that we compile for the occasion. We mingle our futures as we exchange the vows we've composed. The ceremony elicits sweet tears from us and many of our sixty friends and family.

Our reception is a potluck in the same yard. A good time is definitely had by all and I am mind-bogglingly happy.

All the while, I have a strange feeling that my mother is also in attendance. Suddenly, I get that it's because Sat has flown in from Australia to be my best man. He is much more than my best man. He is the tremendous friend who was like a psychological mother to me during our time together there. For years, he effortlessly gave me the unconditional positive regard and encouragement that Helen could not. In honor of that, I dedicated my first book to him.

As a logical extension of our vows to work on evolving together, Sara and I commit to weekly co-counseling. In this venue, we help each other to manage our flashbacks and work through the ever-shrinking vestiges of our childhood traumas.

For the last fifteen years, co-counseling has helped us immeasurably to grow and develop. It has also greatly fertilized the creativity in both of our lives, and taught us a great deal about working through normal differences.

Jaden: The Ultimate Creativity

I meet my son for the first time in the operating room, as his head pops out of the C-section incision in Sara's belly. Shocked, raptured and eyes leaking, I suddenly find myself cutting his umbilical cord. With every nano-particle of my being, I welcome him into the world – somehow not dissociating from him being all slimy and smeared with blood.

I am instantly in love with this new person who miraculously arrives on the scene, seemingly out of nowhere. Two days later, I am a stunned mullet when the nurses step aside as they hand us our swaddled baby to take home.

This feels so unreal...much more daunting than either of us imagined! We keep looking around to see if someone will stop us. Maybe I'm flashing back into the imposter syndrome. Sara says: "Where's the instruction manual?" I quip: "Yeah and where's the cadre of instructors to walk us through the first few months?" Thankfully we get great guidance from *The Attachment Parenting Book* by Dr. Sears and The Berkeley Parent Network website

We immediately commit to quality- and *quantity*-time parenting. We cannot give him too much attention with no extended family in the area to help. Not that you can give a baby too much attention.

Maybe I can do double duty? I'm old enough to also give him grandfathering.

From day one, Jaden is priority number one. I want to witness every burp and gurgle, so I radically prune my schedule. I steal time from my job, my garden, my artwork and sadly my friends. Doting on him also eases my guilt about having him so late in life...about putting him at risk of being fatherless at an early age. To obviate this, I stick with basketball. I must stay agile and healthy.

For the first few years Jaden is always with at least one of us – including both of us at night in the family bed. I take him everywhere. Carrying him like a headlight in his Baby Bjorn carrier fills me with contentment. He's Master Mellow, checking out the sights wherever we walk.

When Jaden turns three, Sara reprises her private practice part-time, and we stagger our work days so he is still always with one of us.

Keeping My Vow: The Buck Stops Here

I know that raising Jaden will not be as simple as doing the opposite of my parents in a black-and-white sort of way. On the other hand they sure set some glaring examples of how not to do treat a child. In a phrase, they raised me and my sisters on fear and shame instead of love and support.

Sara and I dedicate ourselves to love Jaden in a trove of affection, encouragement and playful banter. We childproof our home to let the boy roam – to support his instincts to check everything out – to support his mastery of his immediate environment.

Jaden's confidence grows as we let him make as many choices as safety permits. Yesterday I had to stop him though. "Jaden, I'm taking this fork away from you because if you stick it in the plug hole, you'll go PSSSTTT!!!" He thinks that's hilarious. Later I'll buy some outlet protectors at the hardware store.

To protect him from the legacy of my parents' perfectionism, we never punish or shame him for mistakes. He just knocked his cereal off his high chair table. I flinch remembering being smacked for "spilt-milk" crimes. Somehow I am able to join him in laughing. *I'll have to buy that bowl with a suction cup on the bottom that I saw online this morning.*

We also honor Jaden's protests when they meet the criteria of fairness-to-all. "You're right! It's not fair! I put my leftovers in the compost. You don't have to eat it all [like I gaggingly had to]!" I bring the compost urn over to his high chair. "You can dump your leftover broccoli in here."

On the other hand: "Jaden, bringing food into the living room is not fair to Mommy and Daddy. It's too hard to clean the rug when it spills." We balance extensive freedom with a minimum of rules.

We use timeouts as the logical consequence for his infrequent acting out. I tell him: "Even adults get timeouts. When they are unfair, other people don't want to be with them. When they're very unfair, they get put in jail."

Jaden is also welcome to question rules until we come up with a reason he can understand. No Walkerville "Because I said so."

Jaden's just turned three and I remind him for the fifth time not to leave his Legos in the doorway. When I say: "You never clean up your Legos," he starts bawling angrily: "I clean them up. I CLEAN THEM!"

I'm puzzled at first. I know I've spoken gently...but suddenly I catch his meaning. He's responding to my all-or-none use of *never*. He doesn't have the adverbs yet to tell me that he *mostly* puts the Legos away now. He has been getting better about it.

I sit down and put him on my lap and cuddle him. "I'm so sorry Jaden. You're such a good boy and you hardly ever leave the Legos there anymore. Thank you for all the times you do put your Legos away."

Meanwhile, Sara reminds me for the fifth time this month to put the lid back on the kitchen compost container: "Pete, don't you notice how it makes the kitchen smell?"

As usual, she says it nicely, but this time my tone gets bristly. "I don't know why I keep forgetting. Probably because of how little sleep we get with Jaden waking us up all the time. But I'M TRYING!"

By the last phrase I hear my tone. I take a mini-timeout to collect myself, and realize I'm being unfair. I come back into the kitchen: "Sara, I'm sorry about all that tone. I do appreciate you reminding me...and it's unfair that I keep forgetting. I'll put a post-it on the container to remind me."

This interaction is emblematic of our evolving conversations around conflicts. With time, we each ongoingly shrink our occasional use of inflammatory anger.

I believe anger is normal between loved ones, but loud anger is generally abusive – and counter-productive. Volume blurs the message – scares the other into scrambling for a response rather than fully listening.

I rarely raise my voice with Jaden, but apologize when I do: "I'm really sorry I just barked at you Jaden, but it's dangerous to run up to the street like that. You could easily trip and fall in front of a car."

Whenever practical, Sara and I use *The Techniques for Lovingly Resolving Conflict* [Appendix 4 of my *Complex PTSD* book]. We powwowed about these a great deal when we first met, and continually grow in our ability to use them. I also use a simplified version with Jaden, because kids do what we do, way more than what we say.

What good fortune that Jim Buser and I still meet for weekly basketball workouts. It's been over ten years and Jim has a six-year-old daughter. After playing we often rap about the joys and hardships of parenting. "It's so inspiring!" "It's so exhausting." For both of us, it's so much of the former.

As a devoted father, Jim runs his business from home to maximize time with Elise. He inspires me to cut down my work days even further. I squeeze my private practice into two long days a week.

And I am double-lucky because my hiking buddy, John Barry, also raises his son holistically. I often explore parenting uncertainties with him that he's already weathered with Sean.

Sara and I read to Jaden for hours every week. Around eighteen-months-old he falls in love with library picture books. I enjoy the books as much as he does. Kid's books have evolved quantum levels since the Dick and Jane days.

One night I read *Goodnight Moon* to him and my inner child. Afterwards old grief leaks out about no story-time for me as a kid. *No wonder it took me so long to discover the joys of reading.*

Jaden is soon gobbling up books like they are candy. Between eight and ten he reads the Harry Potter series five times. Sara and I are unsure of its appropriateness at first, but its richness impresses us as we read excerpts of it to him.

Before we know it, we are reading the speaking parts with accents that match the characters. Sara's the most multi-lingual. Jaden does a great Cockney, as well as a condescending upper class Brit, and I give Ron Weasley an Aussie twang. *How disappointing that the movies hyperbolize the scary aspects of the books.*

Playing games is *Bonding-Central* in our family. Early on, I often play down to Jaden's level – to teach him to be a good winner as well as a good loser. To the degree that I win and lose gracefully, he generally does the same.

I rarely play down to Jaden's level anymore. He's luckier with the throw of the dice and the draw from the deck than I am. Sometimes, I wish he would let me win a little more often. The tradeoff is that he likes reading the directions of new games and is a great teacher. I haven't completely worked through my conditioning that *real men don't read no stinkin' directions*. Sara says this is more about me being somewhat ADD.

From five onwards, Jaden unearths my unconscious Know-It-All complex. He brings facts home from school that I'm sure are incorrect. When I take our disagreements to court, Google usually proves him right.

Fortunately I am not delusional enough to claim that the facts have changed since I was in school. Over time, I become more realistic about the accuracy of my database, and have less need to eat humble pie.

Nowadays, I usually assume he is right about empirical facts, but occasionally double-check when he goes to bed. Rarely do I turn out to be *Smarter than a Fifth-Grader*. We do however keep up with the new, newer and newest math by doing lessons together on the brilliant and free online school: Khan Academy.

Here is a snapshot of Jaden at nine years old. Unprompted and unedited he writes in his Mother's Day card: "Dear Mommy, I love you and want you to know it. You are wonderful, and make every day of my life shine. Your kindness rubs off on everybody else. Be happy on your special day. Be Happy, Be Joyful, Be Kind, enjoy yourself. Happy Mother's [that's you] Day! Love, Jaden Walker."

He also makes my day with a Father's Day card thanking me: "I love you. You always do what you say you will." *How wonderful! I didn't think he'd noticed.*

Recently he made me laugh, as he often does, by quoting this joke he read in a magazine: "Politicians and diapers need to be changed often for the same reason."

Here is a poem I wrote to give to Jaden someday.

I choose to love you my son
As heartily as I know how.
Without limit I invest my love…
Daily for nine years now.

I choose to love you
Even knowing with my PhD in loss
That I will lose you
To college, or even high school,
And once and for mostly to marriage.

You don't choose to love me back.
You can't help it.
Your child heart matches
My love with your own instinctive caring.

Unknowingly you fully invest and love me back
Not grasping that you will
Lose me one day
When it's my turn to run out of breath.

Here in 2017, I still read to Jaden a great deal. New books – chockablock with juicy issues to discuss – keep falling off the library shelves. Great middle school authors like Jason Sonnenblick, Josh Berk, David Lubar, Louis Sachar and Varian Johnson create sympathetic misfit protagonists who defy the odds and make good. Their poignant, humorous stories are often wise morality plays about the richness of diversity.

I enjoy their writing as much as Jaden and love the rich repartee it inspires between us. How grateful I am that it extends my tenure as one of Jaden's teachers. And, if I get too didactic, Jaden gently breaks the gravity with a bit of Cockney: "Please Guv'ner, can we get on with the bloomin' story!"

A final proud parent offering: Others often tell us he is "a good kid". *Kind, smart* and *funny* are common adjectives that they use. Yesterday he came home from school with this joke: "And God said: 'Jacob come forth and receive eternal life.' But Jacob came fifth and only received a toaster oven."

I remember when he was three and ambivalently fascinated by pirates. He loved how they looked but didn't like that they killed people. Eventually he brainstormed: "I know! Let's play *Kind Pirates*." And we did…a great deal over the next few years.

We've always encouraged his kindness, except with people who are unkind to him. The hard knocks of being exploited by three spoiled friends in early elementary school have anchored that lesson for him.

So now his friends are also a boon in our life. It is especially easy to love his sweet inner-circle: Daniel, Jude, Jacob, Marquez, and Sebastian.

Jaden's social ease has always exceeded mine. His love of teamwork has him comfortably ensconced in many healthy circles.

My friend Sat recently jibed me: "So Pete, you must be surfing the Dark Net. Where'd you get the teenage hormone-blocker drugs?"

Of all the vulnerability in this book, my critic stirs the most when I write about Jaden. Very weak now, the critic threatens me in a mumble: "How dare you imply that you are doing a good parenting job?"

"What a surprise I hardly hear from you anymore, Helen, now that I've disowned you for over twenty years."

Out of curiosity I let her go on a bit: "You just wait and see Peter! You think you're a better parent than me. But you are digging your own grave. Jaden will soon become one of those sullen angry teenagers, and he will rebel against you – leave you just like you left your father and me!"

Suddenly laughter erupts from way down deep inside me. *Wow, her words just don't get to me!* I really have established *psychological safety*, as well as the physical safety that Judith Herman stresses.

My psyche is so user-friendly now that I don't need my anger to stop her anymore. She just cannot find any purchase. Just recognizing that it's Helen "talking" is enough to turn her judgments aside.

But, just for old time sake, I give her a lighthearted jab: "Who couldn't be better at parenting than you, Helen? Sure Jaden may do some normal teenage distancing. But it'll only be a stage. He'll come warm again like every grown child who gets good enough parenting."

I even let her reply: "Look who's the narcissist now. You think you're so perfect!"

"Oh please, mother-not-so-dearest! Stop projecting. I've only exorcized you and your toxicity. The good old healthy critic, my superego, functions well now, and lets me know when I have made a real mistake and need to apologize and make amends. I can tell when criticism is healthy by its authentically gentle and helpful tone."

—⚉—

So! What a blessing to care for children – whether they are ours or someone else's. Jaden is of course the peak of all my child-rearing experiences – inner and outer. I need no more proof of my belief in Humanism. Human beings are born loving, and remain so with good enough caring.

CHAPTER 23

Regenerating At The Hub Of Relational Healing

The Hub of Relational Healing

Meandering into the Role of Therapist

HERE IS THE trajectory of my journey to become a therapist as viewed through my retrospectoscope.

HOMESTEADING in the CALM EYE of the STORM

I was in a decades-long game of Blind Man's Bluff unknowingly searching for what I wanted to be when I grew up.

Early on in my ambitionless journey, I frequently fell into informal counseling roles...without even knowing what a therapist I was. From six until eighteen, I was off to an early start as my mother's de facto therapist. From then on I had various people acting as if they were my clients.

In the army, several fellow soldiers surprisingly and flatteringly spilled their guts to me about their fears of dying in Viet Nam. Then, during my years on the road, various travelers unburdened their inner sufferings upon me. I typically felt fascinated and honored.

When my travels ended and I finally became bored with life in Darwin, I felt lost for something else to do until I was lit up by the thought of going back to school. Australia offered free higher education to all citizens and even to migrants like me. I enrolled in the Social Work Program at Sydney University and qualified for a monthly government stipend, as well as money from Uncle Sam via the G.I. Bill. I conceived of hitting the books again as an all-expenses paid entertainment.

What a boon! Overnight, I went from no benefactors to two corporate sponsors. Even better, my love of psychology resurfaced, even though I had no real interest in becoming a therapist. I could not imagine that I would ever be good enough for that.

As my social work internships accrued, I realized that people in crisis seemed to sense my capacity to provide a calm eye in their storms. *Maybe I did have a bit of the therapist in me?*

When I graduated, I got my first paid position as a telephone crisis counselor in Sydney. One afternoon, I spent a harrowing half hour with a bloke who called me from a train platform. Every time I heard a train coming into the station, he threatened to jump onto the tracks. As the din of the engine obliterated our conversation, I felt panicky that when the clamor subsided I would not hear his voice again.

In a flash of calm lucidity, I realized he was in unbearable pain; so I said: "Mate, you must be so bloody hurting right now! Please tell me about it."

Within seconds he was ranting and crying out his pain. And then like magic, he told me: "I'm *awlright* now, mate! Thanks cobber!"

WOW! Verbal ventilation saved that guy's life. He let his emotions saturate his words, and his pain was released.

I left the phone-counseling job after two years however, because the boss was a narcissist of historical proportions. I couldn't, however, find another social work job that was not in a dehumanizing institution. So, I defaulted into doing psychological astrology. I wanted to work with people who still had the potential to grow.

I loved helping people via discussing their horoscopes, but the performance anxiety was hell. To get help with this, I continued to pursue every new spiritual and psychological fast fix that I could find. My pain-driven passion for relief made me as persistent as a yellow jacket, no matter how weak each new fix turned out to be.

Nonetheless, I rose out of the ashes of each failed panacea to pursue another elixir for my horrible angst. For a long time, I had no idea that silver linings were accruing and morphing into valuable skills and experience…that one day, I would synthesize this bag of disappointments into an effective therapeutic approach.

When I felt that I had exhausted the therapeutic possibilities Down Under, I looked toward San Francisco for further help. A wonderful book by Will Schutz convinced me to enroll in his Master's Degree program in Humanistic and Holistic Psychology. I immediately loved it, but still felt too much like an imposter to make it as a therapist. Nonetheless, I stuck with my introspection-oriented studies because I was a glutton for self-improvement.

Four years of intense graduate studies elapsed, and I finally got my Master's degree from JFK University and became a *registered* intern-therapist working with a full client load.

My client work often made me feel like I might have the makings of one of those *nothing's-too-heavy* therapists. I easily accompanied clients into the darkest abysses of their pain – perhaps because I had hung out in and survived similar places in myself.

But even though my clients clearly benefitted from our work, I still could not imagine myself in this career. Imposter syndrome and performance anxiety were nasty spoilers that still held my ambition in check.

Eventually, reparenting work helped me realize that my sense of purpose in life had never had a chance to bloom. My belief in my own worth was still hibernating, waiting for me to address even earlier developmental arrests. Until I sufficiently resuscitated my capacity for self-compassion, self-care, and self-protection, my foundation would be too shaky to see myself as a good enough helper.

Finally, several more years of depth work and inner child work united me with my core desire to be a therapist. Once this epiphany stood the test of time, I felt ecstatic that I had found my path. In a moment of lighthearted self-mockery, I celebrated by asking my friend Jim to make a button for me: "Nearly Normal Now". I had good fun wearing it in certain appropriate venues, like my ACA support group where it always garnered some empathic laughs.

Soon after, I turned forty-four. My stunning and shocking birthday present was that I finally felt like an adult! At least much of the time. And, I not only knew my career, I knew my specialty: Helping childhood trauma survivors to grieve through their pain and meet their developmental arrests.

Developmental Arrests! Could there be a concept more central to CPTSD?

Fast forward to 2015. The diagnosis of CPTSD has already been rejected for the DSM, and leading lights in the trauma field resubmit it as *Developmental Trauma Disorder. What a great additional name!*

Unfortunately, it is also rejected for DSM inclusion. The insurance companies that now control psychological benefits are apparently just not going to accept diagnoses that require long-term therapy.

Yet it is as clear as ocean air to me that if CPTSD survivors do not resolve their developmental arrests, they will recurringly feel stuck in shame, fear and depression. The more survivors open compassionately and vulnerably to their child selves, the more they naturally become motivated to care for and protect themselves. Without self-kindness and a felt-sense of safety, life has sparse moments of contentment and fulfillment.

Not Toeing the Line of Melanie Klein

I am doing more post-graduate work, studying both traditional Psychoanalysis [Freudian-based] and modern Relational Psychoanalysis.

Relational psychoanalysis is the new wave. Relational therapists are warm and engaging. They believe that healthy interrelating is the heart of psychotherapeutic healing.

Compare this with Kleinian psychoanalysis, the most popular school of traditional psychoanalysis. Kleinians use a "blank screen" approach – a cauterized type of relating. They blunt their presence by interacting minimally and impersonally. Some still sit behind the client, unreachable for eye contact.

I am especially put off by the Kleinian insistence on never "gratifying" clients. A Kleinian consultant tells us: "Don't be friendly, don't give supportive feedback and don't self-disclose." Another Kleinian critiques my colleague as being "gratifying" for smiling at a client, implying that this is a sexual act.

I flash back to a therapy I had before Gina. I saw Dr. L, a Kleinian, twice a week for two years. Over and over, Dr. L refused to answer my questions. Instead she scrutinized the motive behind my questions, typically interpreting it as evidence of my pathology.

She also repeatedly refused to reassure me when I said I felt disliked by her. At the end of this desiccated therapy, I complained about her aloofness, and she sardonically replied: "You see me as the therapist with the dry tit." *Not any more*, I thought, as I crawled out from under her microscope for the last time.

Silver lining? "Therapy" with Dr. L showed me further how much emotional neglect had damaged me in childhood. Acceptance of neglect was so ingrained in me that it took me two years to realize that Dr. L was a reenactment of my stingy and cold-hearted mother!

What an expensive way to learn about the counter-therapeutic effect of the blank screen approach. I wish I could have a refund for every time I left feeling ashamed for wanting a smattering of empathy.

More importantly, I felt fully validated in rejecting the "old school approach" along with her. I unambivalently embraced the dawn of Relational Psychotherapy – a sweet descendant of my beloved Humanistic Psychology.

A decade later, I felt further confirmed while reading the results of a large survey of psychotherapy patients. In rating the effectiveness of their therapy, the most cited factor was: "Feeling that the therapist cared about me". This was true regardless of the therapist's theoretical approach!

Mutual Relational Healing

> *Effective therapy involves the transformation of both people in their engagement with one another.*
>
> – Dr. Stephen Mitchell, Guru of Relational Psychoanalysis and Psychotherapy

Let me recount a pivotal session with a client over twenty years ago.

Lorna comes into her therapy session distraught: "I'm such a hopeless case! I've been coming here for over a year and I just can't...or won't stop hating myself. I wish I was dead! I try and I try, but I can't get a moment's rest from my critic. I truly am defective! How can you stand to be in the same room with me?"

I feel so much sorrow for her. It wasn't that long ago that I often felt like she does. I flash to a mental image of Will Schutz crying at Antioch in that first encounter group. Tears begin to brim in my eyes in empathy. For once I don't stop them. I don't actually cry but I let my eyes well up.

With full eye contact I say: "I'm so sorry. I really know how you feel. I've been there so many times and thank god I discovered that having a good cry often resolves it."

Alright! I can see her whole body relaxing. And now the damn bursts. She weeps into what is clearly relief, and then says: "Thank you so much for telling me that, Pete. It helps so much to know that you understand that place and won't hate me for it. I feel so much better now."

Man Oh Man! That was my most therapeutic vulnerable disclosure yet. I feel comforted by it too. Whenever the timing and situation is right, I will allow my eyes to well up. Sharing my vulnerability is clearly healing.

Ongoing versions of this session convince me that emotionally reverberating with some clients helps create a hub of relational healing. And at the best of times this healing is mutual. In the session above, Lorna had an enormous release from toxic shame, and I too felt a release from the shame that had stopped me from welling up with empathy in previous therapy sessions. At that moment, I became a person who could now show empathy more completely, and benefit from the mutual trust that created.

Over time, vulnerable self-disclosure becomes one of my most potent tools for helping clients to deepen their recovery work. Modeling emotional authenticity without shame invariably proves helpful. I do not, however, use this technique until I sense that the client is developmentally ready for such help.

When I do disclose, I show similar emotional pain to what they have just shared. Here are some examples: "Yes my mother was mean like yours, and Mother's Day makes me very sad too" or "I hate that he did that; bullies like your father and mine really piss me off" or "Yeah, me too. I still find new situations scary" or "Yes I hear you. Waking up depressed is one of my most unfavorite things" or "Wow! That happened to me too once. I ran into the car in front of me when I was spacing out...I was so mortified and scared!"

Via this kind of practice, clients talk about and emote out their pain more easily. As the therapeutic relationship matures, clients who have never felt human support gradually open to being soothed by my empathy.

I'll never forget the glorious session when that first happened in my own therapy with Gina. For the first time ever, I *got* and *let in* the warmth of her empathy for *my pain*. What a therapeutic landmark! I cried perhaps the sweetest tears ever!

As the client gets used to my empathy, we may one day resonate about our mutual suffering. Most commonly, this occurs when I commiserate something like: "You know I still get flashbacks sometimes too." When the timing is right, this helps ease his or her shame about having CPTSD. One lovely day I joined a client in bemoaning the pain of feeling triggered. Simultaneously we both exclaimed: "God, I hate flashbacks!" and we both teared up laughing.

Such exchanges can revive the survivors' unmet childhood need for *mutually* supportive relationships. Practicing commiseration with me often sets the template for finding this type of mutuality outside of therapy.

The benefits and limits of relational healing are explored in greater detail in Appendix 2. I especially recommend reading it if you have been exploited by a narcissistic therapist who made this process all, or too much, about her/him.

I myself have benefitted greatly over the years from reverberating empathically with clients in their emotional pain. Mutually resonating in vulnerability is healing for both the client and me. Both of us simultaneously de-shame each other. Shame is a nasty, humongous onion with myriad layers to be peeled.

I believe regular immersion in mutuality also explains why I have not experienced any significant burnout or compassion fatigue in my career. What a boon! A job helping others that also helps me...and often leads to them helping others in kind. This is how all human service work should be. Good for the served and good for the served.

As I look back, I feel beyond lucky to have stumbled into being a relational therapist. I feel impossibly fulfilled by the many successful therapies I have shepherded.

While confidentiality dictates that I cannot write in detail about anyone's therapy, there are two general positive outcomes that always warm me.

In the first, clients gradually eke out a supportive relationship with themselves. By the time they leave, their toxic critic is progressively shrinking, their self-esteem is steadily growing and their flashbacks are decreasing in frequency, duration and intensity.

In the second, improved self-esteem also promotes success in other relationships. Clients shed toxic people and find safe social harbor – unlikely to ever be captured again by an abuser. Many cut off or dramatically reduce contact with traumatizing family members, and relationships that mimic them. *What could be better than seeing bullies lose their scapegoats!?*

Moreover, improved self-protection often makes them feel safer and less triggered by human contact. With enough time, truly supportive relationships come their way.

Sometimes these bonds are human and sometimes they are with pets. My client, Mary Alice, told me about the mutually healing relationship she has with her three dogs: "I, the groomer, have also become the groomed."

Such mutual benefit is further borne out by research showing that dogs and other mammals can create favorable neuro-chemical changes in their owners' brains. Pets stimulate the release of oxytocin, the "love hormone" that fosters bonding; they also lower cortisol levels, a stress hormone that can damage brain tissue. For some survivors like me, having a loving relationship with a pet can be a transitional stage for finding one with a fellow, safe-enough human being with whom one can share these neuro-chemical benefits.

HOMESTEADING in the CALM EYE of the STORM

Writing *COMPLEX PTSD: From Surviving to Thriving*

Reading Judith Herman's book, *Trauma and Recovery*, makes me realize that my diagnosis is more severe than PTSD. I have Complex PTSD [CPTSD]. CPTSD is a more virulent and ingrained type of PTSD, unique to childhood trauma and other traumas that occur on a long term, daily basis.

Over the next five years I use the CPTSD diagnosis to guide my own and my clients' recovery work. I then attend seminars with renowned traumatologists Bessel Van der Kolk and John Briere who brilliantly describe the CPTSD syndrome. Yet, I am disappointed at how little they have to say about effective treatment. Even Herman's book is somewhat light on how to help.

On the other hand, I have been getting good results treating CPTSD with the practical techniques described in my *Tao of Fully Feeling* book. So, I begin writing articles about my insights for *The East Bay Therapist* and several other therapy periodicals.

As a family-first dad, I have no large blocks of time to write. I snatch scraps of time while my young son is sleeping or absorbed in a playdate. I often sit down totally exhausted and am amazed when I emerge from the fog into the lucid company of my Muse…often within a sentence or two.

The on-switch of my laptop seems to turn on my clarity, and I record insights I know but rarely feel clear enough to access or articulate.

On the downside, my Muse bypasses punctuation and only speaks to me in endless run-on sentences; for example: *Oh my word…WORDS! Way too many words. What kind of rat's nest is this?* Siamese quintuplets of complex ideas haphazardly connected and littered with modifiers that upon re-reading seem to be orphans separated from their relatives by many lines.

Writing the new stuff takes no time at all. But editing it into *readable* takes forever! I endlessly trim the fat, trying to turn it into muscle. I endlessly polish…at times not sure whether I am actually smudging.

In the early stages of writing, I have an epiphany about a phenomenon that I name *emotional flashbacks*. Unlike PTSD, an emotional flashback is rarely visual. Instead it is a painful reliving of the overwhelming feelings of being an abandoned child. Abandoned children often feel excruciatingly afraid, ashamed, depressed, helpless, and/or hopeless.

Eureka! This is a key missing piece. Emotional Flashbacks are a fundamental dynamic of CPTSD! I did not clearly identify them earlier because I was so often in their grip. Now that I have more respite from flashbacks, I have more perspective on them...understand them more clearly.

In celebration, I write my pivotal article: *Emotional Flashback Management in Complex PTSD*. In it, I condense my treatment approach into 13 steps, tools and perspectives that have brought considerable relief to me and my clients. [*The 13 Steps* and many of my other CPTSD articles can be downloaded for free from my website: www.pete-walker.com.]

My emotional flashback article gets picked up by the E-zine, Psychotherapy.net. Soon the number of grateful emails from clients and therapists quadruples. The most amusing response is: "Your article is an oar in my hands, and I don't feel so defenseless on shit creek."

Numerous respondents also tell me they carry a copy of the 13 steps with them because it is so helpful in triaging their flashbacks.

All this validation is a psychic surgery that removes the cataracts that made me unsure of my understanding in *The Tao of Fully Feeling*. Now upon hearing a detailed sketch of a client's traumatic childhood, I typically can predict the characteristics of their suffering and prescribe an approach to alleviating it. And not uncommonly, I get an early and accurate picture of key themes of their abuse/neglect.

Throwing caution and my critic to the wind, I decide to expand my articles and findings into a book. Moreover, I am so fortified by readers' gratitude for my vulnerable self-disclosures in *The Tao*, that I illustrate the new book with vignettes about my recovery journey.

In the process I also realize that most of my early dietary and somatic explorations were actually helpful. I could not see it at the time because of my all-or-none perfectionism. Now however, I realize that my physical health subtlely began improving back then. Forty years of healthy eating, stretching and exercising must account for some of the spring that I still have in my step.

I publish *COMPLEX PTSD: From Surviving to Thriving* in late 2013 with a shocking absence of trepidation. It soon goes viral through many online recovery websites. As of this writing, over 30,000 copies have sold – without any advertising other than my e-mail blast and my website. Perhaps there is a dysfunctional parenting epidemic in Western Cultures!

I have also been blessed by thousands of positive responses to my CPTSD book. Amazon lists 300 five star reviews and Goodreads.com lists 250. Because of my past, it is still sometimes difficult to fully let this in. But more and more I am moved and comforted by readers' gratitude.

I see this as an example of the *mutuality* that is fundamental to *Regenerating at the Hub of Relational Healing*. On a daily basis I feel *healed* by messages of gratitude for the *healing* the book has reportedly brought to my respondents! Their reports of growing improvement on-goingly fertilize my own recovery.

Lucky me indeed! All this feedback fills me with inspiration to finish and publish this third book…and to up the ante on my self-disclosure. And yes, exposing myself even more vulnerably than before has triggered more than a few flashbacks. Thankfully, none anywhere near as intense as with *The Tao*.

I recommend that survivors read *Complex PTSD* first, even though *The Tao of Fully Feeling* precedes it by eighteen years. The *Tao* is best used as its sequel because it focuses on crucial Flashback Management Step 9. As such, it is an in depth guide to identifying and grieving the losses of childhood. Without such work, emotional recovery is usually quite limited. Emotionally based self-compassion and self-protection may remain undeveloped.

CHAPTER 24

Thriving Surpasses Surviving

I always saw my family life as a sinkhole
I tried to climb out of. But more
It was a vacuum, a grave that needed dirt to fill it in

— IRA SADOFF

DAILY ABUSE FROM both my parents drove me into *learned helplessness*. I was stuck in a day to day struggle of surviving the impossible requirements of my tormentors.

Some freedom came when my unconscious started calling the shots. Breaking out of one jail into another, I drunkenly drop-kicked myself out of Pre-Med into the Army. At the time, I was way beyond imagining that could ever have a silver lining.

But what a shift in trajectory! Unleashing my *Id* for less than hour and breaking all those windows rerouted me from my mother's dream of Med School to my father's sentence of cannon fodder for the military. Paradoxically, the military gave me some room to begin to expand and grow, albeit haphazardly.

The general theme of *directionless-ness* rules the first half of my life. Happenstance is in charge. And I am constantly on the move to outdistance my pain.

I am in survival mode much of the time. But as I shuck off bosses, there are days and rare weeks of thriving.

As I move into the second half of my life, periods of thriving increase. By my fifties, I have broken out of the tiny jail cell of black-and-white thinking, either-or choosing and all-or-none doing. I have escaped my inner boss [the toxic critic] to a large degree. Thriving far outweighs surviving. I no longer pursue the shibboleth of "Don't worry, be happy." The sentiment of the book, *Want What You Have*, has become mostly true for me.

Now my response to the "Stress" in Complex Post Traumatic Stress Disorder automatically shifts from my critic's militaristic rag: "Drop and give me ten [pushups]" to compassionate encouragement: "Stop and give me ten breaths [deep and slow]." Torqueing quickly turns into tweaking. *Drive and strive* increasingly shift into *ease up* and feel the soft massage of the breath.

The Breath is headquarters central of my ongoing recovery process. If something upsets me, I look for a place to sit and slowly count ten breaths. I count repeatedly until I get ten deep slow ones in a row without being distracted by thought, urge or fantasy. This usually correlates with restored serenity. At its best, I feel as if each breath is soothingly stroking my whole body from the inside out.

Breathing still occasionally uncovers upset feelings. At such times, feeling into those emotions often releases restorative tears. When this does not help, I usually need to verbally ventilate. Most often my wife or another close friend helps me with this.

My thriving continually increases as my flashbacks diminish. Now my primary source of flashbacks is sleep. Every so often I awake as my inner child… dreading going down to breakfast where I knew I would be abused.

In the old days, I dealt with this by unconsciously shooting adrenaline and speeding off into productivity. Now I feel blessed to know it's a flashback. So I go inside and invoke various combinations of the 13 Flashback Management steps. Typically I land on step 7 and fully feel the sensations of the underlying dread, deadness and depression.

As I do this I talk comfortingly to my child: "I know this is how you felt every morning, every day, week, month and year of your imprisonment in Walkerville. God it was awful going down to face cranky mommy and daddy.

"I'm so sorry you had to bear that for so many years…that I wasn't there to protect you. But I'm here now and I love you even more for what you suffered. I will lay here a while with you and help you feel through these feelings which were their fault not yours.

"And afterwards, we'll go be with Sara and Jaden. They are so loving, and always make us feel safer and like we belong."

Rarely does this type of flashback last for more than thirty minutes. But whether or not it subsides, I'm grateful that I can still connect comfortably with my family, my clients and intimate others. I do not have to get pumped up to be worthy of their company.

My ultimate struggle was to channel *Love* into self-acceptance. I choked on my parents' perfectionism for forty years – perpetually postponing self-kindness.

I wrestled with a garbage truckload of impossible goals until I discovered my healthy loving anger. It armed me for a million battles against my parents' evil offspring: the critic.

Over and over, I angrily renounced my parents' curse. *I will not go to my grave like you without ever tasting self-kindness.* Finally – All Praise to the Powers of Persistence – I attained the ultimate loyalty of unflinching self-support.

Now, I experience myself as thriving a high percentage of the time, even though it is at times tired and thriving. Even better, I rest in self-compassion nearly all the time.

I am enormously grateful for finding a route out of the maze of CPTSD. Now when I temporarily flashback into that maze, I quickly find the trailhead.

I was branded a "disgrace" by my parents and the nuns. I suffered decades of thinking people saw me as "a bad egg." It felt so unfair. I always wanted the best for almost everyone. But, over and over, when something went wrong, I was sure that everyone thought it was my fault, and instantly sunk into guilt and shame.

Some twenty years ago – without even noticing it – I stopped having this toxic shame flashback. Since then, when something goes wrong, I rarely think anyone is silently accusing me. If the thought occurs however, my self-protective subpersonality jumps in: *No Way! People look to me for help when things get hairy.* How wonderful that my toxic shame is now largely historical.

So little wonder that in contemplating my childhood, I picture the inside of my house as dark and dingy – like an aged black-and-white photo, while the world outside is bright, colorful and filled with the promise of discovery and opportunity.

My Introvert Emerges from a Chrysalis of Extroversion

Now that I have been around the block seventy times, it seems that accepting my introversion was the skeleton key to my recovery.

Introversion can be measured on The Myers-Briggs scale – a continuum that runs between the extremes of extroversion and introversion. I am well polarized towards the introverted end and was deeply ashamed of that for much of my life. I frequently overcompensated and tried to live as if I was *Mr. Outgoing*.

As my recovery progressed, partying gradually lost its shine, but I still hated my introversion. My toxic shame flared whenever my effervescence dwindled. Even after I gave up relying on alcohol for a boost, I still hunted thirstily for the fountain of extroversion.

Thankfully, as my recovery matured, I began to appreciate solitude. Three steps forward, two steps backward of course.

When I finally stopped using adrenaline to pump up my expressiveness, my dream of being a human power transformer and a social butterfly gradually expired. *Oh! But what a long, drawn out painful death it was.*

Now I rarely try to tweak my energy when my sociability goes walkabout. What a relief to easily bypass socializing when I am not in the mood.

My son and wife help me greatly with this. They model easy acceptance of their fluctuating extroversion and energy levels.

I am so grateful to at last value being an introvert. Now I finally get why it puzzled me that solitary confinement was considered the worst punishment.

I am also a bit stunned that I feel sorry for extreme extroverts these days instead of envying them. [This may partly be retroactive sorrow for my old over-compensating self.]

There are some manic extroverts at my gym who squirm when they cannot wrangle someone into a talk-fest. They remind me of winos sparechanging for a drink. What a freedom to easily resist the pressure to swap clichés – to high five-jive some guys I barely know every time I'm in the gym.

Thank god that my long painful crucifixion into forced extroversion is over. I wish I had marked the date so I could celebrate the recovery of my developmentally arrested introversion…with a small, temperate party.

And of course it's not all-or-none. My extrovert subpersonality is still a significant part of me, which I enjoy when it shows up naturally.

Beginning with my first begrudging nod to introversion, my peace of mind gradually improved. Nonetheless, I must occasionally rescue myself from the shame that society heaps upon us introverts. At such times browsing Susan Cain's brilliant book, *Quiet*…or re-listening to her stunning *Ted Talk* reminds me of introversion's gifts (www.ted.com/talks/susan_cain_the_power_of_introverts).

The Right to Feel Bad

As I learned to make peace with my introversion, I also came to accept normal human depression. This began long ago at a garage sale when I stepped on the book, *The Right to Feel Bad,* by Lesley Hazelton. At first glance, I thought: *Right! What moron would consider that a right? It ain't a right. It's a plight!* Yet the book screamed out to me: "Buy me, I'm only 25 cents!"

What a find! Reading it served up an ongoing banquet of liberating insights. I eventually became convinced that it is normal to occasionally feel down. "Everyone has recurring bouts of low energy and *anhedonia* [the feeling of not being able enjoy one's usual pleasures]."

Feeling low is so less painful now that I rarely fight it. When I go with this part of my emotional flow, it is typically easy to wait out the blahs. Many times I just cruise through them.

And sometimes, *Lo and Behold,* my depression contains nuggets of startling emotional intelligence. Leaving Brenda, and then Lynn, were priceless jewels of instinct – born out of staying attuned to the lingering depression that accumulated from being committed to someone incapable of mutuality.

When I do not relax into feeling my depression, it typically morphs into *depressed thinking*. For much of my life unprocessed depression fueled painful negative thinking. How endlessly I perseverated on my inadequacies and those of others, and life itself when I was depressed!

The Right to Feel Bad launched me into a decades' long quest to soothe this core wound of CPTSD. I have made great progress in accepting my share of the doldrums and the blues. Less and less do I anxiously distract myself from feeling down. Rarely do I die into shame from feeling unhappy. Now my inner and outer critics are emaciated…too weary and listless to do any real damage.

My depression grows milder and scarcer every year. When it does fog over me, it is often a feeling of boredom (a euphemism for depression) or waking up in the doldrums of a flashback.

At such times, I almost always short-circuit self-criticism by introverting – by going internal as soon as possible to practice kindness and self-soothing. Typically I disarm the critic in less than twenty minutes, and then ride out the blahs in an hour or two. During this time, I slow my pace, reduce my productivity expectations and, when I have the time, sit and continue to relax into the tired sensations of the depression until they morph into peacefulness.

On rare occasions my depression sets in with that old feeling and color of cement. At such times, my "bad" emotional weather does not mimic San Francisco's morning fog and burn off in the afternoon. In that case, I treat the gloom like a temporary death…the death of being glad to be alive. [I also often treat lingering fear or anxiety like a death – the death of feeling safe.]

From this perspective, I use the four processes of grieving to work through what is usually an especially intense flashback to my early abandonment. Often it is enough to just [1] *feel through it* as described in the "Minding the Body" section of Chapter 19.

Other times I need to [2] *verbally ventilate* with a supportive witness like my wife and other best friends. Often, just naming and "confessing" to feeling bad de-shames me and allows my feeling-scape to shift into another tone.

When feeling down is most stubborn, I may need the <u>emoting</u> processes of grieving to move through it. This can be [3] *a good cry* and/or [4] *an angry vent* at the critic who has snuck back in with a new disguise to pathologize me about being in the dumps.

I love the irony that now that I have the right to feel bad, I seldom do. I generally move through depression so easily that I spend more time than ever feeling mellow and appreciative of the ordinary facets of everyday life. And thanks to my wife and son, I laugh so much more at the funny and silly sides of things.

Hand in glove, I've largely learned to tackle the hardest things on my daily agenda first. Rarely do I waste time procrastinating or worrying about how hard some task will be. As a kid, I tortured myself forever perseverating about jumping into the cold pool. Now I just dive in, like I do three mornings a week when I swim laps. It always amazes me that before the first lap is done, I am no longer noticing the cold.

In this regard, I have been guided by Scott Peck's dictum of "work before play" for three decades, and now know indubitably that it creates much more time for carefree play.

Countering Counterphobia

Understanding counterphobia was also a key to my recovery. After the army, I traveled the world searching for meaning. But I had no compass. I counterphobically barged through any open door – the more ominous, the better.

In moments of hesitation, I'd shore myself up with: *What's the worst that could happen!?* Once my critic blasted me: "You could die you idiot!" Unhesitatingly, a voice deep inside quipped back: *Well, I bet that will have the ultimate silver lining.*

It seems my counterphobia was wed to my death instinct. Freud called the pull toward death: *Thanatos*. Throughout my *On the Road* phase, Thanatos and counterphobia repeatedly led me into situations that had death written all over them.

It was a long time before I understood my counterphobia. Now I realize that facing external danger back then felt less scary than avoiding it.

Confronting an externally fearful situation usually resolved my felt-sense of fear more quickly. But hesitating in the face of it activated my underlying sea of internal, unconscious fear and made me feel more afraid.

I learned to sidestep internal overwhelm by confronting what looked like external danger. Like Don Quixote, I tilted my lance at outer fears to distract myself from inner fear. The danger I could see typically felt like the lesser of two evils – usually less daunting than what lay buried inside me.

My reckless abandon sometimes looked like courage to others, but it was actually fear of my own fear. When I finally understood this, I bristled at FDR's homily that: "The only fear is fear itself." He used the phrase in a way that created widespread fear of fear. Not only should people be afraid of becoming fearful, but they should also be ashamed of it when they do!

This command trickled into the collective mind as a patriotic duty to deny and repress inner fear. What a catastrophe this is and was for our emotional intelligence. Being out of touch with our fear prevents us from understanding that fear is sometimes a life-saving instinct. Fear can be a first level warning about situations and people that are dangerous to us. Without access to this all important information, many survivors spend their lives in trauma bonds with people every bit as toxic to them as the parents that gave them CPTSD.

Fear of our own instinctive fear also blocks us from recognizing and working through old, now-unnecessary, childhood fears that we have relegated to our unconscious minds.

Realizing all this left me "struck" by this irony: *Counterphobic Pete Walker was running away from his own fear!*

But of course I couldn't help it. My dissociative freeze response was so weak that my anxiety was not fully unconscious. It constantly jangled like choppy waves of angst on the surface of a terrifying underlying sea.

What could I do but keep rowing? Thankfully I finally docked in grief-work. Grieving gradually evaporated my hidden sea of unworked through fear into a puddle. Nothing releases fear like tears. Now, it rarely accumulates enough to activate my counterphobia or busyholism.

The greatest benefit from my counterphobia was that it pushed me into Life's terrifying social arena. Had it not, I might have been a hermit. When I was young, I often fantasized about desert islands, monkish hermitages and log cabins in the boonies.

Like many Complex PTSD survivors, I was unconsciously afraid of everyone. Anyone could trigger me into intense fear, especially unknown people. Through my recovery work, through persistent counterphobic socializing, and through the grace of running into many benevolent people, I got better at navigating the frightening land of other humans.

My intense fear of people "guided" me throughout my life and I gradually found people with whom I increasingly felt comfortable.

An essential part of this process was using my counterphobia to enter the hell of fear inside me. For years, I then rushed headlong into my painful memories and emotions. Eventually I found ways to metabolize and integrate them.

Besides helping myself in the process, I also aided many therapy groups to deepen. I was typically the first one to spill his guts – just to get the trepidatious process over with. But gratefully, over time, hovering at the hub of mutual healing gradually became a comforting place to be. My being vulnerable became easier and often helped others to therapeutically and shamelessly do the same.

Not As Good As I Hoped – Better Than I Expected

My life was *not as good as I hoped* until I consciously enlisted my counterphobia in the service of addressing my developmental arrests. Since this redirection, my life has increasingly become *better than I expected*.

I feel like I've come an epic distance from lost in time and space to feeling abundant fulfillment as a therapist, family man, friend and world citizen.

And how amusing that I have also come full circle and become a priest of sorts! I hear confessions, sermonize about charity to oneself, and celebrate the sacraments of grieving, gratitude and relational healing.

I love how Denise Levertov, describes the grace of grieving:

<u>Talking to Grief</u>

Ah Grief I should not treat you
Like a homeless dog

Who comes to the back door
For a crust, for a meatless bone.
I should trust you
I should coax you
Into the house and give you
Your corner,
A worn mat to be on,
Your own water dish.
You think I don't know you've been living
Under my porch.
You long for your real place to be readied
Before winter comes. You need
Your name, your collar and tag. You need
The right to warn off intruders
To consider my house your own
And me your person and yourself
My own dog.

—m—

As a youth I didn't understand "Be careful what you wish for." I wished to never need anything from anyone. How lucky I was that LSD and subsequent teachers taught me to wish for love.

Little by little, I found comfort in relationships. Insisting on *mutuality* eventually pared down my reenactments. Corpses of relationships with narcissists litter the road behind me. And now I often feel loved and loving enough…even though I still at times feel lonely…like all human beings.

> I wished to vanquish my introversion
> > but now I treasure it.
>
> I wished to celebrate every moment,
> > but who knew that routine could so reward, and naps be so delicious?

I wished to become enlightened and free of suffering,
but who knew there were such riches embedded in pain?
Who knew that shame could morph into healthy pride, and fear into courage?
Who knew that vulnerability could create uplifting intimacy?

When I was stuck in Walkerville and when I aimlessly followed my nose around the world, time dragged by like a one legged man climbing a sand dune. But now in my senescence, life is pregnant with meaning and fulfillment. Time has sped up and flows by way too quickly...perhaps, because I am more often like a child at play.

After flirting so much with death, and after promising myself euthanasia at age 70 if life was still too misery-laden, I have never valued life more. I cherish being here so much of the time that I hope to be above ground long enough to have grandchildren to care for.

A Final Parental Appraisal

My poor parents! They didn't know love from liver. Even though Helen and Charlie did mellow some, I would not leave my son alone with them for a minute if they were alive today. Their lack of remorse could easily cause them to regress into abusiveness.

Hence and sadly, I am relieved that they are dead. I will never again be triggered by live interactions with them. I do, however, think and hope they are in a better place.

But were there any silver linings to having such poor excuses for parents?

Their genes were good in many ways. Both my parents were smart. I have my father's strong constitution, and he lived to 81 without paying any mind to diet or exercise. *God! I'll be here forever.*

I also inherited some of his self-discipline and persistence. And to his credit, he became less rigid after my mother died. He even became a world traveler, which was a delicious irony.

My mother loved flowers, birds, words and music. These are splendors that I have enjoyed all my life and she was the first person I ever saw enthuse about them. She was also funny, despite the destructive sarcasm that often besmirched her humor.

So in the final tally I am grateful that my parents had me and my lovely sisters, even though they had no business having children. And although I may have wished I were dead too many times early on, my gratitude about being alive has grown for decades.

Onward and Where-ward?

> *The woods are lovely, dark and deep*
> *But I have promises to keep*
> *And miles to go before I sleep*
>
> — ROBERT FROST

I'm seventy now – way past my anticipated expiration date – and I cannot imagine retiring. I would miss my work too much. Forty years of poignant and uplifting human connections are hard to beat. Even in the years of struggling with the imposter syndrome, I typically found the calm eye of the storm – the hub of psychological healing – within five or ten minutes and cruised critic-free for the rest of the session.

A session ending in those days, however, was a gangplank for the critic to climb back on board. My hindsight then was not 20-20, but microscopic – a mutinous search for evidence of my fraudulence.

Nowadays, the critic is a wisp and I have uncommon job satisfaction. Nonetheless therapizing is not always coasting. If I am tired, under the weather or in a flashback, sessions can be difficult – especially when I am too fuzzy to find the words I am looking for. Thankfully this problem has ebbed greatly over the years, and I typically do good enough work even when my brain is not fully online.

So I am where I want to be much of the time, and I hope for that to continue. I also hope to continuously evolve as a person. Jaden will be off all too soon, but the silver lining of that heart-rending loss will be time for me to resume teaching.

I don't hope to write another book, but perhaps I'll find a way to blog that won't dominate my time too much.

Now and then I fantasize about being a foster parent. Maybe, at my age, it will have to be a dog. And I bet I'll find some new or old enriching form of volunteer work.

Whatever happens, I wish for an ongoing increase in my ability to relax and savor everyday blessings. I love music, flowers and color more than ever. And I love fixing anything I can save from being thrown out... like the "oink-oink" voice box of Jaden's stuffed piggy which has survived the recycling of most of his stuffed animals.

I love "fixing" my anger too. I have recycled it into fighting my toxic critic for decades.

Narrative Therapy

Narrative Therapy research shows that recovery from trauma is encoded in a survivor's story about that trauma.

As the theory goes, survivors are recovered to the degree that they relate the full story of their suffering – accurately, sympathetically and with appropriate affect.

Narratives that are expressed with self-hate, shame or inconsonant affect [e.g., laughing mockingly about one's difficulties] typically show areas of unfinished business. Likewise, recounts that rush over or dissociate from feelings or themes of trauma show where more work is needed.

Said another way, autobiographical accounts that are devoid of empathy for the self often show where self-esteem needs more repair.

—∞—

So thank you for reading my memoir. If you need it, I hope it helps you to take a quantum leap into greater self-kindness.

I also hope my story shows that traumatized people can and do go on to live fulfilling enough lives. And, if you would like to know more about what helped/helps me most in my recovery please continue to Appendix 1.

As I spread my wings,
    releasing heart scars and curses,
        The buzzards of lonely decades
            egress in purple flight.

Free time
    Spreads its cherry blossom minutes
        randomly
            like a Zen poem-painting,
where time is not the essence,
    and spontaneity flows like honey
        from the peaks of peace
            to the vales of fully feeling.

APPENDIX 1

Navigating CPTSD: My Top 10 Practices

MANY READERS WRITE to me asking about the key to CPTSD recovery. As I wrote in *Complex PTSD*, I think there are many keys. Here are the top ten practices of my ongoing recovery. Thankfully the amount of time I need to dedicate to them has steadily decreased over the years.

I use the words "practices" to emphasize that there are no fast fixes, singular solutions or final arrivals in CPTSD recovery. As unfair as it often seems, recovering is ninety percent perspiration and ten percent inspiration.

Milking Self-Kindness and Self-Protection out of Grieving

I go on endlessly about grieving because it's brought me unparalleled relief. Most of the silver linings that I discovered about my trauma appeared on the other side of grieving.

I am often tickled by the irony that a good cry leaves me feeling stronger and more confident. For decades, my tears dissolved my fear and confusion, and left me with a clear and hopeful sense of direction.

When I was 29, I was devastated when I saw my beautiful black Labrador, George, die under the wheels of a car. *George! How I wished back then for someone who felt as safe and comforting as him.* Miraculously, the overwhelming pain of his brutal death was washed away by a monsoon of tears.

George's demise opened me to the value of emoting. Previously my emotions were a great source of fear and shame. I almost always avoided them with a desperate repertoire of tricks.

When my tears sprung forth that day, I was baptized with the Holy Spirit of grieving. Never again did I resist my tears. From then on I hungered for them until they became easily accessible.

When I was 39, my mother and my best dog, Herbie, died in short succession. My grieving for Herbie, who unconditionally loved me for ten years, totally eclipsed my grieving for Helen. In the heart of my mourning, I wrote this poem.

> Herbie died and left me to find a new ride…
> Left me with a precarious lead off first base…
> Left me yearning to be picked off.
>
> I see the pitcher chuck a knuckler
> And mesmerized, I watch its loco dance.
> I hear the stitches tumble a tune upon the air:
> "Hey Pete, it sure is sweet and free up here."

I never dream of my mother, but my Dreamtime has been graced generously over the years with comforting visits from Herbie.

I well up now with tears of gratitude for Herbie, my high-grade social lubricant. *Kind* people were continuously drawn to this boddhisatvic dog…this mottled cattle dog of alluring homeliness. Herbie helped me many times to connect easily with her admirers.

A few tears escape their wells as I remember her being lost in transport on a plane. The Airline kept sending her to the wrong airport, and I goose-chased her for two days from city to city before we reunited.

When I opened her kennel, she sped around the airport floor in circles, skidding on the slippery linoleum in long tangents...then scrambling back into circling.

She ran in unbridled joy at our reunification. Unable to contain her feelings, she manically lapped the waiting area a half-dozen times.

As I write, I flash back with compassion to my six-year-old hyperactive self – running around a car for an hour to escape the bully, Michael Carmody. He couldn't catch me and I dared to laugh at him in his frustration. Sweet tears of grief sweetened with relief hallow the rebooting of these memories.

My tears – from the first drenching onwards – reliably rebirth me out of flashbacks. Crying is my get-out-of-jail-free card. It still occasionally rescues me from the death-pall of the abandonment depression, and revives my appreciation for being alive.

I'm sure that grieving saved me from an early grave. Before my tears were easily accessible, I only had "accidents" and risks gone bad to release my pain. As my knack for grieving grew, my recklessness dried up and blew away.

Yet no matter how wise my choices, how mindful my actions and how supportive my friends, life will deal me, like everyone else, an unfair slew of upsetting surprises.

Grieving is my tool kit *par excellence* for dealing with fortune's outrages. Over and over, I find refuge In the Calm Eye of the Storm... of tears.

Whittling Down the Critic

My critic ruled the roost of my early life. Denial and minimization were its allies, until I realized I had become numb to its domination. In one transformative epiphany, I flashed: *Oh my God! This critic is so hellaciously huge that it is the boss of me!* I am perpetually over-focusing on the negative!

Something powerful awoke in me and I thought: *This is unacceptable!* I will take back control of my mind...become the captain of my brain... exorcise the internalized drill sergeants of my parents and the Catholic Church.

I will no longer salute the twisted flags they have brainwashed me to enshrine! No more unconsciously locking into step with the critic's commands and judgments.

And NO to perfectionism and its all-or-none thinking! NO to all those false alarms of seeing danger everywhere! NO to only seeing what's wrong with me, with others and with life.

Early on my rebellion against the critic seemed hopeless. For a long time it seemed that all my efforts were making it worse. In truth, I was stuck in a gradually unfolding process of discovering its enormity.

Like many of my clients, this failure created new reasons to hate myself: "I can't do anything right. What's wrong with me? Why don't I just choose to love myself."

After breaking the record for spinning out in that nasty whirlpool, I finally saw my self-hate as my parents' most poisonous legacy. Being continuously hated by them trained me to hate myself. "The gift that keeps on giving" has many references, but no "gift" is worse than being inculcated with an inner critic that eternally frowns at you with disgust.

During the early years of critic work, I gave up the fight many times. How could I hope to conquer this multifaceted foe! Maybe I should just go back to joking about being *so* self-critical, like Woody Allen and everyone else. Who could blame me? As my client, Mary Alice, once said: "That sucker has so many different ways of attacking you, it's like playing whack-a-mole!"

Many tools eventually helped, especially grieving self-compassionate tears. But shrinking it was glacial until I shifted into angrily counter-attacking it whenever I caught it biting me.

The success of this fighting increased dramatically when I started visualizing the critic as an ugly two-headed beast: Charlie on the left and Helen on the right. I brought in the big guns when I added disgust to my anger – imagining that I was contemptuously giving them back their shame as well as their intimidation.

Innumerable times, I "dissed" them scornfully: *Piss off Charlie and Helen! You heartless a-holes! You're a nasty pair of cowardly child-beating bullies. Shut The F UP!*

Over and over, I countered the critic with contempt, mostly in the silence and privacy of my own mind. Over and over I imagined myself screaming at the critic with my parents' favorite insults.

Before long this practice spontaneously triggered deep empathy for my child-self. I then translated this empathy into contradicting their slurs. After a moment or two, I'd move from anger into compassion for myself. I uttered many versions of: *I love you little Pete. You're a good kid. You're smart, witty, resourceful, and so on. I am here for you and on your side no matter what.*

I repeated versions of this two-step process full-heartedly at least ten times a day, and within months the critic began to noticeably abate. Within a few years it disappeared for lengthening periods.

One day as it tried for an encore, I saw it as a one winged fly that could not lift itself off the floor. I laughed at it: *You're a pathetic envoy of Helen and Charlie. Do you really think you still have any "cred" with me!?*

On another memorable morning, I awoke in an intense flashback of self-disappointment and was soon rescued by this unprompted self-defense: *So Herr Critic, aka Helen and Charlie, you used to run the show all the time. Now you're lucky to get a few seconds. You used to be a class-5-rapids, but now you're a seasonal trickle in a place where it rarely rains! So, PLEASE, let me invite you to GET THE HELL away from me!* And POOF! Like magic, I was back on my side again.

Now it is almost always easy to dismiss the critic. It's so weak, I rarely need the empowerment of anger. When it occasionally rearises, my current favorite response is a condescending response: *Oh! It's Mr. & Mrs. SMALL POTATOES again...trying to make a crisis out of something minuscule...something that truly is just SMALL POTATOES.* I co-opted this phrase from my mother who used it to put down anything I did well. I use it instead as a reminder that her criticism is next to nothing to me now.

O, how far I've come! My mindfulness usually spots toxic criticisms immediately and I effortlessly let them wither away. Simply noticing the critic lures it into the quicksand of my healthy self-protection. I have whittled it down from commander-in-chief of my psyche to a mere shadow of its former self.

Now and for the last two decades I almost always feel like a good enough person.

Flight-into-Light

Like many survivors, my recovery process began unconsciously with a spiritual quest. I needed to find something profoundly good about life to counteract the soul crushing effects of my family.

But striving for enlightenment was a salvation fantasy, and only helped marginally with my CPTSD. My Icarus-like flights into the Light did however give me powerful subjective experiences of a *Benevolence* at the core of life.

Trying to permanently merge with this Light however, melted my waxen wings and repeatedly sent me plummeting into the sea of my abandonment depression.

The Icarus in me won some and lost some. When I caught enough glimmers of the Light to know that an ultimate good exists, I felt buoyed enough to journey inside – to search for something worthwhile at my psychological core. When I finally learned to meditate effectively, I gradually found Spirit within.

Now my flights-into-light are sojourns inside to find an inner glow. My ongoing meditative practice regularly brings me helpful insights, restores my equanimity and self-acceptance, and occasionally provides me glimpses of THAT which is so much greater.

My ultimate flight-into-light was an eight hour Enlightenment experience with LSD – an experience of feeling transcendently at one with a loving God that permeated everything. [What a surprise years later to read that Freud knew of this experience: "…the *oceanic feeling*…the sensation of harmony and interconnection with the universe."]

This LSD journey, described in Chapter 6, impassioned me to search for permanent enlightenment. Luckily my quest short-circuited two years later, but I had enough tastes of *God as Love* to convince me that life is a stunning gift from an unfathomable and generous *Creator*. Like Walt Whitman and other poets, I increasingly saw love and beauty in life's ordinary and myriad details.

Delusional or not, I feel lucky to believe in a Benevolent Creator. This is not a choice but a profound subjective sense of knowing. The years before my huge epiphany – especially the Catholic ones – were desolately empty without this deep sense of a Higher Power.

And even if in death, my light is completely extinguished, I gained immeasurably from this vision. It blessed me with an increasing capacity to appreciate being alive.

Bibliotherapy

Books were my first teachers. They "introduced" me to compassionate adults who helped me with their wise and kind words. For decades I read my way into a better relationship with myself.

The book that took the lid off my denial about my childhood trauma was Alice Miller's *The Drama of the Gifted Child*. Reading it also took the floor out from under me, and dumped me into the bottomless basement of my abandonment depression:

> An emotional maelstrom
> Squared, cubed and taken to the highest Parental power.
> A childhood full of hunger
>   unsootheable by food
>   cranking in the canyon of my belly.
> Hunger born in an emotional famine
>   suffered in solitary confinement
>   behind the bars of a prison crib.

As horrible as the discovery of this unresolved pain was at the time, the ensuing Dark Night of the Soul awakened me to the grievous damage caused my parents' abuse and neglect. Denial died, and I was lost in a sea of overwhelm for months.

Recovery by Gravitz and Bowden subsequently gave me a sextant to begin navigating this sea.

John Bradshaw's books and videos released the pause button on my arrested development. His PBS videos on the dysfunctional family and inner child work were like a series of waves that I rode deeper into recovering.

Working with this material helped me recognize how often I went down the rabbit hole of self-hate. How awful that this eventually devolved into hating myself for hating myself.

Thankfully, I finally realized that self-hate had been a childhood requirement rigorously enforced by my parents and the clergy. *No wonder this habit was so hard to break!* Gradually it began to crumble as I forgave myself over and over for repeating their brainwashing, and then invoked unconditional self-acceptance.

Other recommendations that I have for Bibliotherapy are contained in Chapter 15 of my CPTSD book. Let me also note that I am sure that many other valuable trauma-recovery books are now available, but I have not had the time to explore them.

Writing that Helped Me To Right Myself

Journaling was *loving mothering* and *therapy* for me. I could always bring my whole self – as small as it was as at first – to my journal and explore all my concerns. To this day, I still occasionally journal to plumb a gnarly issue.

Journaling taught me to bear witness to myself – to validate that I was born innocent – unfairly deprived of a child's birthright to be loved. Through no fault of my own, I got the joker from the parenting deck. Journaling helped me grieve this terrible loss. My four foot stack of journals is in many ways a history of how I reparented myself for fifty years.

I love writing. It feels like flirting with the unconscious – and on lucky days connecting with the Higher Self. My Muse often surprises me with unbidden jewels. Occasionally, they scintillate and make me teary.

These wondrous and numinous tears feel like proof of God's existence. A Jew or a Christian might say: "God created us in his own image… wanting us to also be creative."

Occasionally an inspiration makes me laugh aloud: "I didn't know I knew that." Wherever this inspiration comes from, I'm sure it's not only my ego coughing up a new mixture of ideas it has heard before.

Meditation: There's No Boogeyman in My Inner Closet

At my first ten day meditation retreat I was cooped up inside myself without distraction or diversion for ten straight days. *Damn! That was intense.* But it left me knowing – at least most of the time – that there was nothing wrong with me – nothing inside me that I had to flee, hate or be ashamed of.

Ten years later, during my second ten day retreat, I anchored that understanding by practicing... 24/7... *this* guidance from Galway Kinnell:

What Is
Is
Is what I want
Only that
But that

From that time on, I learned to use Vipassana to rescue myself from thousands of flashbacks. For me, the quickest way back to calmness is to fully feel what I am most reluctant to feel.

Now when I get triggered into a flashback, my dominant urge is to find a safe place to meditatively feel into the sensations and emotions of my upset as fully as I can. Within twenty minutes, the flashback almost invariably resolves and I am once again at peace with myself.

Stephen Levine's *Who Dies* and Jack Kornfield's *A Path with Heart* are two great books that teach this invaluable skill.

Getting and Giving Individual & Group Therapy

I needed to be reassured by many good-hearted authors before I could face the fear of seeking help from a stranger. I was a client of various therapists off and on for twenty-five years. Without that experience, my effectiveness as a therapist would have been quite limited.

Receiving and providing therapy have been the yin and the yang of my ongoing training...training that informs me about what can and cannot be accomplished in psychotherapy.

INDIVIDUAL THERAPY

Numerous helpful short-term therapies, and co-counseling with my friends Randi and Nancy, made me want long-term, depth-work psychotherapy.

As described earlier, my first foray with Kleinian Dr. L was awful. To avoid repeating this, I had test- sessions with seven highly touted therapists.

In one interview-session after another, each renowned therapist tried to distract me from venting pain. It was so hard to believe. Each paid lip service to welcoming grief, but when my feelings surfaced, they apparently could not go where they had not been.

After the sixth, I despaired about finding a therapist who would welcome my emotional pain. I reread some of the therapist-writers who insisted that shame about emotional pain could only be worked through with a supportive witness. I scheduled a seventh appointment and mercifully I finally found Gina.

Hundreds of sessions with her over five years brought me profound relational healing. My toxic shame lost its life support system. My toxic critic became an endangered species, and at times I almost disliked automatically shooting it on sight.

Through my experiences as a client, I discovered in the laboratory of my own psyche what actually helps. What especially struck me was that all my helpful therapists reparented me to some degree.

As an extra bonus, many also served as role models on how to do therapy. Thank you, thank you, thank you Derek, Bob, Randi, Nancy, Gina and Sara for your psyche-renovating help – for helping me truly befriend myself.

As a therapist I noticed that most clients suffer shame and self-hate over similar issues. I heard endless self-flagellation over the same minor flaws, "bad" feelings, taboo fantasies, and small potato mistakes. So many humiliated confessions about such common harmless human imperfections!

How tragic that perfectionism shames us into hiding the same innocuous "shady secrets." As I consistently felt no judgment about my clients "flaws", the glacier of my own self-judgment gradually melted into a snowball.

I have facilitated more than thirty thousand therapy sessions, and frequently experienced healing in the manner I describe in Appendix 2. How blessed I am that I have had so many clients who I easily care about and respect.

A great turning point occurred decades ago when I learned to quickly nudge bona fide narcissists out of my office. Dyed-in-the-wool narcissists do not seek transformation. They only want adoring listeners whom they can control and suck dry. Too many become even more entitled from the process of therapy – believing that everyone owes them fifty minutes of uninterrupted listening.

Group Therapy

What a boon that so many of my university courses featured group therapy. Sydney University was way ahead of its time.

Antioch was the most profound. At Antioch, Will Schutz taught me to do anger work in a way where no one hurt themselves or anyone else. I often left group feeling purified by the cleansing flame of therapeutic angering. What a privilege to pass this gift onto others!

My disappointment in the poor quality of JFK groups was tempered by the sheer quantity of experience. JFK shortcomings matched the old saying: "Good and bad experiences are like the right and left hand. The wise person uses both to his/her benefit."

From JFK, I learned to avoid the mistakes that commonly spoil group therapy. I guarded my groups from being hijacked by narcissists. I immediately stopped shaming and scapegoating behaviors, and divvied up the time so that all members shared equally.

I was also a member of many support groups. Really liking and being liked by others with similar vulnerabilities helped pry perfectionism off my self-esteem.

My men's support group was the heart of my created family for fifteen years. My imperfections were met with nothing but kindness. *I cannot thank you guys too much for your healing support!*

This all culminated with an ACA/Codependency/CPTSD support group that I lead for twenty-five years. It was by far my most potent experience of *the hub of mutual relational healing* [see Appendix 2]. Members often grieved together about the pain caused by their selfish parents.

They cried together and they angered together. They healthily blamed their parents for forcing them to fawn and abandon themselves – for making them easy pickings for exploitative narcissists.

The group's mutual empathy shrunk their inner critics and bred self-kindness. Most members went on to find at least one other island of human safety in the world outside of the group.

I was not a "working member" of the group, but often felt vicariously comforted and healed by group commiseration. I treasure everyone who "graduated" from this group. I wish I could name them for posterity, but of course confidentiality prohibits.

Sometimes when I flash back into alienation, I remember all the groups that gave me their esteem when "mortified" was my middle name. Accordingly, I often advise survivors to join a support group – on line or in vivo. Many respondents to my writings have testified to the helpfulness of such connections.

Self-Reparenting: Finding an Inner Mom and Dad

I am forever indebted to John Bradshaw for exposing the epidemic of traumatizing parents. Such parents create children who grow up developmentally arrested in myriad ways. Bradshaw gave us many reparenting tools to meet the unmet needs of survivors of such abandonment.

Over time, I also discovered tools of my own which I used to reparent myself and my clients. I taught many clients through modeling to take over the job of ongoingly mothering and fathering themselves.

In my own recovery, my critic upped its scoffing to a new level when I first heard about inner child work. I had to bypass my inner child at first and just work with the concept of healing my developmental arrests.

Thankfully I eventually whittled down my critic and built a profoundly therapeutic relationship with my developmentally arrested, infant, toddler, preschooler, primary schooler and adolescent.

Through continually evolving my ability to nurture, love and protect myself and my various child selves, I customarily feel a sense of safety and of *belonging* in the world. [Guidelines for this process can be found in Chapters 8 & 9 and Appendix C of *The Tao of Fully Feeling*.]

The Created Family: Healing the Loss of Tribe

The love of my grandmothers and my sisters, Pat, Diane and Sharon, helped keep my heart alive despite all the parental and clerical abuse. Growing up in New York City as a baby boomer gave me access to a wealth of kids on the street, and I had many safe enough friends, although I also had to learn to steer clear of numerous bullies.

Moving to Dover, New Hampshire as an adolescent opened the door to more supportive friendships, especially the one with my lifetime friend, Bruce McAdams.

Even the army brought me many good enough friends. I also met many kind and respectful people during my travels. All this gradually restored my trust in human nature.

Communal living greatly bolstered this trust. Fifteen years with kind roommates soothed me with relational healing. How lucky I was to come of age during the hippie times. I was especially fortunate to live for a decade in Australia while the Hippie Zeitgeist of loving cooperation still endured.

During this time, many layers of my deep CPTSD fear of people dissolved. Empirical proof accumulated that destructive narcissists like my parents were a small part of the population. I bet they are less than ten percent.

Sadly, communal living ended for me thirty years ago. Happily, it was gradually replaced with a looser sense of tribe. I experience my current clan as concentric circles of intimacy. My inner most circle is my wife, son and a handful of close friends with whom I can easily be my whole self.

The next circle is a group of old friends I see infrequently but immediately feel close to when I do.

Outside that circle is less intimate friends and family members with whom I am usually comfortable via many years of safe interactions.

A final superficial but warm circle is safe-enough acquaintances from my neighborhood, my son's school and my membership in community organizations.

Intermingling with various arcs of this circle are the many people I no longer see but still hold dear in my heart.

When I am actively engaged in flashback management, I sometimes visualize a human mandala of all these circles as Step 10 [Seek Support].

Pete Walker

Gratitude: A Realistic Approach

Yesterday I laughed aloud at a cartoon in *The New Yorker*. Moses, with the Ten Commandments in hand, was looking up toward God and calling out: "Now, how about some affirmations to balance out all this negativity."

Twenty years ago I began my end-of-the-day gratitude practice. Upon laying down each night I spend five minutes using my breath to relax me. To better appreciate the day, I then recall ten things for which I am grateful. Even on gloomy days, I usually find ten worthwhile things.

Usually it's simple stuff: an especially sweet pear, something funny that Sara or Jaden said, a new flower that bloomed in my garden, a cloud with a striking shape, a sense of being healthy when I stretched, a dull radio background sound that suddenly morphed into a tune that begged for my accompaniment.

Gratitude is a thought-correction practice that gradually eroded the negative noticing of my toxic critic. Now, I refuse to let all-or-none thinking throw out the baby of daily niceties with the bathwater of normal disappointments.

Here is how I keep this practice fresh. I accept that I do not always *feel* gratitude while I am expressing it. As I argue in my first book, our feelings are rarely a matter of choice. But gratitude is more than a feeling.

Gratitude is also a health-inducing perspective that with enough practice grows into a belief. So while I may not *feel* grateful for my wife while we are struggling about something, I almost always know she is a blessing in my life. And although life can bring unpredictable difficulties, bounteous wonder usually tips the scale and makes me grateful to be alive.

Sometimes I have difficulty with the homily "Stop and smell the roses." In my old all-or-none days, I was bitter when their perfume did not rescue me from feeling bad. Nowadays though, I still love flowers even when they do not move me. And, I still dislike it when someone tries to fast-fix my pain by pointing them out.

On a larger scale this is true of gratitude and love in general. At times Monet's paintings, my favorite songs or even kindnesses from others do not impact me.

Yet, in a wider spiritual sense, I am always grateful for these gifts because I know from experience that sooner or later I will fully appreciate them again.

So, I accept the cyclical nature of *feeling* love and gratitude, knowing that I will repeatedly be moved by the bounty of the world. Color, flowers, nature, food, panoramas, music, movies, kindnesses, pets, and so on, will inevitably move me again even when they momentarily leave me cold.

Back in the late twentieth century, the practice of *Be-Here-Now* [based eponymously on Ram Das's book] was considered to be the height of wisdom in many spiritual circles. Invoking "Be Here Now!" was supposed to make you instantly return to feeling grateful and loving.

I soon came to hate this phrase however, because I hated myself for not being able to do it on command. Even worse, *be-here-now* was often callously shoved in the face of anyone who was having a hard time.

Once in a JFK group, a student sporting an *ascended master* persona told a woman distraught about the recent demise of her twenty year marriage: "If you weren't so attached to the past, you wouldn't be so upset. Try to Be Here Now!"

Over time, "be-here-now" morphed into "just be grateful!" which in turn acquired a flight-into-light subtext: "If you just get your mundane head out of your unspiritual ass, and flip the *gratitude* switch, your pain will instantly vanish."

Unfortunately I still regularly see this shaming use of gratitude…especially in Marin County, the nesting place of the world's largest population of flight-into-lighters.

For my own use, I have ironically converted be-here-now from an elixir to a reminder: *Be here now, Pete. Drop down into that pain and feel your way through it.* Usually this soon restores me into authentically being here now.

Don't Sweat the Small Stuff is a more modern version of be-here-now. It's a great book title and idea by itself, but it's instantly ruined by the book's small print subtitle: *And it's All Small Stuff.* Hopefully at this point I don't need to explain the nonsense in that.

An anonymous reader sent me this poem.

> *In which I count to ten, grateful that:*
> *Spider webs catch sunlight and moonbeams.*
> *Long-lost lovers sometimes reappear.*
> *Women make an art out of friendship.*
> *Wisdom wanders the world planting stories.*
> *People transform pain into blues.*
> *Weather changes.*
> *Sloths are not extinct.*
> *Turkey contains serotonin.*
> *Frequently accidents are not as bad as they might be.*
> *Love abides.*

APPENDIX 2

Three Dimensional Relational Healing *

"IN ANY EFFECTIVE psychological treatment the doctor is bound to influence the patient: but this influence can only take place if the patient has a reciprocal influence on the doctor." – Carl Jung

Stephen Mitchell echoes this wisdom throughout his book, *Relational Concepts in Psychoanalysis*. His work fortified me to use my vulnerability in therapy sessions to foster relational healing.

It has also been my great fortune that many clients and readers have thanked me for my openness. Many report that my vulnerable disclosures help them to let go of their shame about similar suffering. Without their validation, I would not feel strong enough to challenge Mainstream Psychotherapy's taboos about therapists being self-disclosive.

Self-Compassion, Empathy, Mutuality

In my client work I use a model of three *interwoven* levels of relational healing to address the many developmental arrests common to Complex PTSD. Here is the model in a nutshell.

On the first level, <u>Self-Compassion</u>, I help survivors improve their *relationships with themselves*. This addresses the developmental arrest of their *self-care*.

On the second level, _Empathy_, survivors gradually open up to being comforted by my caring. This level addresses their developmentally arrested need to *benefit from another person's support*.

On the third level, _Mutuality_, feelings of *mutual empathy* naturally arise that benefit both the survivor and myself. This revives the client's developmentally arrested capacity to form *intimate relationships based on reciprocal caring*. It also activates the client's dormant capacity for *relational efficacy* – the spiritual/emotional experience of seeing that one's caring has a positive effect on others.

Healing Developmental Arrests in Complex PTSD

Here is a more detailed sketch of what this three dimensional healing looks like in practice.

Self-Compassion   On the *first level*, I aid clients to awaken their developmentally arrested instincts of self-compassion, self-protection and self-care. To accomplish this, I use psychoeducation, critic-shrinking techniques, reparenting, unconditional positive regard and compassion. All the while I foster the creation of enough safety for them to grieve the losses of their childhoods. Some clients work exclusively on this level; others grow into the next levels at varying rates.

Empathy   On the *second level*, my favorite tool is to show clients that as well as being kind to them, I am kind to myself when I am in their current state of emotional pain. I model shameless-ness about suffering to teach them to treat their own suffering kindly. This helps show that my compassion for their pain is real...not just a pose of kindness.

Let me restate some earlier examples of how I empower my empathy with vulnerability: "Yes my mother was mean like yours, and Mother's Day makes me very sad too" or "I hate that he did that; bullies like your father and mine really piss me off" or "Yeah, I hear you. Waking up depressed is one of my most unfavorite things" or "Yes, I also once ran into the car in front of me when I was spacing out...I was so mortified and scared!"

When the timing is right, I may also sparingly allow my naturally occurring tears about their pain to well up in my eyes as proof of my caring.

Over time, my self-disclosure sometimes further evolves into a version of this: "I still get flashbacks too. But, the type of work we are doing has ongoingly decreased their intensity, duration and frequency."

It is important to emphasize that I only self-disclose in response to cues from the client. I must sense that they are developmentally ready for and open to this type of help.

The use of vulnerable self-disclosure can shrink the dynamic whereby clients see me as perfect [as their parents pretended to be] and themselves as defective [as their parents saw them]. If this shame-generating dynamic is not worked through, clients often drown in toxic shame during the session, and feel too unsafe to access their real vulnerability.

Moreover, as work on the second level matures, client *experiences of self-care* [level one] and *receiving my care* [level 2] interweave in a yin/yang process that increases their capacity to be self-nurturing.

Mutuality   On the *third level* of healing, the developmental arrest of *mutual caring* begins to shift. The client's growing self-compassion slowly grows into empathic feelings toward the therapist.

Two people experiencing deep self-compassion naturally open their hearts to each other. When both parties are emotionally grounded in self-kindness, a healing biofeedback loop of unconditional positive regard may momentarily open. This loop of mutual empathy reminds me of a luminous infinity symbol.

Mutuality is an intersubjective process of relational healing – a reciprocal process that occurs regularly between a good enough mother and her child – and between two people with a healthy attachment bond.

This circular connection of mutual compassion gives birth to feelings of trust and safety. Feeling full acceptance ultimately stimulates a client to love in return, if s/he has not been traumatized into an extreme narcissistic defense.

Mutuality is a process by which two attuned people de-stress and comfort each other. Modern neuroscience is beginning to identify the physiology behind this unique process of mutual human healing. Some think it may be mediated by the brain's mirror neurons.

Working at the mutuality-level heals the developmental arrest of growing up in a family devoid of mutual love and empathy. In its most remedial moments, mutuality cocoons both parties in healthy attachment feelings such as warmth, trust, and appreciation.

Good enough parents regularly bathe their children in this exchange and are warmed by it themselves. Over time, these children grow up to later form new healthy attachments as they "pay" this process forward.

In a similar way, mutually reverberating in anger or sadness also enhances feelings of healing connectivity. We soothe and co-regulate each other when we are mad or sad together about the same injustice. How tragic it is that, *commiseration* – the most transformative of all intimate connections – is so rare in Western cultures!

Perhaps the most powerful mutuality occurs when therapist and client resonate in fear and/or depression in a way that heals the common shame that typically attaches to these feelings.

In one such interaction, my client free-associated to a pithy saying she once heard: "This depression feels like a seed in me that is collecting potential energy." *How sweet to be reminded of this on a day when I regressed into feeling grumpy with myself for feeling down.*

The culmination of the third level occurs when clients disclose their anger or disappointment with me. This allows me to model an *intimacy-deepening* process for resolving normal relationship frustrations.

During this process, I sometimes help clients identify and remove contempt from their anger. Contempt, a mixture of anger and disgust, is the intimacy-destroying process that was modeled by their parents. I help them be angry with me in a way that does not hurt me or them, or the good will between us.

In doing this, I use the "Tools for Lovingly Resolving Conflict" [Appendix 4 of my *CPTSD* book] to guide our process. This then helps them to cultivate their developmentally arrested conflict-resolution skills.

Decades of working with clients' anger in sessions has helped me grow a great deal. At key junctures a few emotionally astute clients upgraded my anger work skills. *Mutuality* typically builds emotional and relational intelligence in both the client and the therapist!

Relating in the mutuality zone can also spontaneously triggers upsurges of insight, equanimity, light-heartedness and humor in both me and the client.

I call all these instances of psychological interconnectedness *regenerating at the hub of relational healing* – which is not infrequently *regenerating in the calm eye of the storm*.

Marvelously, *healing mutuality* is not exclusive to therapy. When I consider all the great nurses I've known – like my sister – a capacity for mutuality might be the common denominator in their excellence.

In fact, any two individuals with enough emotional and relational intelligence can co-create mutuality, like my friend Randi and I did in co-counseling back at Antioch University. Those who get enough of it growing up naturally do.

In therapy of course, the focus of sessions always needs to be on the client's concerns. A long period of focusing singularly on the client's psyche, however, is often necessary in the beginning.

Some precocious clients quickly move into working on all three levels. They slide easily from one level to another as needed. It is important to note that clients still typically do a high percentage of the talking on level three, even during the development of the arrested ability to be *dialogical*. Dialogicality is an easy conversational balance between talking and listening. Therapists enable this by keeping their self-disclosures "short-winded"…non-monological…and always in service of the client. [Guidelines and limits to using self-disclosure are in Chapter 13 of my CPTSD book.]

In order to model self-compassion, therapists must of course hold their own suffering with kindness. Therapists from dysfunctional families [*Are there many who aren't?*] must effectively address their own family-of-origin pain before they can authentically open their hearts to similar pain in their clients.

Moreover, introspective therapists also know that they suffer many commonalities with their clients. Life intrinsically brings suffering to everyone. Loneliness, loss, world chaos and bad luck are existential issues for us all, not just survivors whose parental abandonment is the ultimate loneliness, loss and tragic luck.

Finally, those rare therapists who have had good enough parenting may be less suitable for this work. The stubborn, ingrained pervasiveness of the toxic critic and toxic shame may be beyond their ken.

*CAVEAT: I believe that this three dimensional process of relational healing can help most CPTSD victims, but not all. Some survivors were too traumatized to ever trust again. I also think some individuals, traumatized or not, are born so polarized to introversion that they have little drive or need for human interaction. However, in both cases, these individuals can usually benefit by working on the first level of my relational model – improving their relationships with themselves.

APPENDIX 3

Psychedelic-Assisted Therapy

PLEASE GET PROFESSIONAL guidance if you decide to explore psychedelics. I am very lucky to have come out of my experiences *relatively* unscathed. My friend, Dave, was tripping when his high-on-acid buddy dove off a twenty story building. Dave instantly dissolved into a psychotic break and was hospitalized for two weeks. As you saw earlier in my story, Dave himself suffered devastating LSD flashbacks two years later.

That being said, there is currently a "second coming" of the therapeutic promise of psychedelic pharmaceuticals. The US government has reauthorized the supervised use of psychedelics in a number of university research programs.

Tom Shroder, editor of *The Washington Post Magazine*, wrote a compelling book: *Acid Test: LSD, Ecstasy and The Power to Heal*. It presents scientific, evidence-based research [Harvard, NYU, UCLA] on the effectiveness of treating anxiety disorders, including PTSD, with psychedelics.

NYU and The California Institute of Integral Studies [S.F., CA] now train therapist-guides in the art and science of *psychedelic therapy*. More information about this can be found in Michael Pollan's article "The Trip Treatment." Pollan is a renowned author who teaches journalism at UC Berkeley. You can search for his article at www.newyorker.com [2/9/15].

In his article Pollan describes a study in which psychologists measured significant increase in *openness* more than a year later after a single trial with a psychedelic substance. Openness is a psychological quality that includes aesthetic appreciation, imagination, creativity and tolerance of other's viewpoints.

Pollan also quotes Harvard researcher, Walter Pahnke: "The experiences of eight who received the psilocybin were indistinguishable from, if not identical with, the classic mystical experiences reported in the literature by William James [The Father of American Psychology]."

Michael Pollan's concluding comment about psychedelic therapy is that: "Many of the researchers and therapists are confident that psychedelic therapy will eventually become routine."

The prestigious *Journal of Psychopharmacology* also published an article entitled: "Psilocybin [a naturally occurring psychedelic] can occasion mystical-type experiences having substantial and sustained personal meaning and spiritual significance" [2006]. Two thirds of the study's participants rated the experience in their top five spiritually significant experiences, and a third as their top.

On a more subjective level, let me overemphasize that psychedelics are best used for self-transformation, not partying. I went on to experiment with psychedelics about twenty times after my initial life-transforming experience. Only a few times, did I replicate a lesser version of the first experience. Moreover, as time passed, my psychedelic experiences became increasingly troublesome.

Like many others I know, too much use eventually produced a bad trip. I had two bad trips that were the most painful experiences of my life – eight hellish hours of full blown schizophrenia. Fortunately for me these psychotic breaks ended when the drug wore off. I have met too many people who were not that lucky.

For most people an opening of *The Doors of Perception* [book by Aldous Huxley about psychedelics] is time-limited. Most of my friends stopped tripping after a year or two. It seems as if the insight that comes through this drug enlightens us in a way that can then guide our spiritual evolution without the need for further use.

LSD consciousness-expansion seems to be a window that stays open briefly for most people. Lasting consciousness-expansion is a slow and gradual evolution that ensues from effective, ongoing psychological and spiritual work.

A Caution about Cannabis

My experiences with LSD paralleled my experiences with marijuana – a psychoactive drug of much lower potency that can be significantly mind-expanding and growth-inducing. Unfortunately for many users, this effect gradually diminishes or disappears. Fortunately, like many of my friends, pot started to trigger paranoia relatively quickly in me, and it never became something that I habitually used.

In guiding others in their recovery, I do not take an all-or-none stand against cannabis except in two instances. First, I believe that children and teenagers should never use it. There is a huge amount of compelling scientific evidence that pot *physiologically* interferes with healthy brain development in those under eighteen.

Second, though marijuana is widely touted as non-addictive, there is a significant subset of individuals who become psychologically addicted. Whether they start as teenagers or as adults, any mind-expanding effect slowly gives way to ongoing dumbing-down. This effect is sadly glamorized in several teenage movies that star stereotypically stupid stoners.

Only the most exaggerated stereotypes belie the truth. Most of the strikingly dumb or common sense-challenged potheads whom I have met started smoking as young teens or earlier. In my hippie days, these were not infrequently the hippies who devolved into using heavier drugs, and who regressed into the excessively narcissistic behavior that gave hippies such a bad name.

It is important to note that as with alcohol, many people can use marijuana recreationally – and sometimes therapeutically – without harm. I have seen considerable evidence however that excessive use of either drug may stimulate dissociative or narcissistic behavior and cause more harm than benefit in any age group.

Made in the USA
Middletown, DE
12 May 2023

30420243R00209